Designing Effective Legislation

Designing Effective Legislation

Maria Mousmouti

Lecturer in Law, Institute of Advanced Legal Studies, University of London, UK and Executive Director, Centre for European Constitutional Law, Greece

Edward Elgar
PUBLISHING

Cheltenham, UK • Northampton, MA, USA

© Maria Mousmouti 2019

All rights reserved. No part of this publication may be reproduced, stored in a retrieval system or transmitted in any form or by any means, electronic, mechanical or photocopying, recording, or otherwise without the prior permission of the publisher.

Published by
Edward Elgar Publishing Limited
The Lypiatts
15 Lansdown Road
Cheltenham
Glos GL50 2JA
UK

Edward Elgar Publishing, Inc.
William Pratt House
9 Dewey Court
Northampton
Massachusetts 01060
USA

A catalogue record for this book
is available from the British Library

Library of Congress Control Number: 2019945331

This book is available electronically in the **Elgar**online
Law subject collection
DOI 10.4337/9781788118231

Printed on elemental chlorine free (ECF)
recycled paper containing 30% Post-Consumer Waste

ISBN 978 1 78811 822 4 (cased)
ISBN 978 1 78811 823 1 (eBook)

Printed and bound in the USA

Contents

Acknowledgements ix
Introduction x

1 The 'mechanics' of effective legislation 1
  1 Introduction: on lawmaking and lawmakers 1
  2 Any principles to guide lawmaking? 4
  3 Efficacy, effectiveness or efficiency? 9
  4 The fundamental elements of effectiveness 12
    4.1 Purpose of legislation: the benchmark of effectiveness 13
    4.2 Content of legislation: the 'heart' of effectiveness 14
    4.3 Overarching structure or superstructure: the context of effectiveness 15
    4.4 Results of legislation: the 'measure' of effectiveness 15
    4.5 Interaction between the elements 16
  5 Conclusion: the lawmaker as the 'designer' of effective laws and the effectiveness test as a thinking process 16

2 Legislation and its purpose 17
  1 Purpose in the life cycle of legislation 17
  2 Challenges for lawmakers 18
    2.1 The unclear boundaries between reasons, justification and goals 18
    2.2 What objectives? 20
    2.3 The vague language of legislative objectives 22
    2.4 The location of legislative objectives 25
    2.5 Too much information on objectives 30
  3 Purpose and objectives in effective lawmaking 33
    3.1 Objectives need to be the starting point in lawmaking 34
    3.2 Specific, measurable and well-formulated objectives 35

		3.3	Objectives as benchmarks	36
		3.4	Traceable objectives	37
	4	Conclusions: purpose as a benchmark for effectiveness		39

3 The content of legislation — 40

1. Lawmaking challenges when designing the content of legislation — 40
   - 1.1 Selecting substantive rules — 41
   - 1.2 Compliance and enforcement — 45
   - 1.3 Communicating the law — 48
2. Effective legislative mechanics — 51
   - 2.1 A clear legislative strategy — 52
   - 2.2 Clear mechanics — 53
   - 2.3 Choices informed by evidence but selected on the basis of effectiveness — 54
   - 2.4 Anticipating compliance — 57
   - 2.5 Consideration of enforcement and implementation — 58
   - 2.6 Clear messages for clear communication — 59
   - 2.7 Experimentation — 60
3. Conclusions: the importance of legislative design — 61

4 Legislation and its context — 64

1. Why context matters — 64
2. Superstructure and the transmission of legislative messages — 66
   - 2.1 The 'all-in-one' message — 67
   - 2.2 'Diffuse' messages — 69
   - 2.3 'Fragmented' messages — 71
   - 2.4 'Patchwork' messages — 74
   - 2.5 Delivery options and their implications — 78
3. Delivering the message effectively — 79
   - 3.1 Informed choices on superstructure — 79
   - 3.2 Accessibility — 80
   - 3.3 Coherence — 81
   - 3.4 Consider how the changes will be appraised — 82
4. Conclusion — 83

5 The implementation of the law: results, impact and effectiveness — 84

	1	Legislation, results and lawmaking	84
	2	Challenges for lawmakers	85
		2.1 What kind of results does legislation produce?	85
		2.2 How can results be anticipated and measured?	87
		2.3 Review	89
		2.4 Horizontal questions: when, how and who will record and measure results?	98
	3	Results in effective lawmaking	101
		3.1 Clearly defined results	101
		3.2 Anticipating implementation	102
		3.3 A clear monitoring, review and evaluation framework	103
		3.4 Clear and specific monitoring, review and evaluation clauses	104
	4	Conclusions	107
6	Which tools for effective lawmaking?		108
	1	Introduction	108
	2	On toolkits, tools and lawmaking	109
	3	A closer look at the contemporary lawmaking toolkit from the perspective of effective lawmaking	112
		3.1 Impact assessment	112
		3.2 Consultation	116
		3.3 So, does the toolkit contribute to lawmaking?	118
	4	Adding 'effectiveness lenses' to existing tools: the effectiveness test	119
		4.1 The effectiveness test	120
		4.2 The structure and elements of the 'effectiveness test'	121
		4.3 'Testing' the effectiveness test: three case studies	124
		4.4 Usefulness, relevance, advantages and limitations	127
	5	Conclusions	128
7	Legislative failure		129
	1	Failure and legislation	129
		1.1 Understanding failure	130
		1.2 A typology of legislative failure	131
		1.3 The timing and actors of a diagnosis of failure	136
	2	Responding to failure	137

		2.1	Amendments: a panacea or a curse?	137
		2.2	Simplification	139
		2.3	Codification	140
		2.4	Law reform – looking at the whole picture	141
		2.5	Effectiveness of the responses	143
	3	Anticipating and avoiding future failure		143
		3.1	Strategic approach to the diagnosis and analysis of legislative failure	144
		3.2	Strengthen the 'immune' system of the legal order	146
		3.3	Learn from failure	147
		3.4	Invest in effective lawmaking	149
	4	Conclusion		149
8	On lawmakers, lawmaking and effectiveness			150
	1	So what about effectiveness?		150
	2	Lawmaking in practice: top down or bottom up?		155
	3	A typology of lawmakers?		156
		3.1	The intuitive lawmaker	157
		3.2	The reflective lawmaker	157
		3.3	The lawmaker that 'muddles through'	158
	4	Cognitive biases in lawmaking?		158
		4.1	Legislative styles, drafting conventions and regulatory culture	159
		4.2	Path dependence, habitual action and legislative 'patterns'	160
		4.3	Borrowed, imported and supranational rules	162
	5	Effective lawmaking		163

Bibliography 164

Index 191

Acknowledgements

This book would have been impossible without the inspiration, support and encouragement of several people. My first round of thanks goes to Professor Dr Helen Xanthaki for her sharp ideas and for cheering me on, when I most needed it. Helen, I value your warmth and positivity and I am proud to count you among my colleagues and friends. Another round of thanks goes to Dr Constantin Stefanou and my colleagues at the Institute for Advanced Legal Studies of the University of London for offering me the academic space to teach, reflect and cross fertilise my ideas. I am also greatly indebted to my colleagues at the Centre for European Constitutional Law, and especially Professor Dr Xenophon Contiades, for their cooperation and companionship for almost twenty years now. My work at the CECL exposed me to real legal problems around the world and has shaped not only my thinking but also my preference for pragmatic and effective solutions.

My family has always been a source of genuine love and support, no matter the circumstances. Mama, Baba, Lydia, Taki, Nikola, Louka my heart warms up when I think of you. Thank you for everything. My dear friends Tamara and Max and their lovely daughters, Zoe and Alia, generously offered not only their friendship but also the warmest London home ever. Tamara and Max, you are family to me. My close friends Alex, Venou, Dimi, Niki have been my safety net through the twists and turns of life that coincided with the writing of this book. Girls, I deeply cherish your friendship. A broader circle of friends helped me, each in their own way, achieve the discipline and focus required to respond to a complicated life of writing, travelling and working. I am indebted to you all.

Writing a book is a unique journey. Intense, overwhelming, consuming but extremely fulfilling. The thoughts of many people have been woven into the fabric of the end result and it has been my intention to acknowledge them as best as I could. Any errors and mistakes remain entirely my own.

Introduction

During recent decades, effectiveness has become a popular topic associated with legislation. The word appears in many places: legislative texts use the adjective 'effective' or the adverb 'effectively' in their substantive provisions; international organisations claim the need for effective laws to ensure the achievement of policy commitments; documents setting quality standards or offering guidance to legislative drafting refer to effectiveness as an aspect of legislative quality; politicians require effective laws to satisfy their electorates; citizens to ensure enjoyment of their rights. Despite the rhetoric, however, the fact remains that we know little about what effectiveness is and even less about how we can produce effective laws.

This book puts forward the idea that effective legislation is not a utopic pursuit: instead, it is the result of complex 'mechanics' in the conceptualisation, design and drafting of legislation and the result of conscious decisions around four elements inherent in every law: purpose, content, context and results. Why is this hypothesis worth exploring? And what makes it novel?

The question of what makes law effective is by no means new. It has been lingering in the writings of legal philosophers and sociologists, scholars in the study of regulation and legislation and in the concerns of practitioners for years, but so far without a concrete answer. Compliance and enforcement are important aspects of it,[1] clarity of expression is another, but no definite formula or solution is proposed as to how to achieve it. Why? The first reason is, in my view, a question of perspective: effectiveness has been considered mainly an implementation issue, a measure of the success of legislation in achieving its goals. But do effective laws materialise magically? My claim is that this cannot happen unless laws are designed and drafted with the specific aim to be effective. Using effectiveness as a lawmaking principle marks a subtle but important shift in legislative decision making: from the abstract use of rationality and evidence based methods[2] towards their purposive use consciously

---

[1] H. Jones, *The Efficacy of Law* (Rosenthal Lectures Northwestern University Press 1968) at 4; A. Allot, *The Limits of Law* (Butterworths 1980) 11; Lawrence Friedman, *Impact. How Law Affects Behaviour* (Harvard University Press 2016) at 44–72.

[2] J. Rachlinski, 'Evidence-Based Law' (2011) 96 Cornell Law Review 901 at 910.

oriented towards effectiveness. A second reason is the fact that the concept of effectiveness itself remains largely abstract and ambiguous. What is it that makes a law effective? And can the relevant factors be proactively engineered to lead to effective laws? Disciplinary barriers and lack of clear focus have failed to give it a clear operational content. So, although the starting point of this study is by no means novel, the approach is fresh in terms of perspective: it looks at the potential of effectiveness to proactively guide lawmaking.

Hence, the focus is on lawmaking, and the lawmaker. Against the traditional focus of legal studies on black letter law and the perspective of the implementer or the judge,[3] the spotlight is now on the lawmaker, as an autonomous actor with the leading role in the early stages of the life cycle of the law. But who exactly is the lawmaker? Depending on the jurisdiction, the answer will vary: it might be policy makers, professional drafters, experts, civil servants, drafting committees, parliamentarians or combinations of the above.[4] My approach is a functional one: it is the job description rather than the job title that matters. My focus is on the individuals whose role is to conceptualise and 'engineer' rules and give shape and form to legal norms, independently of where they are placed within the system. Lawmaking is a global enterprise and despite the differences that make legislation jurisdiction and legal system-specific, the conceptual dilemmas of lawmaking are common – and unique – to those involved in their design and drafting.

Lawmaking on the other hand, as the 'enterprise of subjecting human conduct to the governance of rules'[5] is a complex process that entails the transformation of an idea into binding norms and its consequent exposure to the cruel test of reality. This transformative process is a constant interplay between substance and form,[6] a dialogue of minds, disciplines, languages and mindsets[7] and a decision-making process during which political concepts are transformed into legal material and rules acquire concrete shape and form. Contemporary lawmakers have a triple role as *'policy translators'*, *'design-*

---

[3] K. Tuori, 'Legislation Between Politics and Law' in Luc Wintgens (eds), *Legisprudence* (Hart Publishing 2002) 99; Luc Wintgens, 'The Rational Legislator Revisited. Bounded Rationality and Legisprudence' in Luc Wintgens and A. Daniel Oliver-Lalana (eds), *The Rationality and Justification of Legislation* (Springer 2013) at 3.

[4] Constantin Stefanou, 'Comparative Legislative Drafting. Comparing across Legal Systems' (2016) 18:2 European Journal of Law Reform 123, 124–34.

[5] Lon Fuller, *The Morality of Law* (revised edn, Yale University Press 1964) at 106.

[6] A. Seidman, R. Seidman and N. Abeyesekere, *Legislative Drafting for Democratic Social Change. A Manual for Drafters* (Kluwer 2001) 26.

[7] Helen Xanthaki, *Drafting Legislation. Art and Technology of Rules for Regulation* (Hart Publishing 2014) 22.

ers' of effective legislation and *'communicators'*. Balancing the competing demands of this complex role requires a clear focus, and, most importantly, a clear method.

But why effectiveness? Several values have been signposted as indicators of a 'good' law, for example legality, legitimacy, legal certainty or proportionality. Compared to them, effectiveness is 'humble' in terms of origin and aspiration. It has a managerial descent,[8] is 'neutral', relative and fluid, 'empty' in terms of substantive content and highly contextual: it can reflect distinct angles (macro or micro), can be formal or substantive, and can raise different questions depending on the standpoint.[9] Why is effectiveness, as the capacity of the law to achieve its objectives, so important? Its main strength is its straightforward logic: does the law work? Does it have the capacity to work? How can it be designed to work? Its value lies in adding rationality to legislative decision making by ensuring the connection between objectives and results,[10] rather than indicate which objectives or which results. Other values with a similar rationale, like efficacy and efficiency, are either too broad (efficacy), hence beyond the realm of the law, or too 'coined' in their focus towards costs[11] (efficiency). So far as legal systems are purposive[12] and legislation is a 'goal-oriented' intervention,[13] effectiveness is the value that best captures firstly, the capacity of legislation to function as a *system*; secondly its *mechanics* as the controllable factor that can influence the achievement of results; and last but not least, the items that fall within the mandate and the decision-making powers of the lawmaker. The thinking process that leads, or can lead, to effective legislative decision making is what makes effectiveness a fascinating topic of study.

A disclaimer: effectiveness is not a measure of perfection. From the proactive perspective of the lawmaker, effectiveness requires the lawmaker to do the best they can with what they have. Reality cannot be magically changed and the law is no miracle worker. Resources are not infinite. Circumstance is not

---

[8] Ulrich Karpen, 'Efficacy, Effectiveness, Efficiency: from Judicial to Managerial Rationality' in Klaus Messerschimdt and A. Daniel Oliver-Lalana (eds), *Rational Lawmaking under Review. Legisprudence According to the German Federal Constitutional Court* (Springer 2016) 304.

[9] Maria Mousmouti, 'Introduction to the Symposium on Effective Law and Regulation' (2018) 9:3 European Journal of Risk Regulation 387–90.

[10] Alexander Flückiger, 'Effectiveness: a new Constitutional Principle' (2009) 50 Legislação: cadernos de ciência de legislação at 190.

[11] Wim Voermans, 'To Measure is to Know: The Quantification of Regulation' (2015) 3:1 The Theory and Practice of Legislation 91 at 110–11.

[12] A. Allot, *The Limits of Law* (Butterworths 1980) 11.

[13] Gunther Teubner, 'Substantive and Reflexive Elements in Modern Law' (1983) 17:2 Law & Society Review 239–85.

always opportune. People might not comply or comply creatively. The 'implementation game'[14] is complex, dynamic and can always evolve in unanticipated ways. Effectiveness is not a magical solution: instead, it is a realistic and grounded criterion for making decisions in a context of 'bounded' rationality,[15] with the view of delivering results.

Despite the rhetoric, the conceptual content of effectiveness remains fragmented, unsystematic and abstract. Compliance and enforcement are positively linked to it, yet is that all there is to effectiveness? Far from it. In my view, effectiveness is the 'functional link'[16] between four fundamental elements that are present in every law: objectives, content, context and results. Why these elements? Because they explain the why, the how and the what in relation to legislation. Purpose sets the benchmark for *what* legislation aims to achieve; the content of legislation (i.e. choices in substance, form, structure and language) determines *how* the law will achieve the desired results and how its messages will be communicated; context determines *how the provisions will integrate the legal system*; and, results indicate *what has been achieved*. These four elements, I feel, are the elements inherent in every law that make the concept of legislative effectiveness concrete and tangible. Each in isolation and all four in conjunction shape the invisible mechanics that lie under the surface of any law. And although reality can interact with legislation in unexpected ways and bring unfortunate surprises, these elements are what the lawmaker has at hand when putting together a law.

So, if effectiveness can be consciously 'engineered', what conceptual and methodological insights are needed to guide the choices of lawmakers? Two important aspects are missing, in my view, from existing scholarship and practice: firstly, the emphasis on legislative *design*. Although an unusual term to associate with legislation, it is the process of making strategic choices about legislation as an instrument that intervenes in social and legal reality, the required elements and their role. It is the process of designing the 'formula' according to which the law will intervene. The process of design involves thinking, reflecting, analysing and coming up with a strategy on how the law will change the status quo. Design allows the elements of the final product (the law) to make sense and to have, at least conceptually, the potential to produce results. The second element are *mechanics*. They are not about intuition, circumstance or luck but about selecting the right ingredients and mixing them in the appropriate dosages. What kind of ingredients? The lawmaker's

---

[14] E. Bardach, *The Implementation Game: What Happens after a Bill becomes a Law* (MIT Press 1977).

[15] Wintgens (n 3) at 14.

[16] Mauro Zamboni, 'Legislative Policy and Effectiveness: A (Small) Contribution from Legal Theory' (2018) 9:3 European Journal of Risk Regulation 416–30.

toolkit includes legislative techniques, doctrinal and legal concepts, drafting principles, structure, language, form, even layout. Out of these, the lawmaker will have to choose the right ones and articulate them into a coherent whole. The 'effectiveness test', a simple thinking process, proposes an open set of questions to prompt the lawmaker to think around their choices and the use of the tools to ensure mechanics that allow the law to be effective. Effective legislation does not need only bright ideas or minds, imaginative or ambitious strategies, but also skilful mechanics.

Last but not least, effectiveness lies at the intersection of theory and legislative practice. It is an interdisciplinary concept that, like legislation, evolves in two parallel universes: conceptual choices put to the test of reality. Theories offer particular lenses on social reality and legal practice has inescapable theoretical dimensions.[17] Any attempt to deal with effectiveness has to involve both: looking at concepts and how they work in practice; looking at legislative choices, how people reacted to them, what worked well, what not and why; learning from patterns, identifying limitations and automatisms and factoring them into the process. My effort is to nurture this dialogue around the four elements of effectiveness. I look at theory, I look at practice and try to figure out what could work.

Against this background, I am not proposing any grand, all-encompassing new theory of effectiveness. My aim is much humbler: I test the elements of effectiveness in theory and practice. I explore the ways in which content, structure, language and form can be used to formulate solutions that have the potential to be effective. My focus is not on fixed and abstract solutions but on the questions that need to be asked and criteria on the basis of which to make decisions. Between the choice of an approach and the choice of precise words for the product, lie a number of critical decisions to be made.[18] Which requirements will best achieve the goal? How specifically should these requirements be framed? Who should be responsible for implementing the legislation? What sort of enforcement strategy should be employed? How will results be monitored and reviewed? For this set of questions, modern scholarship and practice provide no comprehensive answer.

The book has the following structure: Chapter 1 explores the fundamental theoretical questions around effectiveness and its position and role in lawmaking. It focuses on its evaluation evolution along the life cycle of legislation, its potential and limitations as a lawmaking principle and identifies its four fundamental elements: objectives, context, content and results. The following

---

[17] C.R. Sunstein, 'On Legal Theory and Legal Practice' (1995) 37 Nomos 267–87.
[18] E.L. Rubin, 'Legislative Methodology: Some Lessons from the Truth-in-Lending Act' (1991) 80 Geo. L.J. 233.

chapters take a closer approach to the design and the mechanics of the elements of effectiveness in legislation. Drawing on examples from distinct jurisdictions to illustrate the diversity and wealth of lawmaking, they evolve around the main challenges that lawmakers have to address.

Chapter 2 focuses on the role and function of purpose in legislation. Purpose is an internalised benchmark for every law (and its effectiveness) yet a notoriously amorphous and shapeless concept. This chapter takes a fresh approach to the debate around purpose and the challenges of how to shape, phrase and locate purpose. It argues that in effective lawmaking purpose needs to be an objective, rather than subjective, concept that clearly identifies the functions, aims and intended effects of legislation and sets a clear benchmark for the effectiveness of every law.

Chapter 3 looks at the challenges involved in designing the content of legislation. The formulation of the content of the law is the 'heart' of effectiveness and involves complex decisions on the appropriate type of rules, compliance motivations, enforcement mechanisms and conscious choices on how to communicate the law in a context of bounded rationality. The chapter concludes that effective formulation of content requires a clear process of legislative design, decisions grounded on reality and evidence, consistency and coherence in the formula designed, openness to innovation and experimentation, and most importantly, learning from experience and legislative practice rather than automatically replicating existing legislative patterns.

Chapter 4 focuses on the context of new legislation, as the broader framework within which laws operate. Adopting the perspective of a communications medium, I examine how legislative messages can integrate legal systems and the impact of different choices on accessibility, coherence and effectiveness. The chapter puts forward a strong argument that lawmakers need to consider superstructure when deciding how to 'package' the legislative messages and consciously select the choices that best promote accessibility and coherence.

Chapter 5 explores results. It addresses the fundamental questions of what kind of results can be expected from legislation, how these can be monitored, and when, how and by whom they need to be appraised. The chapter concludes that results need to be clearly identified when laws are designed, and need to be framed by appropriate mechanism to monitor implementation and evaluate results.

Moving from the theoretical challenges of lawmaking to the actual business of policy and lawmaking, Chapter 6 critically considers the usefulness of practical tools like Impact Assessment and Consultation in the design of effective legislation. The main finding is that both tools contribute to legislative design but fail to go into the detail required for the design and drafting of the mechanics of legislation, while they lack an explicit focus on effectiveness.

The 'effectiveness test' is proposed as a solution to add 'effectiveness lenses' to the existing toolkit and examine the selected formula from this perspective.

Chapter 7 tackles an issue rarely addressed in academic literature on legislation: failure. It examines fundamental, yet difficult, questions: when has a law failed? Who is in the position to say so? What are the reasons for failure? What comes after? Ultimately, can future failure be avoided? The chapter concludes that failure is intrinsically linked with the objectives and anticipated results of the law: the clearer they are the more realistic the expectations of what the law can and cannot do and although it can never be excluded scepticism and analysis, proper consideration, holistic approaches and learning from past experience are the main ways to set solid foundations for the future.

Connecting the threads running along the previous chapters, Chapter 8 wraps up the findings of this journey. Firstly, that legislative decision making in practice has two distinct starting points: as a 'top down' process that transforms ideas or ideals *to* specific rules or as a 'bottom up' process that attempts to deal with real life situations and problems *through* rules. The critical difference between the two is their connection to reality: the former favours more abstract and 'intuitive' choices, while the latter is more 'grounded' and open to evidence and knowledge. However, both might be necessary. Secondly, lawmakers differ in the way they approach decision making: they can be 'intuitive', if they rely more on abstract assumptions or automatisms when designing the law, they can be 'reflective' to the extent that they engage in an active thinking process during lawmaking or might just 'muddle through' doing what they are asked to do, without much thought. Thirdly, lawmakers are limited in their decisions by heuristics and cognitive biases[19] – unique to their trade – that often appear to prevail over reflection: legislative styles and traditions, drafting conventions, legislative 'patterns', path dependence, borrowed or imported solutions replicated without consideration, in fact any automatism that goes unquestioned, limits the scope of choices of lawmakers. Last but not least, practice confirms that effective lawmaking requires more than good engineers: it needs a genuine commitment to make the law work, a clear thinking and learning process and a method.

---

[19] R.H. Thaler and C.R. Sunstein, *Nudge* (Penguin Books 2009) at 21–3.

1. The 'mechanics' of effective legislation

> Laws are like sausages. It is better not to see them being made
> Attributed to Otto von Bismarck[1]

1. INTRODUCTION: ON LAWMAKING AND LAWMAKERS

Lawmaking is serious business. Subjecting human conduct to the 'governance of rules'[2] is a continuous to-and-fro between form and substance[3] that transforms ideals, ideas, assumptions and solutions into rules. This 'transformation'[4] depends on the features of legal systems, constitutional frameworks, political and social structure, culture but also on a number of other factors.

The most challenging aspect of lawmaking is its *prospective* nature. Karl Llewellyn wrote that 'one of the statutory draftsman's major problems is to look into existent behavior beforehand, to make sure that his formula, when it becomes an official rule, will not merely bask in the sun upon the books. He must so shape it as to induce its application... or else... his blow is spent in air'.[5] To devise this *formula* and *induce its application*, lawmakers have to rely on implicit or explicit assumptions about social reality and social problems, the ways in which they are expected to evolve, how the law will affect them[6] and how people will react. The need to anticipate is the more creative, but also the more uncertain, part of lawmaking. Uncertainty arises not only from the

---

[1] https://quoteinvestigator.com/2010/07/08/laws-sausages/
[2] L. Fuller, *The Morality of Law* (Revised edn Yale University Press 1964) at 106.
[3] P. Zumbansen, 'Law's Knowledge and Law's Effectiveness: Reflections from Legal Sociology and Legal Theory' (2009) 5:2 CLPE Research Paper 11/2009 11.
[4] M. Zamboni, *The Policy of Law. A Legal Theoretical Framework* (Hart Publishing 2007) 91.
[5] K. Llewellyn, 'A Realistic Jurisprudence – The Next Step' (1930) 30 Colum L. Rev. 431.
[6] A.D. Oliver-Lalana, 'Due Post-Legislative Process? On the Lawmakers' Constitutional Duties of Monitoring and Revision' in K. Messerschmidt and A.D. Oliver-Lalana (eds) *Rational Lawmaking under Review. Legisprudence According to the German Federal Constitutional Court* (Springer 2016) 259.

obvious limitations in human capacities and limited information but also from the lack of time, pressure for results, limited resources, among several other factors.

The second challenging aspect of lawmaking is that legislation is – and always will be – the 'baby' of both politics and the law. As the product of this intercourse, legislation is governed by different types of rationality: political, legal, cultural, operational, and internal.[7] Combined with the distinct functions of the law (as a heuristic mechanism, as a social coordinative, power – limiting or justificatory function[8] or as a symbolic or educational instrument) and the interaction with reality they might generate significant clashes. So, apart from anticipating the future, an important aspect of lawmaking is to balance these distinct logics.

It is obvious that lawmaking is far from a clinical experiment. It takes place in a dynamic environment. It is complex in terms of content, management, organisation, coordination and implementation. It is highly contextual. Several actors are involved, several processes take place in parallel or consequently usually under extreme time pressure. Pressure comes in many shapes and forms. Further, it is not static. The life of the law is an eternal cyclical[9] process of action, reaction and more action that shapes its content. In this highly volatile context, lawmakers have to give shape and form to the law. How can they be guided in this task? How can they make the best possible decisions? But first of all, who are these 'lawmakers'?

It is an oxymoron, but lawmakers, the individuals who actually design and draft legislation, are a notoriously obscure actor in the lawmaking process. Why? Firstly, because the 'pre-legislative' phase when laws are actually drafted remains esoteric, but also because there has been little emphasis on the lawmaker as an autonomous actor in the lawmaking process, the spotlight being primarily on the implementer or the judge.[10] As a result, despite the importance of legislation, the persona of the lawmaker remains highly enigmatic. So, who exactly are the the lawmakers? There is no definite answer. Depending on the jurisdiction, the answer will vary: it might be policy makers,

---

[7] Paul Wahlgren, 'The Legitimacy Sphere: Between Law, Culture, Politics and Enforceability' (2010) 56 Scandinavian Studies in Law 428–39.

[8] Dirk H. van der Meulen, 'The Use of Impact Assessments and the Quality of Legislation' (2013) 1:2 The Theory and Practice of Legislation 205–325.

[9] P. Noll, *Gesetzgebungslehre* (Rowohlt, Reinbeck 1973) 314.

[10] K. Tuori, 'Legislation Between Politics and Law' in Luc Wintgens (ed) *Legisprudence* (Hart Publishing 2002) 99–107, 99; Luc Wintgens, 'The Rational Legislator Revisited. Bounded Rationality and Legisprudence' in Luc Wintgens and A. Daniel Oliver-Lalana (eds), *The Rationality and Justification of Legislation* (Springer 2013) at 3.

professional drafters, experts, civil servants, drafting committees, parliamentarians or combinations of the above.[11] In any case, a number of individuals, no matter what their function within a jurisdiction is, are responsible for conceptualising, 'engineering' and giving shape and form to legal norms, independently of where they are placed within the system. But how do they actually do that?

Understanding lawmaking requires moving away from the focus on black letter law and judicial thinking towards the anticipatory thinking that lawmakers are involved in. Despite the alleged alliance in terms of aim and technique between judicial and legislative processes,[12] there are important differences: judges interpret or engage in post factum critique of established law while lawmaking involves weighing and balancing, hence discretion. Further, their position differs in institutional and deontological terms (the judge as a stable actor versus the legislator in the service of political power), in the type of deliberation involved (consensus versus negotiated compromise) but also in the type of reasoning required (subsumptive reasoning versus open and 'practical' reasoning directed to the future and dependent on causal factors that cannot be established in a normative way).[13] Last but not least, the questions tormenting the lawmaker and the judge differ in nature, texture and scope and the challenges are fundamentally different: the judge has to address procedural, jurisdiction, evidence or interpretation questions, while the lawmaker deals with open-ended questions associated with the features of a specific problem, normative solutions, appropriate and adequate measures, the aims to be achieved and so forth.

If the main role of a lawmaker is to establish and delimit the law in a way that gives precise legislative shape to policy[14] and 'draw the line' between the two then their role is increasingly complex: they have to 'master' their circumstances, receive diverse input, understand, analyse, 'converse' with different interlocutors, and finally design a solution that serves policy objectives and has the potential to work. This combines at least three distinct functions: that of a *policy translator* charged with the task to transform political concepts

---

[11] Constantin Stefanou, 'Comparative Legislative Drafting. Comparing across Legal Systems' (2016) 18:2 European Journal of Law Reform 123, 124–34.

[12] J. Landis, 'Statutes and the Sources of Law' in *Harvard Legal Essays Written in Honor and Presented to Joseph Henry Beale and Samuel Williston* (Harvard University Press Cambridge Mass 1934).

[13] M. Atienza, 'Reasoning and Legislation' in L. Wintgens (ed) *The Theory and Practice of Legislation. Essays in Legisprudence* (Ashgate 2005) 297–318, 300–313.

[14] H. Xanthaki, *Drafting Legislation. Art and Technology of Rules for Regulation* (Bloomsbury Professional. 2014); Stephen Laws, 'Drawing the Line' in C. Stefanou and H. Xanthaki (eds) *Drafting Legislation. A Modern Approach* (Ashgate 2008) 19–35.

into legal material; that of a '*designer*' of workable (effective) rules and that of a '*communicator*' that effectively transmits the 'message' of the law to the targeted audiences.

Giving centre stage to the lawmaker and approaching lawmaking from their perspective is not only a novel endeavour but, most importantly, marks a change of perspective: the question – and the challenge – is no longer whether or how the law works in practice, but instead how it should be designed in order to work. What kind of guidance do lawmakers have in this complex task? How can they make the best possible decisions in this fluid, complex and uncertain environment?

2. ANY PRINCIPLES TO GUIDE LAWMAKING?

For years, there has been no comprehensive theory or analytical formula for lawmaking. Disciplines working with the law remained restricted within their disciplinary 'silos' with limited cross fertilisation of knowledge that could generate more holistic approaches. Legal theory and legal sociology focused on the operation of the law in the outside world and its applicability, observance, enforcement,[15] the relation between law in paper and law in action and legal behaviour in reaction to it.[16] Political scientists focused on processes, institutions and the emerging dynamics, while law and economics approached rules as structures of incentives[17] whose efficiency (maximisation of expected costs and losses) depends on the type of rules and enforcement.[18] Behavioural law and economics highlighted the role of cognitive biases in decision making[19] and further possibilities to model behaviours. The study of regulation touched upon both design and delivery but at the level of regulation. Factors relevant

---

[15] H. Kelsen, *Pure Theory of Law* (translated from the 2nd revised and enlarged German edition by Max Knight, The Lawbook Exchange 2009) 11; H.L.A. Hart, *The Concept of Law* (2nd edn Oxford University Press 1997) 103; H. Jones, *The Efficacy of Law* (1968 Rosenthal Lectures Northwestern University Press) 4, 5, 14–21, 76.

[16] A. Sarat, 'Legal Effectiveness and Social Studies of Law: on the unfortunate resistance of a research tradition', Legal Studies Forum (1985) IX 1 23–31 at 23; A. Allot, *The Limits of Law* (Butterworths 1980) viii, 28, 30.

[17] D. Friedman, *Law's Order* (Princeton University Press 2000) at 11.

[18] C. Veljanovski, 'Economic Approaches to Regulation' in R. Baldwin, M. Cave, M. Lodge (eds) *The Oxford Handbook of Regulation* (OUP 2010) 17–38 at 28.

[19] J. Wright and D. Ginsburg, 'Behavioral law and economics. Its origins, fatal flaws, and implications for liberty' in A. Hatzis and N. Mercuro (eds), *Law and Economics. Philosophical issues and fundamental questions* (Routledge 2017) 297–331, 300ff; Ch. Jolls, C.R. Sunstein, R. Thaler, 'A Behavioral Approach to Law and Economics' (1998) 50 Stan. L. Rev. 1471; C.R. Sunstein, 'Behavioral Analysis of Law', 64 U. Chi. L. Rev. (1997) at 1175.

to lawmaking, related to content, purpose, fit with the legal and social context, implementing processes, language, incentives and enforcement are highlighted with little, if any, systematisation. Further, all disciplines retain their ad hoc focus on legislation and offer little insight on how rules can be generated.

So, is lawmaking a completely liberal and anarchic process? On what bases are legislative decisions made? Is it circumstance and intuition? What kind of guidance does the legal system offer?

Constitutions reluctantly, if at all, and with very few exceptions,[20] express a clear theory to guide lawmaking, beyond the formal adoption of rules. Constitutional law on the other hand discusses principles of proper lawmaking[21] that encompass proportionality, legal certainty and legality or substantive principles (rule of law, social state, etc.), among several others. These principles are indubitably relevant, but how concretely can they proactively guide legislative decision making?

There are two main concerns with the usefulness of abstract substantive principles (like proportionality or legal certainty) from a lawmaking perspective. The first is that they retain the ad hoc focus on the law. The impact of a rule on legal certainty or legality is considered after a norm has been enacted. Yet, as discussed before, norm formulation is fundamentally different from norm interpretation. The thinking process behind delivering a judgment or assessing the constitutionality of a law is different to the proactive thinking required in lawmaking. Let's take for example the proportionality test, which is used to 'correct' the rationality of lawmaking by examining whether a measure serves a legitimate purpose, whether it is rationally connected to the purpose, is the least restrictive of all equally effective means, and is not disproportionate in the strict sense.[22] This ad hoc 'balancing exercise' looks at lawmaking in the light of the facts of a specific case. Can it also, and to what extent, proactively guide lawmakers to make more proportionate decisions? The proactive use of judicial tools (and thinking) in lawmaking is an issue that deserves closer study and attention in the future. However, at the moment, it does not offer a concrete solution.

---

[20] Art. 170 Constitution of Switzerland; art. 24 Constitution of France.
[21] P. Popelier, 'Legal Certainty and Principles of Proper Law Making' (2000) 2:3 European Journal of Law Reform at 321; U. Karpen, 'Introduction' in U. Karpen and H. Xanthaki, *Legislation in Europe. A Comprehensive Guide for Scholars and Practitioners* (Hart Publishing 2017) 1–16 at 12.
[22] N. Petersen, *Proportionality and Judicial Activism. Fundamental Rights Adjudication in Canada, Germany and South Africa* (CUP 2017) at 2.

Secondly, abstract standards like the ones mentioned above are elusive, relative and vague.[23] Legal certainty, that advocates for a coherent, simple and complete set of clear legal rules in terms of predictability and foreseeability can be deconstructed in a myriad of different dimensions.[24] Substantive standards like democratic legitimation, functionality, completeness and coherence, understandability and accessibility and legistic or procedural standards often lack concrete content, contradict each other and are challenging to operationalise.[25] And although their overall relevance in lawmaking is beyond doubt, the concrete proactive guidance they can offer is not evident. Without undermining their potential to assist lawmakers, these principles need further elaboration and operationalisation in order to reflect the concerns of the lawmaker in the early stages of lawmaking.

From another viewpoint, constitutional provisions enriched with judicial doctrines offer an emerging normative approach to lawmaking.[26] Constitutional (and other) courts are increasingly assuming a role as regulatory watchdogs[27] and attempt to place themselves in the prospective position of the lawmaker. Courts review the substantive and procedural rationality in lawmaking,[28] operate as an additional layer of scrutiny[29] and obligate lawmakers to anticipate judicial objections and incorporate judicial norms into legislative decision making. The German Federal Constitutional Court has 'constitutionalised' major tenets of rational lawmaking into judicial review standards, for example, the choice of options when legislating, the justifiable nature of data and prognoses, the duty to give reasons, consistency and coherence in the design of

---

[23] H. Schulze-Fielitz, 'Paths Towards Better Legislation, Detours and Dead Ends' in K. Messerschmidt and A.D. Oliver-Lalana (eds) *Rational Lawmaking under Review. Legisprudence According to the German Federal Constitutional Court* (Springer 2016) at 36.

[24] P. Popelier, 'Codification in a Civil Law Jurisdiction: A Northern European Perspective' (2017) 19:4 European Journal of Law Reform 253–61 at 259.

[25] Schulze-Fielitz (n 23) at 35–6.

[26] D. Oliver-Lalana and K. Messerschmidt, 'On the Legiprudential Turn in Constitutional Review: An Introduction' in K. Messerschmidt and D. Oliver-Lalana (eds) *Rational Lawmaking under Review Legiprudence According to the German Federal Constitutional Court* (Springer 2016) 1.

[27] P. Popelier and A. Mazmanyan, 'Constitutional Courts and Multilevel Governance in Europe. Editors' Introduction' in P. Popelier, A. Mazmanyan and W. Vandenbruwaene (eds), *The Role of Constitutional Courts in Multilevel Governance* (Intersentia 2013) 13.

[28] R. Ismer and K. Messerschmidt, 'Evidence-based judicial review of legislation: some introductory remarks' (2016) 4:2 The Theory and Practice of Legislation 91–106, 92.

[29] I. Bar-Siman-Tov, 'The role of courts in improving the legislative process' (2015) 3:3 The Theory and Practice of Legislation 295–313, 312.

laws,[30] to name only a few. Other Constitutional Courts are still reluctant or even unwilling[31] to acknowledge this relationship and role and involve themselves into the 'interna corporis' of legislative decision making.

Several questions remain with regard to evidence-based review of legislation,[32] including its nature as a duty or a prudential obligation, methodological uncertainties,[33] its borderline relation with judicial activism, and, most importantly, the democratic legitimacy of courts to deduct and control a lawmaking method from the constitution.[34] No matter how actively courts engage in this process in the future, their constitutional role will always be that of a guardian rather than a 'reformer' of the law.[35] Constraints on the role of courts as agents of law reform include their attachment to precedent, the limitations of the litigation process, the lack of legitimacy to change the law, the lack of resources to examine problems of law comprehensively, the fragmented nature of information they are presented with and the limited scope of interpretation powers.[36] This evolving discussion, although inconclusive, highlights however the need to make legislative decision making less obscure. There is little doubt that the dialogue between judges and lawmakers merits more attention with regard to the ways in which it can proactively contribute to lawmaking.

Legislative studies or legisprudence[37] is the only discipline that acknowledged the role of the lawmaker as an actor with an autonomous sphere of decision making.[38] In this context, the focus is on ways to improve quality, make legislators more 'intelligent' and receptive, the process more legitimate and the

---

[30] See the contributions in K. Messerschmidt and D. Oliver-Lalana (eds) *Rational Lawmaking under Review Legiprudence According to the German Federal Constitutional Court* (Springer 2016) passim.

[31] P. Popelier and Josephine De Jaegere (2016) 'Evidence-based judicial review of legislation in divided states: the Belgian case', 4:2 The Theory and Practice of Legislation 187–208; R. van Gestel and Jurgen de Poorter (2016) 'Putting evidence-based law making to the test: judicial review of legislative rationality', 4:2 The Theory and Practice of Legislation 155–85; P. García-Escudero Márquez, *Técnica legislativa y seguridad jurídica: ¿hacia el control constitucional de la calidad de las leyes?* (Cuadernos Civitas Thomson Reuters 2010).

[32] Ismer and Meßerschmidt (n 28) 91–106.

[33] A. Daniel Oliver-Lalana, 'On the (judicial) method to review the (legislative) method' (2016) 4:2 The Theory and Practice of Legislation 135–53.

[34] Oliver-Lalana and Messerschmidt (n 26) at 2.

[35] Peter Sales, 'Law Reform Challenges: The Judicial Perspective' (2018) 39:3 Statute Law Review 229–43.

[36] Ibid.

[37] Karpen, 'Introduction' (n 21) at 3; L. Mader, 'Evaluating the Effects: A Contribution to the Quality of Legislation' (2001) 22:2 Statute Law Review 119–31, 120.

[38] Wintgens (n 12) at 3.

end product simpler and easier to comply with.[39] Legislative studies approach lawmaking from two distinct perspectives: at theoretical level through the emphasis on rational or evidence-based lawmaking and at another level, through the emerging, and more applied, discipline of legislative drafting.

Rational lawmaking is concerned with procedurally and substantively rational laws[40] by emphasising two complementary elements: the well-grounded design of legislation through fact finding, analysis of means and alternatives, legislative balancing, smart goal setting and decision making (anticipation)[41] and the appraisal of the actual impacts of legislation to ensure responsiveness to changing circumstances (retrospection).[42] In its anticipatory aspect, law informed by reality – as opposed to intuition – is assumed to produce better laws.[43] In its retrospective aspects the need to monitor and correct legislation is the only way to ensure that laws perform as expected and do not produce harmful effects. Even though the link between legislation and logic is contested[44] and the direct connection between evidence-based lawmaking and evidence-based law is difficult to prove[45] rational lawmaking is more pragmatically oriented towards 'neutralising' the predominantly 'intuitive' effects of the political process with legistic quality.[46]

Legislative drafting on the other hand deals with the actual process and intricacies of laying down the law. It approaches it as a dynamic process driven by practical, 'applied' wisdom, guided by theoretical principles and complemented by evidence, analysis and creativity. The aim is to make conscious and evidence-based decisions in the process of drafting a specific legislative text.[47] It explores choices in structure, language, syntax, form and expression. Although overall complementary, these two strands have a large gap between the mostly theoretical (and abstract) focus of rational law-making on evidence

---

[39] Karpen, Introduction (n 21) at 3; Mader (n 37) at 120.
[40] Ismer and Meßerschmidt (n 28) 91–106.
[41] Oliver-Lalana (n 6) at 286; Oliver-Lalana (n 33) at 136.
[42] Oliver-Lalana (n 6) at 259.
[43] J. Rachlinski, 'Evidence-Based Law' (2011) 96 Cornell Law Review 901–23 at 910.
[44] J. Hage, 'The (Onto)logical Structure of Law: A Conceptual Toolkit for Legislators' in M. Araszkiewicz and K. Pleszka (eds) *Logic in the Theory and Practice of Lawmaking* (Legisprudence Library Vol. 2 Springer 2016) 3–49.
[45] Rachlinski (n 43) at 912.
[46] H. Schulze-Fielitz, 'Paths Towards Better Legislation, Detours and Dead-Ends. An Appraisal of Consultation and Independent Experts, Justifications for Legislation, Impact Assessments and Controls of Efficacy' in K. Messerschmidt and D. Oliver-Lalana (eds) *Rational Lawmaking under Review Legiprudence According to the German Federal Constitutional Court* (Springer 2016) 33–57, 34.
[47] Xanthaki, *Drafting Legislation* (n 14).

and anticipation and the mostly practical approach of legislative drafting with little in-between on the numerous substantive legislative decisions that need to be made. The 'operating arm' of evidence-based lawmaking, originating from public policy and law and economics, regulatory reform programmes have contributed structures, processes and instruments to make lawmaking evidence based.[48] The broad framework is in place (anticipation and retrospection), the practical aspects are in place, the tools are in place. But what about the vast space in-between?

However, another important contribution of legislative studies to lawmaking, and the most important from the perspective of this analysis is the introduction in the discussion of principles of economic or 'managerial' rationality,[49] such as efficacy, effectiveness and efficiency to strengthen and complement the rational aspects of lawmaking. These principles interact with substantive ones[50] and add neutrality, objectivity and a 'managerial' rationality to the decision making process. However, even this, the triad, is not free of conceptual and operational challenges when considered from the perspective of lawmaking.

3. EFFICACY, EFFECTIVENESS OR EFFICIENCY?

None of these principles are new. Yet different disciplines prioritise and rate them differently: legal theorists 'prefer' efficacy,[51] sociologists effectiveness,[52] law and economics scholars and scholars of regulation efficiency.[53]

A first problem is the conceptual confusion between these concepts and especially efficacy and effectiveness. Effectiveness was initially considered a condition of validity of a norm,[54] a link that was later rejected.[55] Efficacy (rather than effectiveness) was chosen to indicate the conformity of actual behaviours to the standards or models of behaviour prescribed by the law.[56]

---

[48] P. Popelier 'Management of Legislation' in U. Karpen and H. Xanthaki (eds) *Legislation in Europe* 53–72, 53, 56.

[49] U. Karpen, 'Efficacy, Effectiveness, Efficiency: from Judicial to Managerial Rationality' in K. Messerschmidt and A.D. Oliver-Lalana (eds) *Rational Lawmaking under Review. Legisprudence According to the German Federal Constitutional Court* (Springer 2016) at 304.

[50] Karpen, 'Introduction' (n 21) at 12.

[51] H.L.A. Hart *The Concept of Law* (2nd edn OUP 1997) at 103.

[52] Allot (n 16) at 11.

[53] R. Baldwin, M. Cave and M. Lodge (eds) *Understanding Regulation. Theory, Strategy and Practice* (2nd edn OUP 2012) at 25–31.

[54] Kelsen (n 15) at 11.

[55] Hart (n 15) at 103; J. Raz, *The Authority of Law* (2nd edn OUP 1980) at 87.

[56] Jones (n 15) at 4.

The relationship between these two principles remains particularly controversial even today. Mader linked efficacy to the achievement of the goals of legislative action and effectiveness to the correspondence between the attitudes of the target population and the normative model. Karpen and Xanthaki follow this definition.[57] Fluckiger claims the opposite: he considers measures efficacious if applied and followed, efficient if the cost is proportional and effective if they achieve their objectives.[58] On the other hand, legal sociologists associate effectiveness (rather than efficacy) with the goals of legal policy and the results produced by a norm.[59] Allot defines an effective law as one that can do what it was designed to do and effectiveness is the degree of achievement of its objectives.[60] Efficiency, a term with economic origin, has clearer – and less disputed – content as it looks at costs in relation to outcomes.

The confusion especially in the definition of efficacy and effectiveness and the relation between them emerges both because the terms are used interchangeably but also because they are associated with sub-concepts that remain equally vague. Do both concepts link the goals of legislation with its results and effects? Is compliance a criterion of efficacy, effectiveness or both? Do goals and results coincide with compliance and observance? What kind of goals? What kind of results? Are the two synonymous? If not, what is the difference between them?

This controversy can be resolved if we accept that the three principles are mutually complementary and reflect different functions of legislation. Efficacy is the concept that focuses on the broader functions of legislation and the extent to which it contributes to broader policy or societal goals (the question being: *has the law achieved its broader objectives on the legal system or the society, for instance, to promote equal opportunities?*). Effectiveness on the other hand focuses on results directly associated with the rule and its mechanics (the question being: *does the law work as planned? Does it achieve its direct goals?*) while efficiency looks at objectives in relation to costs (the question being: *does the law achieve maximum benefits with the least cost?*). Seen in this light, each principle reflects a different function of a legislative text: achievements in the legal or social arena (efficacy), application and observance of the law and achievement of direct results (effectiveness) and the cost-effectiveness of the solution (efficiency). From this perspective, the three principles operate

---

[57] L. Mader, 'Evaluating the Effects: A Contribution to the Quality of Legislation' (2001) 22:2 Statute Law Review, 119–31 at 126. See also Karpen (n 49) at 304–8.
[58] A. Flückiger, 'Effectiveness: a new Constitutional Principle' Legislação: cadernos de ciência de legislação (2009) 50, 183–98, at 190.
[59] Sarat (n 16) at 23.
[60] Allot (n 16) viii at 28, 30.

in synergy to allow a multidimensional understanding of legislative quality. Xanthaki's pyramid of virtues[61] reflects the different scope of each principle.

This 'solution' shows firstly, that out of the three values effectiveness is the most suitable to encapsulate the internal systemic consistency, coherence and purposive nature of legislation; and, that it is the primary expression of legislative quality that lawmakers can realistically pursue within their mandate.[62]

There are several reasons for this. On the one hand, efficacy (as the connection between the law and regulatory goals) is too broad as it goes beyond the scope of the law in the realm of policy; efficiency is guided by a narrower, 'coined' rationality looking at resources in relation to outcomes but downplaying important substantive elements which are not valued by cost-related concerns. Despite its advantages in terms of objectivity and inclusivity, the prevalence of cost-related arguments in legislative decision making can over-technify decisions, obscure broader impacts which are not easily quantified, cannot always weigh all effects (and especially social impacts) and, most importantly, can oversee public interest elements which go beyond the economic, but are nonetheless important in lawmaking.[63] Effectiveness on the other hand, as a concept tailored to the measure of the legislative text or rule, contributes a layer of rationality by setting clear benchmarks[64] and connects them to the mechanisms introduced, the results prescribed by the legislator and those achieved in real life. Further, it renunciates a thinking primarily oriented towards numbers to include consideration of social, psychological and political effects.[65] Effectiveness as the capacity of legislation to do the job it is meant to do, reflects the *mechanics* of legislation and its *systemic* capacity to work.

Hence, effectiveness combines many features which are particularly relevant in the anticipatory aspects of lawmaking; first, it is a *purposive* concept that reflects the orientation of legislation towards specific goals. Second, it is 'neutral' and 'empty' in terms of substantive content (it does not tell us what to do) but highlights the 'link' between ideals, situation and results.[66] Third,

---

[61] H. Xanthaki, 'On Transferability of Legislative Solutions' in C. Stefanou and H. Xanthaki (eds) *Drafting Legislation. A Modern Approach* (Ashgate 2008) 1–18 at 17; H. Xanthaki, *Drafting Legislation. Art and Technology of Rules for Regulation* (Bloomsbury Professional 2014) at 7.

[62] H. Xanthaki, 'Quality of Legislation: An achievable universal concept or a utopia pursuit?' in L. Mader, M. Tavres de Almeida (eds) *Quality of Legislation. Principles and Instruments* (Nomos 2011) at 80–81.

[63] W. Voermans, 'To Measure is to Know: The Quantification of Regulation' (2015) 3:1 The Theory and Practice of Legislation 91–111 at 110–111.

[64] Flückiger (n 58) at 187, 189.

[65] Karpen (n 49) at 306.

[66] Mauro Zamboni, 'Legislative Policy and Effectiveness: A (Small) Contribution from Legal Theory' (2018) 9:3 European Journal of Risk Regulation 416–30.

it is *systemic* to the extent that it reflects the *mechanics* of legislation and its capacity to function as a 'system'. Fourth, it is element inherent in every law and defined to an extent (but not exclusively) by the substantive choices made by the lawmakers. Fifth, effectiveness evolves together with the rule from a *prospective* to a *real* dimension (and hence captures both aspects of rational lawmaking): the former expresses the extent to which legislation is conducive to the desired results (can a law achieve the desired results?), which is pertinent to lawmakers, while the latter expresses the extent to which the attitudes, behaviours, results and outcomes correspond to those prescribed by the legislator (has a law achieved the desired results?). The answer to these questions and their interrelation is an indicator of the effectiveness of a rule.

However, even if we accept that effectiveness best reflects the tangible aspects of the quality of a rule that falls within the making scope of the lawmaker, this solves neither the question of how it can be operationalised nor how it can serve as guidance to lawmaking. Does effectiveness have concrete content? Can lawmakers consciously work towards effectiveness? How? Which legislative choices promote effectiveness and which ones do not? Can effectiveness move from an abstract and theoretical principle into one that guides legislative decision making?

4. THE FUNDAMENTAL ELEMENTS OF EFFECTIVENESS

Taking a closer look at effectiveness, existing scholarship and practice fail to offer a convincing answer to the question what makes a law effective. Rather, they highlight a number of elements. Philosophers acknowledge the link of effectiveness to the communication of the legislative 'message', supportive action in courts and society, enforcement and motivating compliance in the subjects of the law.[67] Legal sociologists acknowledge vaguely its links to the content of the law, the character of norms, the clarity of purpose, the interaction and fit of the law with other components of the legal system and the social context, implementing norms, institutions and processes, language, the audiences, deterrents and enforcement mechanisms.[68] Overall, emphasis is placed on the deterring function of sanctions, compliance and enforcement but goes in little depth on all other issues. So is effectiveness about the content, the process or the results?

---

[67] Jones (n 15) at 5, 14–21, 76.
[68] Allot (n 16) viii at 13.

If legislation is a to-and-fro between form and substance[69] and the lawmaker has to transform ideals, ideas and assumptions into effective provisions using concepts, the law, language, structure and form, effectiveness has to comprise four fundamental elements that are present in every law: objectives, the 'solution' expressed in the content of the law, results and context (overarching structure or superstructure).[70] Each element plays a distinct role: purpose sets the benchmark for *what* legislation aims to achieve; the substantive content determines *how* the law will achieve the desired results and how this will be communicated to its subjects. The results of legislation indicate *what has been achieved* while context (overarching structure of legislation) determines *how the law integrates the legal system and interacts with it*.

Seen as a synthesis of these elements, the content of effectiveness is no longer abstract. On the contrary, it becomes specific, concrete, tailored to specific elements present in every legislative text, and, most importantly tangible because the four elements fall within the decision making sphere of the lawmaker. This is a good starting point for operationalising effectiveness as a concept to guide lawmaking. But let us take a closer look at each element and try to identify the lawmaking challenges associated with them.

4.1. Purpose of legislation: the benchmark of effectiveness

Purpose dominates the life-cycle of legislation: when a rule is conceptualised and drafted, purpose is the 'link' between the specific problems addressed, the broader policies of the government and the means chosen to address them; when a law is interpreted, purpose helps diagnose the intention of the legislator to interpret vague provisions. Further, purpose is the obvious starting point in the effort to connect legislation with its results and determine what a law has achieved. Objective-setting is the obvious starting point of every rational decision-making process. However, when it comes to lawmaking, objectives remain notoriously vague.

The purpose of a law indicates *what* the law aims to achieve. Obvious as this may sound, the closer one looks at legislative practice the less it appears to mean. Despite its supposedly leading role when designing, drafting and implementing legislation, the purpose of legislation is difficult to trace, and

---

[69] Zumbansen (n 3) at 11.
[70] M. Mousmouti, 'Operationalising Quality of Legislation through the Effectiveness Test' (2012), 6:2 Legisprudence 201; M. Mousmouti, 'Effectiveness as an Aspect of Quality of EU Legislation: Is it Feasible?' (2014) 2:3 The Theory and Practice of Legislation 309–27; Maria Mousmouti, 'Making Legislative Effectiveness an Operational Concept: Unfolding the Effectiveness Test as a Conceptual Tool for Lawmaking' (2018) 9:3 European Journal of Risk Regulation 445–64.

understand. Objectives are often conflated with the justification of legislation; their formulations leave much to be desired and, last but not least, they often do not give clear messages. How can lawmakers use purpose to design legislation which is clearer on what it aims to achieve? How can they formulate clear and meaningful expressions of purpose that set a clear and substantive benchmark for what the law aims to achieve? These issues will be explored in Chapter 2.

4.2. Content of legislation: the 'heart' of effectiveness

The second fundamental element of effectiveness is the content of legislation. Laws often come as a solution to a problem. The 'mechanics' of the solution involve important decisions on the choice of rules and legislative techniques to be used, incentives for the target audiences to comply, enforcement or administration mechanisms and choices in communicating the messages of the law using language, structure, form etc. Seen from the perspective of effectiveness, the content of the law determines *how* it will achieve its results.

The choice of rules determines how behaviours will be directed towards the desired goals, what rights are conferred or obligations are imposed, how the rules will be enforced and the consequences or motives attached to them. Finally, the way in which the 'message' of the law is stated, determines how the targeted audiences will be reached. These choices obviously have a significant impact on the capacity of legislation to achieve results. If the selected rules (or combination of rules) are inappropriate to address the problem or to the audience or do not serve the objective of the law, their design is ineffective; if enforcement mechanisms are inappropriate or implementation is inadequate, enforcement is ineffective; if the subjects of the law do not know how to comply or encounter difficulties in complying or interpreting rules, drafting is ineffective.

From the perspective of the lawmaker, the formulation of the content of rules poses three important challenges: what kind of rules for what kind of problem? How to anticipate compliance? What kind of enforcement? and how to best communicate? These topics, common in the discussion around legislation, are so far treated as implementation problems. However, seen from the perspective of lawmakers they raise questions of distinct texture and content. How can the lawmaker choose rules the subjects are more likely to comply with? How can they anticipate which legislative techniques are more likely to bring the expected results? And what criteria can they use apart from intuition? How can the most appropriate enforcement styles and mechanisms be selected? Not all laws are the same, not all audiences are the same. What can work best in each case? How can language, as the main communications medium of the message of the law, be used to transmit clear signals? Last but not least, what factors might limit the capacity of the lawmaker to make objective decisions? These issues will be explored in Chapter 3.

4.3. Overarching structure or superstructure: the context of effectiveness

Every new piece of legislation, following its enactment, becomes part of the legal system. Every legal system is saturated with legal messages with obvious or hidden interactions between them. Every new Act comes with a new message (or messages) that will compete with those transmitted by other laws for the attention of the end-recipients.[71] The way in which the different messages coexist has an impact on the effectiveness of the message itself, on the capacity of the end-recipient to locate it and understand it and on the capacity of the implementer and the judge to apply and interpret it.

From the perspective of the end-user, the challenge is firstly to identify relevant messages within a complex legal system (identify does not mean understand, it means locate) and secondly, to differentiate a message from competing ones and figure out their relationship. Does the new message change, override, alter or leave pre-existing or competing messages unaffected? How does it affect what we already know? From the perspective of the lawmaker, these considerations translate into three lawmaking challenges: firstly, how to ensure that the message is accessible to the end-recipient within the legal system? secondly, how to ensure that the message is coherent with other messages? and thirdly, how to ensure that the message is identifiable and measurable? These questions will be considered in Chapter 4.

4.4. Results of legislation: the 'measure' of effectiveness

A law is enacted in anticipation of specific results. The relation between the law as a vision and the law in reality is not always linear. The need to learn about the results of legislation is a requirement of democratic governance, a way to prevent adverse effects on fundamental rights and to consistently appraise the responsiveness of the law to the regulated problems and phenomena.[72] However, the legal discipline is not particularly at ease with measurable concepts like results, outcomes or effects. Despite this, it is a fact that every law produces specific results and effects, wanted or unwanted.

---

[71] Allot (n 16) 36.
[72] A. Flückiger, 'L'obligation jurisprudentielle d'évaluation législative: une application du principe de précaution aux droits fondamentaux' in A. Auer, A. Flückiger and M. Hottelier, *Les droits de l'homme et la constitution: études en l'honneur du Professeur Giorgio Malinverni* (Schulthess 2007) at 170.

Information on the results of legislation shows *what has been achieved*. It is critical for effectiveness, firstly because it enables learning about the real-life results and effects of legislation and secondly because it connects the different phases of the life-cycle of legislation and allows the juxtaposition of initial purposes and real-life results. Without information on results, effectiveness cannot be appraised, the self-correcting process cannot be initiated, errors cannot be identified and addressed. This information is an important requirement for effectiveness. From a lawmaking perspective, challenges pertain to the kind of results expected; the design of meaningful monitoring, review and evaluation mechanisms. What can the lawmaker do in anticipation of the real-life results of legislation? These questions will be examined in Chapter 5.

4.5. Interaction between the elements

Needless to say, the four elements are closely interrelated and interact to shape the unique 'working' of every law in a specific context, space and time. How coherent, aligned and mutually reinforcing are these elements? What is their role in making the law effective or ineffective? And how can these be proactively anticipated?

5. CONCLUSION: THE LAWMAKER AS THE 'DESIGNER' OF EFFECTIVE LAWS AND THE EFFECTIVENESS TEST AS A THINKING PROCESS

Lawmaking is a challenging yet fascinating exercise. Effective lawmaking presents the challenge of having to anticipate – to the extent possible and in as much detail as possible – that the choices and solutions considered have the capacity to work. In this effort, effectiveness provides a framework for legislative decisions – and a clear decision-making criterion. The hypothesis is that, following a meticulous thinking process that involves analysis, design and drafting, legislative effectiveness becomes manageable and feasible.

In this process the effectiveness test is a practical exercise that operationalises the elements of effectiveness through a loose set of questions that trigger reflective thinking. The next chapters will take a closer look at each element, their theoretical and practical dimensions, the challenges they raise from a lawmaking perspective, in the effort to identify solutions that promote effective lawmaking. Additionally, the self-correcting process of scientific inquiry and legislative practice are welcome to negate, refine, particularise, test and improve them.

2. Legislation and its purpose

Cessante ratione, cessat ipsa lex[1]

1. PURPOSE IN THE LIFE CYCLE OF LEGISLATION

Purpose dominates the life cycle of legislation: it guides the lawmaking process, serves as a point of reference for implementation and interpretation and sets the benchmark for the legitimacy, rationality, proportionality and effectiveness of the law. Objective setting is the obvious starting point of every rational decision making process. However, when it comes to lawmaking, objectives are notoriously vague, 'slippery'[2] and 'amorphous'.[3] This 'indeterminacy of aim' is, according to Fuller, the reason behind many 'ills and disorders' of a legal system. He claims that 'if each separate law carried its own distinct purpose, plainly stated, these difficulties would disappear' as judges, enforcement agencies and the public would be in a better position to interpret, enforce or understand what is going on.[4] Assuming this is true, what are the reasons behind the mysterious nature of aim in legislation? And how can purpose play a clearer role in the lifecycle of the law?

The importance of purpose in the life cycle of legislation is evident. In lawmaking, purpose is the main compass for shaping the content of the law. It is the link between the problems addressed, the broader policies, the means chosen to serve them and the state to be achieved. During implementation, when law in paper is 'challenged' by reality, purpose is an obvious recourse for the implementer who seeks guidance on the meaning of an unclear or ambiguous provision. Judges interpret statutes based on enacted and unenacted

---

[1] 'When the reason of the law ceases, so does the law itself' is a common law maxim cited in W. Twining and David Miers, *How to Do Things with Rules* (5th edn CUP 2010) 114.

[2] D. Greenberg (ed) *Craies on Legislation. A Practitioners' Guide to the Nature, Process, Effect and Interpretation of Legislation* (9th edn, Sweet & Maxwell 2008) 607, 608.

[3] M. Radin, 'Statutory Interpretation' [1929–1930] 43 Harvard Law Review 863, 872.

[4] L. Fuller, *Anatomy of the Law* (Penguin 1968) 40–41.

intentions and extraneous sources acquire new importance in lack of explicit purposes. Overall, the move towards purposive interpretation has reignited the interest in the purpose of statutes especially when words do not provide a clear solution or are contradictory to enacted purpose. This debate essentially highlights firstly, the difficulties involved in interpretation when no specific purpose is stated in the text and secondly, the challenges that emerge when purpose needs to be deducted or when it is stated in a contradictory manner. In the process of judicial review, purpose is sought when examining the proportionality or constitutionality of legislative measures[5] or when trying to establish the rationality of lawmaking. Last but not least, during post legislative scrutiny or evaluation, purpose is the starting point of any appraisal of the performance of the law.

Despite its importance, purpose obstinately remains an ambiguous concept with an unclear function, location and highly volatile formulation. This chapter approaches the challenges associated with the content, formulation, placement and function of purpose statements in legislation and aspires to explore solutions that will make it a more tangible concept in the life cycle of the law.

2. CHALLENGES FOR LAWMAKERS

The main function of purpose is communication: it explicitly states and communicates the purpose of an Act to the user, the implementer and the interpreter. Three main challenges come in the way of this important function: its vague nature, formulation and location.

2.1. The unclear boundaries between reasons, justification and goals

A former judge of the Federal German Constitutional Court famously stated that 'all the legislature owes to the public is legislation', not the reasons why this is necessary. This rather introvertive view of lawmaking is nowadays openly challenged by the emphasis placed on the justification of the rationality, legitimacy, efficiency, transparency, participation and public interest basis of legislation.[6] Obligations to justify legislation are consolidated in

---

[5] N. Petersen, *Proportionality and Judicial Activism. Fundamental Rights Adjudication in Canada, Germany and South Africa* (CUP 2017) at 2.

[6] P. García-Escudero Márquez, *Manual de Técnica Legislativa* (Thomson Reuters 2011) at 101.

Constitutions,[7] constitutional laws,[8] Rules of Procedure,[9] acknowledged as general principles of law,[10] required in legislative practice.[11] Constitutional Courts have also addressed them.[12] Further, in most jurisdictions nowadays, bills are accompanied by reports that explain and justify legislation. Justification is important for the legitimacy and transparency of the law, no doubt about that. However, it is essentially different to objective setting. The confusion between the two appears to be one of the reasons behind the 'indeterminacy' of aim that Fuller highlighted.

Problem definition and goal identification are also distinct matters. A problem is broader and might highlight a number of reasons why legislation is necessary. A legislative goal on the other hand might target all or only part of the problem (as is often the case with legislation) and essentially indicates what is the state to be achieved with regard to it. In other words, justifying the need to legislate and providing convincing arguments for the solutions chosen is a distinct exercise to determining what the law intends to achieve in the legal and social arena. Although both play an important role in lawmaking, each has a different function. The former responds to the test of necessity (problem/s addressed, link to public interest, legitimacy, political priorities), the second responds to the weighing and balancing of available options (proportionality, cost, rationality), while the latter responds to the need to set out in precise terms the state to be achieved or desired (objective setting). If these merge into

---

[7] Article 88 of the Spanish Constitution; Article 74 of the Greek Constitution; Article 296 of TFEU.

[8] In France, Article 7, Loi organique n° 2009-403 du 15 avril 2009 relative à l'application des articles 34-1, 39 et 44 de la Constitution; see also Premier Ministre, Secrétariat général du Gouvernement, Conseil D'État, Guide de légistique 3e édition mise à jour 2017 (La Documentation française 2017) Section 3.1.1. available at: https://www.legifrance.gouv.fr/Droit-francais/Guide-de-legistique2 (last accessed 8/12/2018).

[9] Par. 43 of the Joint Rules of Procedure of the Federal Ministries (GGO) 2011 available at: https://bscw.bund.de/pub/bscw.cgi/d52920962/120119%20GGO_neu_engl.pdf?nonce=03349cf7faa309dce38778bbd9215cf97cb14c6e (last accessed 8/12/2018).

[10] Joined cases 43/59, 45/59 and 48/59 Von Lachmueller and others v Commission 1960 ECR 989 ff.

[11] See for example, Queensland Government, Department of the Premier and Cabinet, Guidelines for the preparation of explanatory notes https://www.premiers.qld.gov.au/publications/categories/policies-and-codes/handbooks/legislation-handbook/drafting-process/assets/guidelines-preparation-of-explanatory-notes.pdf (last accessed 8/12/2018); Office fédéral de la justice, Guide de législation Modules 'loi', 'ordonnance' et 'initiative parlementaire' 2014 at 36, available at: https://www.bj.admin.ch/dam/data/bj/staat/legistik/hauptinstrumente/module-f.pdf (last accessed 8/12/2018).

[12] C. Waldhoff, 'On Constitutional Duties to Give Reasons for Legislative Acts' in K. Messerschmidt and A.D. Oliver-Lalana (eds) *Rational Lawmaking under Review* (Springer 2016) 129–51 at 132–3.

a single function, reasons and goals get conflated with justifications, are inundated with details and objectives are beclouded. This thorny issue has received little attention in lawmaking literature yet, I believe that much of the confusion around the objectives of legislation derives from the overlap between these three concepts.

The lesson from legislative practice is that while justification is important for legislating, the reasons why the chosen solution is appropriate, and its specific objectives need to be distinctly identified. This is essential not only in order to clear the mind of the lawmaker but also in order to provide clear directions to the implementer and the interpreter. Instrumentality and goals should not be confused.

2.2. What objectives?

Intentions, aims, purposes, goals, objectives, intended consequences, (whether direct, indirect or ulterior and non-consequential), and effects refer to a wide range of situations that need to be differentiated[13] in order to determine their role and usefulness in lawmaking.

A fundamental distinction is between (intended) *goals* and (real) *effects* of legislation. Goals (or objectives) refer to intended conditions or consequences of a law, while effects refer to actual consequences, including intended and unintended ones.[14] In other words, goals express aspirations while effects refer to results actually produced. At the level of aspirations, different types of goals can be distinguished: specific goals or objectives that indicate legal changes directly aimed by legislation. These produce outputs or direct results. For example, the increase in the number of women sitting on company boards is a direct objective of legislation imposing quotas for their representation in corporate decision making bodies. The direct result of this measure will indicate the extent to which this has actually been achieved. Broader objectives on the other hand point toward changes in the surrounding legal and social environment. They lead to outcomes and effects. To revert to the previous example, quotas aim towards the broader objective of a more gender balanced composition of decision making bodies in the corporate sector. Their outcome will be the extent to which quotas have actually achieved this. One intended goal might produce multiple outcomes and vice versa.

---

[13] W. Twining and David Miers, *How to Do Things with Rules* (5th edn CUP 2010) 153.

[14] Mauro Zamboni, 'Goals and Measures of Legislation: Evaluation' in U. Karpen and H. Xanthaki, *Legislation in Europe. A Comprehensive Guide for Scholars and Practitioners* (Hart Publishing 2017) at 98–9.

```
┌─────────────────┐   ┌──────────────┐   ┌──────────┐
│ Specific objectives │ │ Direct results │ │ Outputs │
└─────────────────┘   └──────────────┘   └──────────┘

┌─────────────────┐   ┌──────────────┐   ┌──────────┐
│ Broader objectives │ │   Outcomes   │ │  Impact  │
└─────────────────┘   └──────────────┘   └──────────┘
```

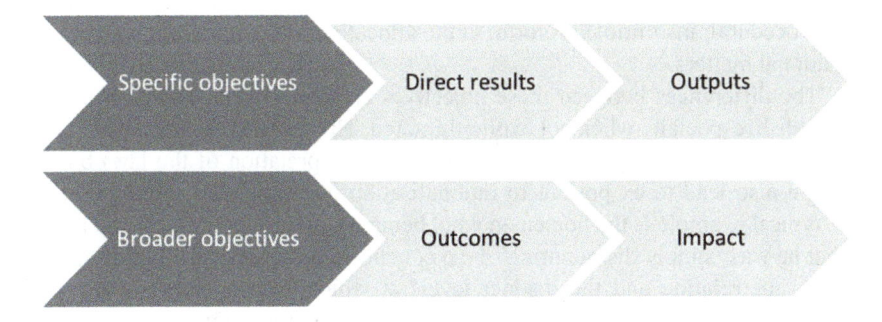

Figure 2.1   Interrelation between objectives and results

Obviously, law can aim towards multiple objectives that differ in scope, nature and texture: they can be *tactical* or *strategic*, to be achieved in a narrow period of time inside and outside the legal arena or over time. For example, the objective to reduce the gender pay gap is a tactical goal that serves the strategic objective of promoting gender equality in employment. Patent goals are formally endorsed by the legislator while hidden goals are informally embraced. Last but not least, micro-, meso and macro goals intend to influence a specific legal arena, an entire legal area or society at large.[15] Differentiating these terms and their content is important in order to place the effort invested in lawmaking at the right level.

A law imposing a 30% quota for positions held by women on boards serves at the same time a number of objectives: the (direct) objective to increase the number of women on boards and several outcomes: to increase the representation of women in decision making bodies in the corporate sector, to ensure a gender balanced composition of decision making bodies in the corporate sector (meso) and to promote gender equality (strategic). These objectives might produce a number of effects: positive ones, for example to increase beyond 30% the number of women sitting on boards, or unintended ones, for example to lower the glass ceiling in gender pay. It might also have negative effects, for example discouraging women or men to take parental leave during their career. The One Child Policy in China that imposed tax obligations on couples having more than one child led to an unintended increase in the level of abortions, as couples who wanted a male child resorted to this solution.

---

[15] Ibid at 97.

To conclude, several objectives often coexist to reflect different functions of legislation as an instrument of policy and social engineering aimed at changing attitudes and behaviours in the medium and long term, as an instrument aimed at procedural, institutional reform, in the allocation of resources and in organisational matters.

The differences between these objectives are often subtle and difficult to establish, especially when not explicitly stated. This leads to the need to deduct them (when necessary for the application or interpretation of the law) but it might also lead to ex post facto rationalisation of unintended consequences. A typical example is the horseman who, being thrown from his steed, declared that he was 'simply dismounting'.[16] To conclude, the objectives of legislation, their interrelation and the distinct levels at which they operate need to be transparent in order to clear the mind of the lawmaker when making decisions and secondarily for serving the goal of assisting the interpreter and the implementer later on.

2.3. The vague language of legislative objectives

A second problem is that objectives, even when stated, are vague. Objectives often linger in the no mans' land between policy and the law or are too narrow. Transforming political material into legal material is the cornerstone of lawmaking[17] and the usefulness of legislative objectives is to make this interrelation evident. Their most important function is to state and express the concrete compromise achieved. This is the only way in which legislative objectives can reduce 'ambiguity' and serve effective lawmaking.

Although few would disagree that every law has a purpose, a closer look at the way this is expressed in practice makes the whole endeavour confusing, to say the least. The hybrid nature of purpose, as a concept with political and legal 'genes' that resonates different types and levels of ambitions, is confirmed by legislative practice, that offers a very diverse picture. The examples below are only meant to highlight different types of challenges associated with different formulations.

A first type of objectives includes broad policy-inspired ones. The Swiss Federal Law (Section 1, Article 1) on the elimination of inequalities affecting people with disabilities reads:

---

[16] R.K. Merton, 'The Unanticipated Consequences of Purposive Social Action' (1936) 1:6 American Sociological Review at 897.

[17] M. Zamboni, *The Policy of Law. A Legal Theoretical Framework* (Hart Publishing 2007) 91.

1 La présente loi a pour but de **prévenir, de réduire ou d'éliminer les inégalités** qui frappent les personnes handicapées. (...to prevent, reduce or eliminate inequalities... – emphasis added)
2 Elle crée des conditions propres à faciliter aux personnes handicapées la participation à la vie de la société, en les aidant notamment à être autonomes dans l'établissement de contacts sociaux, dans l'accomplissement d'une formation ou d'une formation continue et dans l'exercice d'une activité professionnelle.

The Employment Equity Act of Canada reads:

2 *The purpose of this Act is to **achieve equality in the workplace** so that no person shall be denied employment opportunities or benefits for reasons unrelated to ability and, in the fulfilment of that goal, **to correct the conditions of disadvantage** in employment experienced by women, Aboriginal peoples, persons with disabilities and members of visible minorities by giving effect to the principle that employment equity means more than treating persons in the same way but also requires special measures and the accommodation of differences (emphasis added)*

The German General Act on Equal Treatment of 14 August 2006 reads:

*The purpose of this Act is **to prevent or to stop discrimination** on the grounds of race or ethnic origin, gender, religion or belief, disability, age or sexual orientation (emphasis added).*

The Swedish Discrimination Act (2008:567) reads:

*The purpose of this Act is **to combat discrimination** and in other ways promote equal rights and opportunities regardless of sex, transgender identity or expression, ethnicity, religion or other belief, disability, sexual orientation or age (emphasis added).*

These statements might be music to the ear of the inexperienced reader, yet they raise a number of questions to the experienced jurist. They are declaratory, express political ambitions and fall in the realm of policy rather than the law. Can a law 'eliminate' inequalities or 'achieve' equality in the workspace? Effective though it may be, no law on its own can solve, not to mention eliminate, complex and multidimensional social phenomena or problems. These statements have a symbolic and educative function but are too ambitious and broad to be achieved by law alone and set a meaningful benchmark for what a law aims at.

On the exact opposite side of the spectrum one can find objectives with a pragmatic, factual, instrumental rationale: '*to make provision for...*', '*to amend the law...*', '*to transpose in the national legal order Directive...*' or '*to reform and harmonise* equality law'. They often describe the processes initiated by the law: '*to render unlawful* certain kinds of discrimination' or '*to prohibit victimisation in certain circumstances*'... Article 1 of Greek Law 3769/09 reads:

> *The purpose of this law is **to lay down a framework for combating discrimination** based on sex in access to and supply of goods and services, as provided for in the provisions of Directive 2004/113/EC of the Council of 13 December 2004 (emphasis added).*

Accurate as these statements might be, they are descriptive and provide limited information with regard to the substantive objectives of the specific law beyond the obvious: introducing new rules or changing existing ones. The information is descriptive or procedural and not of much use when it comes to the actual content of the law and the state desired. Does it refer to substantive equality? Equality of opportunity or formal equality? Contrary to the previous ones, these statements provide a very narrow benchmark for the law.

A third type includes combinations of the previous formulations. The combination of narrow and broader objectives indicates the legal means used as well as the overall objectives to which they contribute. When narrower statements are linked to (policy) objectives they provide a more meaningful benchmark both for the interpretation and the effectiveness of the law. For example

> *Article 1 Purpose*
> *The purpose of this law is to lay down a general framework for combating discrimination on the grounds of .... with a view to putting into effect the principle of equal treatment.*

Another type of objective, more rarely encountered, includes concrete targets or thresholds to be achieved within a specified period of time. These legislated benchmarks, although often policy related, have the advantage of being measurable and timebound, operationalise objectives and can be useful both to end users and to those involved in appraising or reviewing legislation.[18] They are encountered in legislation on climate change, energy, poverty, etc.[19] but also in other areas of law. For example, the objectives associated to the French law 2006-340 (equal pay) included among other issues:

> *La loi se donne pour objectif, après établissement d'un diagnostic partagé dans les branches et les entreprises, d'arriver par le dialogue social tant dans les branches*

---

[18] A. Lee and J. Leslie, 'Judicial Review of Target-Setting Legislation' (2010) 15:3 Judicial Review 236–41 at 241.

[19] J. Rutter and W. Knighton, 'Legislated Policy Targets' (Institute for Government 2012) at 1.

que dans les entreprises, à la suppression en cinq ans de l'écart constaté. .... ('to reduce in five years the identified gaps in gender pay').

Generalisations are difficult, if not impossible, and the type of objectives and their formulation differs not only within legal systems but also within different laws. However, these examples highlight a number of issues: first, the multiple level playing fields of legislation, the distinct types of objectives that might be pursued and their distinct functions as propaganda, information, pedagogic, instrumental or as meaningful benchmarks for legislation. Can a law 'eliminate' inequalities or 'achieve' equality in the workspace? Is it the purpose of the law just to amend legislation or is this done in the light of a broader outcome? Moreover, to what extent is this information useful to interpreters and appraisers?

The degree of abstraction or precision of legislative objectives affects the life of the law but also the work of the lawmaker, the interpreter and the implementer. Ambiguous and vague purposes leave room for manipulation and interpretation. Clearly formulated and specific objectives provide clear guidance and direction. For purpose to be a clear and objective concept that sets a meaningful benchmark for what the law aims to achieve, it is necessary to connect the specific purpose pursued by the law to the broader policy objective. This is a good way of ensuring that purpose fulfils its function as a link between policy and legislation.

2.4. The location of legislative objectives

A third problem is that legislative objectives are not always easy to locate. Unless explicitly stated in the legislative text, information around it can be found in extraneous material or in several places at the same time raising issues of contradictions and vagueness.

Purpose or objective clauses are the most evident way of expressing purpose in the text of the law. Their function is to state the purpose of an Act, provide an aim to interpretation and state a criterion for the exercise of discretion.[20] Supporters highlight their usefulness in terms of clarity, aiding the understanding of legislative intention and resolving doubts and ambiguities, setting the scene[21] of a statute and aiding the transition from the general to the particular,

---

[20] A. Seidman, R. Seidman and N. Abeyesekere, *Legislative Drafting for Democratic Social Change. A Manual for Drafters* (Kluwer 2001) at 311.

[21] A. Samuels, 'Statement of Purpose and Principle in British Statutes' (1998) 19:1 Statute Law Review, 63–4.

both for the user and the interpreter.[22] They facilitate the communication of substantive provisions, assist comprehension and illuminate the principles pursued.[23] They are relevant to multiple audiences: they 'clear the mind of the legislator, provide guidance to the Executive, explain the legislation to the public, and assist the courts when in doubt about the application of some specific provision'.[24] In other words, they contribute to the communication, the understanding and the interpretation of an Act.

Critics on the other hand focus on the generality of such clauses and the confusion they can cause. Objectives clauses have no normative density (they are not rules per se) and add little to the distinction between the possible from the desirable, the accessory from the essential, the licit from the illicit. Instead, they are declarations or proclamations with no legal impact, of little practical value and do not serve the economy of the legislative text. From a practical viewpoint, they can be extensive, complex and difficult to summarise in a single statement.[25] However, even opponents do not fully negate the usefulness of purpose provisions. Instead, they highlight the need for carefully formulated, specific and clear purpose provisions.[26] A middle ground approach is that these should be used with great caution. Legislative practice varies. Purpose provisions are consistently used in EU legislation and countries including Switzerland[27] or Spain, are avoided in France[28] and several other European countries, 'discouraged' in the United States[29] or left at the discretion of drafters, for example in Canada.

---

[22] R. Dickerson, 'Statutory Interpretation in America: Dipping into Legislative History – II' [1984] Statute Law Review 141, 153.

[23] Garth C. Thornton, *Legislative Drafting* (4th edn, Tottel 1996) at 154.

[24] William Dale, 'Principles, Purposes, and Rules' (1988) 14 Statute Law Review 15 at 24.

[25] Thornton (n 23) at 155; Dale (n 24) at 15; I.M.L. Turnbull, 'Problems of Legislative Drafting' (1986) 67 Statute Law Review 72; Daniel Greenberg, *Laying down the Law* (Sweet & Maxwell 2011) at 259.

[26] Thornton (n 23) at 155.

[27] See for example Loi fédérale sur l'égalité entre femmes et homes (Loi sur l'égalité, LEg) du 24 mars 1995 (Etat le 1er janvier 2017); Loi fédérale sur l'élimination des inégalités frappant les personnes handicapées (Loi sur l'égalité pour les handicapées, LHand) du 13 décembre 2002 (Etat le 1er janvier 2017).

[28] J-L. Bergel, 'Les formulations d'objectifs dans les textes législatifs. Essai de synthèse', Cahiers de méthodologie juridique n° 4, RRJ 1989-4, p. 975–83.

[29] U.S. House of Representatives, House Office of the Legislative Counsel, *HOLC Guide to Legislative Drafting*, available at: http://legcounsel.house.gov/HOLC/Drafting_Legislation/Drafting_Guide.html (last accessed 8/12/2018).

Long titles, used in common law jurisdictions, list the elements of reform introduced by an Act[30] and inevitably communicate information related to the purpose of the law. They are part of the Act and can be used for interpretation[31] but are often descriptive rather than substantive. The long title of the Sex Discrimination Act 1975 (UK) read:

An Act to render unlawful certain kinds of sex discrimination and discrimination on the ground of marriage, and establish a Commission with the function of working towards the elimination of such discrimination and promoting equality of opportunity between men and women generally; and for related purposes.

Preambles introduce the context of an Act, provide information on the legal basis, explain its object or reasons.[32] They are consistently used in countries like Spain, Switzerland, South Africa but are out of use in others. In European legislation, recitals are a 'genuine statement of reasons'[33] frequently referred to by the European Court of Justice to establish the purpose of provisions.[34] However, overall they are considered mystifying.[35] Preambles differ significantly in length, content and function. In Spain, they state the motives behind an Act, the principles inspiring it, its finality and the main novelties.[36] In Switzerland, they only indicate the authority issuing an Act, the constitutional or legal basis and the message of the Federal Court.[37] In Canada, the choice

---

[30] Helen Xanthaki, *Thornton's Legislative Drafting* (5th edn, Bloomsbury Professional 2013) at 229, 253.
[31] Ibid at 229.
[32] Daniel Greenberg (ed), *Craies on Legislation. A Practitioners' Guide to the Nature, Process, Effect and Interpretation of Legislation* (9th edn, Sweet & Maxwell 2008) at 749.
[33] European Commission, *Legislative Drafting. A Commission Manual*, available at: http://ec.europa.eu/smart-regulation/better_regulation/documents/legis_draft_comm_en.pdf at 16 (last accessed 8/12/2018).
[34] L. Humphreys, C. Santos, L. di Caro, G. Boella, L. van der Torre and L. Robaldo, 'Mapping Recitals to Normative Provisions in EU Legislation to Assist Legal Interpretation' in A. Rotolo (ed) *Legal Knowledge and Information Systems* (ebook, series Frontiers in Artificial Intelligence and Applications IOS Press), Volume 279, 2015. See in particular, CJEU judgment dated 24 November 2005, in Case C-136/04, Deutsches Milch-Kontor GmbH and in the CJEU judgment dated 2 April 2009, in case C-134/08, Hauptzollamt Bremen.
[35] T. Klimas and J. Vaitiukait, 'The Law of Recitals in European Community Legislation' (2008) 15:1 ILSA Journal of International & Comparative Law 65–93 at 62.
[36] P. García-Escudero Márquez, *Manual de Técnica Legislativa* (Thomson Reuters 2011) at 101.
[37] Office fédéral de la justice, *Guide de législation. Guide pour l'élaboration de la législation fédérale* (2007) available at : https://www.bj.admin.ch/dam/data/bj/staat/legistik/hauptinstrumente/gleitf-f.pdf point 885, at 390 (last accessed 8/12/2018).

of whether to include a preamble is left open. Overall, although preambles can provide important background information for understanding of a Bill or explain matters, their contribution depends on the information they provide. If it is only a compilation of political declarations of good intentions their practical value is limited and they can prove confusing in the effort to decipher the purpose of the law (and not the reasons behind it).

Extraneous or preparatory material is another source of information on the purpose of legislation whose importance largely depends on whether and where information on legislative objectives is stated. If the text includes no information, extraneous materials become of primary importance. If purpose is explicitly stated, this material becomes an additional source of information. Depending on the jurisdiction, extraneous material can include explanatory memoranda or reports, impact assessments, travaux preparatoirs, etc. or other material, green papers or white papers, commission reports, etc. Such material can be generated at the pre-parliamentary stage, during debates in Parliament (committee reports or debates in plenary) and after enactment (guidance, explanatory notes). Extraneous material is often used as a source of information on the context and the purpose of an Act.

Reports accompanying draft legislation (exposé des motifs, explanatory notes or reports) provide information on a broad range of issues including the purpose, the necessity, the ratio, objectives and the changes introduced by legislation. They often include a wealth of information on historical, international, economic, social and juridical context and a looser presentation of the context of legislation. These reports can differ substantially in length, depth and analysis of the problem to be addressed and the function of legislation in response, even within the same jurisdiction. Even when guidelines are available on how to draft them, diversity is an inherent feature. In some countries, explanatory reports provide a comprehensive overview of the lawmaking choices associated with legislation. For example, in Switzerland, dispatches on Bills[38] include justification, comments on individual provisions and the legal background, impact on constitutional rights, compatibility with superior law and European law; delegation of powers; points of view debated in the preliminary stages, alternatives and the position of the Federal Council; planned implementation, evaluation and assessment; coordination of tasks and funding; consequences for staffing and finances and implementation, methods for meeting the costs, influence on financial planning and the cost-benefit ratio; consequences for the economy, society, the environment and future generations; relation to the planning of legislation; and consequences for gender equality. In Germany, explanatory memoranda must state the expected

---

[38] Art. 141 Federal Act on the Federal Assembly.

regulatory impact (intended effects and unintended side-effects) including the impact on budget and expenditure, compliance costs, impact on unit prices and price levels, consumers and equality, among other issues.[39]

Explanatory Notes are used in the UK as 'aids to understanding'[40] that state the intention of Government.[41] They include a standard disclaimer that states:

> '1. These explanatory notes relate to the .... Act which received Royal Assent on .... They have been prepared by ...... Their purpose is to assist the reader in understanding the Act. They do not form part of the Act and have not been endorsed by Parliament' (emphasis added).

They are informal in style and focus only on points that require clarification, being neither a comprehensive nor an authoritative statement of intentions.[42] Their role, status, nature and true aims were questioned when used by the courts for the interpretation of ambiguous or unclear provisions. Critics point to the fact that notes are drafted by the executive, not endorsed by the legislature, are in tension with theories of legislative intention, are incomplete and insufficient in terms of legal formulation and might require interpretation themselves. Proponents maintain that it is legitimate to use Explanatory Notes that have been before Parliament when provisions were debated and adopted.[43] However, even judges that have used Explanatory Notes to interpret ambiguous provisions clarify that these are useful only to 'cast light on the objective setting or contextual scene of the statute, and the mischief at which it is aimed'.[44] They do provide information on the purpose of an Act.

Impact Assessments are another source of information on the preparatory phases of legislation. Although they are decision making tools rather than aids to interpretation, the analytical effort included there can reasonably facilitate

---

[39] § 44 of the Joint Rules of Procedure of the Federal Ministries (GGO) 2011 available at: https://bscw.bund.de/pub/bscw.cgi/d52920962/120119%20GGO_neu_engl.pdf?nonce=03349cf7faa309dce38778bbd9215cf97cb14c6e (last accessed 8/12/2018).

[40] R. Munday, 'Explanatory Notes and Statutory Interpretation' (2006) 170:8 Justice of the Peace 124.

[41] Report of a Committee appointed by the Lord President of the Council (Chairman Rt Hon Sir David Renton), *The Preparation of Legislation* (1975, Cmnd. 6053) at 94.

[42] Daniel Greenberg (ed), *Craies on Legislation. A Practitioners' Guide to the Nature, Process, Effect and Interpretation of Legislation* (9th edn, Sweet & Maxwell 2008) at 765.

[43] R. Munday, 'Explanatory Notes and Statutory Interpretation' (2006) 170:8 Justice of the Peace 124, 126, 127, 131; R. Munday, 'In the wake of "Good Governance": Impact Assessments and the Politicisation of Statutory Interpretation' (2008) 71:3 Modern Law Review 386.

[44] Westminster [2002] 1 WLR 2956 at 5–6.

the understanding of the reasons behind a legislative initiative.[45] In the UK, Impact Assessments have been used as sources of information in relation to an Act, as expressions of statutory history or as evidence of parliamentary will.[46] However, they are not designed to be aids to interpretation and cannot provide authoritative information on the intentions behind a legislative initiative. Secondly, they are drafted by the executive and are often of doubtful objectivity to the extent that they often aim to justify – rather than guide politically made decisions.[47] And thirdly, IA's become less reliable as a bill moves onto its different phases, since they are not necessarily updated to reflect subsequent changes. They are however, important sources of information with regard to the purposes of legislation and the decision making process during lawmaking. The increasing use of IA's by the courts, including the European Court, confirm this need.

Practice highlights a number of legislative choices with regard to the placement of information on the purpose of legislation. The ultimate choice is jurisdiction specific and its main qualifier is consistency both in the way the information is provided and in its location and unambiguity.

2.5. Too much information on objectives

The indefinite position or formulation of purpose is one kind of problem. The availability of too much information or contradictory information is another. Given the complexity of statutes, the multiplicity of objectives pursued and the variety of jurisdictional practices, purposes might be expressed in different parts of the Act or material related to the Act, often creating inconsistency and confusion or allowing for selective cherry picking.

For example, the long title of the Equality 2010 Act (UK) reads:

> *An Act to make provision to require Ministers of the Crown .... to have regard to the desirability of reducing socio-economic inequalities; to reform and harmonise equality law and restate ... enactments relating to ...; to enable certain employers to be required to publish information about ...; to prohibit victimisation in certain circumstances; to require the exercise of certain functions to be with regard to the need to eliminate discrimination and other prohibited conduct; to enable duties to be imposed ...; to increase equality of opportunity; to amend the law relating to...; and for connected purposes.*

---

[45] Munday, 'In the wake of "Good Governance"' (n 43) at 391.
[46] Ibid at 396–8.
[47] Sophie Denolle, 'Les Etudes d'Impact: Une Révision Manquée?' (2011) 87 Revue française de droit constitutionnel 503, 507, 510; J-P. Duprat, 'The Judicial Review of *ex ante* Impact Assessment in France: an Attempt to Fuse the Principles of Legal Certainty and Institutional Balance' (2012) 6:3 Legisprudence at 389.

The initial Regulatory Impact Assessment of the Equality Act identified three objectives: 'to standardise, simplify and consolidate discrimination law where appropriate, to make the law more effective and to modernise the law'.[48] These objectives were consistently mentioned in consequent IA's until the third version where an additional purpose was mentioned: 'not to hide inequality'.[49] The Equality Impact Assessment stated that the Bill was seen to strengthen the law, streamline it and support wider work to promote equality.[50] The Explanatory Notes on the other hand stated two main purposes: to harmonise discrimination law and to strengthen the law to support progress on equality.[51] Are these statements to be used on convenience? Ensuring consistency between different statements formulated in different phases of the legislative process is a challenging task whose difficulty increases with the number of references made to purpose.

Similar problems arise when preambles coexist with purpose statements and extraneous materials. For example, the Promotion of Equality and Prevention of Unfair Discrimination Act 4 of 2000 (South Africa) includes both a preamble and a purpose statement:

Preamble
The consolidation of democracy in our country requires the eradication of social and economic inequalities, especially those that are systemic in nature, which were generated in our history of colonialist, apartheid and patriarchy, and which brought pain and suffering to the great majority of our people;
Although significant progress has been made in restructuring and transforming our society and its institutions, systemic inequalities and unfair discrimination remain deeply embedded in social structures, practices and attitudes, undermining the aspirations of our constitutional democracy;
The basis for progressively redressing these conditions lies in the Constitution which, amongst others, upholds the values of human dignity, equality, freedom and social justice in a united, non-racial and non-sexist society where all may flourish;
South Africa also has international obligations under binding treaties and customary international law in the field of human rights which promote equality and prohibit unfair discrimination. Among these obligations are those specified in the

---

[48] Department for Communities and Local Government, Proposals to simplify and modernise discrimination law: Initial Regulatory Impact Assessment (HMSO 2007) 13.
[49] Equality Bill Impact Assessment. Version 3 (House of Commons Report Stage) (TSO 2009) 5–6.
[50] Government Equalities Office, Equality Bill – Equality Impact Assessment (TSO 2009) 8–9.
[51] Equality Act 2010, Explanatory Notes (TSO 2010) 3.

Convention on The Elimination of All Forms of Discrimination Against Women and the Convention on the Elimination of All Forms of Racial Discrimination;

Section 9 of the Constitution provides for the enactment of national legislation to prevent or prohibit unfair discrimination and to promote the achievement of equality;

This implies the advancement, by special legal and other measures, of historically disadvantaged individuals, communities and social groups who were dispossessed of their land and resources, deprived of their human dignity and who contribute to endure the consequences;

This Act endeavours to facilitate the transition to a democratic society, united in its diversity, marked by human relations that are caring and compassionate, and guided by the principles of equality, fairness, equity, social progress, justice, human dignity and freedom.

Article 2 Objects of Act

The objects of this Act are-
(a) To enact legislation required by section 9 of the Constitution
(b) To give effect to the letter and spirit of the Constitution, in particular
    (i) The equal enjoyment of all rights and freedoms by every person
    (ii) The promotion of equality
    (iii) The value of non-racialism and non-sexism contained in section 1 of the Constitution
    (iv) The prevention of unfair discrimination and protection of human dignity as contemplated in sections 9 and 10 of the Constitution
    (v) The prohibition of advocacy of hatred, based on race, ethnicity, gender or religion, that constitutes incitement to cause harm as contemplated in section 16 (2) (c) of the Constitution and section 12 of this Act;
(c) to provide for measures to facilitate the eradication of unfair discrimination, hate speech and harassment, particularly on the grounds of race, gender and disability;
(d) To provide for procedures for the determination of circumstances under which discrimination is unfair;
(e) To provide for measures to educate the public and raise public awareness on the importance of promoting equality and overcoming unfair discrimination, hate speech and harassment;
(f) To provide remedies for victims of unfair discrimination, hate speech and harassment and persons whose right to equality has been infringed;
(g) To set out measures to advance persons disadvantaged by unfair discrimination;
(h) To facilitate further compliance with international law obligations including treaty obligations in terms of, amongst, others, the Convention on the Elimination of All Forms of Racial Discrimination and the Convention on the Elimination of All forms of Discrimination against women.

Abundant information is provided in this example. The information in the Preamble is highly political in terms of language and ambition and often of no direct relevance to the specific law. The objectives on the other hand are specific, often too specific or procedural and although constitutional principles are mentioned (under b) the link is not always explicit. Do these distinct parts of the text function as a unity or do they just address different audiences? Where would a judge look for information? Or could they choose the most suitable or convenient objectives? The lesson is that while the absence or scarcity of information is problematic so is its abundance. Balance and constraint in the formulation of objectives emerges as an essential lawmaking quality.

Legislative practice offers a spectacular array of examples of how objectives can be formulated and where they can be placed in legislation. The typology is far from exhaustive: inevitably it will expand with the number of examples analysed. The point I want to make however is that information on the objectives of the law is not only difficult to trace but either scarce or abundant, inconsistent and often useless.

3. PURPOSE AND OBJECTIVES IN EFFECTIVE LAWMAKING

Objective setting is the obvious starting point of every decision making process. In lawmaking, objectives tend to be a mystifying rather than a solid concept. The function of legislative objectives is clear: to state and communicate the purpose of the Act to the user, the implementer and the interpreter, to assist interpretation and provide a criterion for the exercise of discretion[52] and 'bridge' the gap between policy and law. They have additional symbolic, informative and pedagogic functions.[53] If objectives are difficult to trace, vague, ambiguous, too narrow, too broad, or inconsistent, they do not only fail to fulfil these functions, or prioritise some functions over others (eg the symbolic ones), but they negatively affect their usefulness for the function of the law.

From the perspective of effective lawmaking, purpose is not a formality but a point of reference and an operative part of the law that needs to be clear, objectively identifiable and traceable, and set a meaningful benchmark for what a law aims to achieve. Hence, the task of the lawmaker is to formulate a clear and meaningful purpose, that is unambiguous and easily identified, reflects the different levels at which legislation is expected to operate (direct and broader objectives, results, outcomes and effects) and sets a clear and substantive benchmark for what the law aims to achieve. How can this be achieved?

---

[52] A. Seidman, R. Seidman and N. Abeyesekere, *Legislative Drafting for Democratic Social Change. A Manual for Drafters* (Kluwer 2001) at 311.

[53] J-L. Bergel, 'Les formulations d'objectifs dans les textes législatifs. Essai de synthèse', Cahiers de méthodologie juridique n° 4, RRJ 1989-4, at 975.

3.1. Objectives need to be the starting point in lawmaking

The starting point for the design of effective legislation is a legal and social problem and the goals connected to it, not vice versa. Once a problem is identified and its features are analysed, the attention turns to what can and needs to be addressed by legislation. Once this is established, what can actually be achieved? Which objectives can be pursued through legal means? What specific and broader objectives are pursued? How do these interrelate, what is their prioritisation or ranking? How are they connected to broader policy objectives? Undifferentiated objectives do not promote effective design.

The actual process of objective setting remains relatively obscure in lawmaking. Only impact assessments make a clear point about it, but even they might come too late or just justify the objectives already endorsed. *Objective setting is a strenuous thinking process about what the law needs to do and what it can do and how this interacts with the broader policy priorities.* If impact assessments are not used by lawmakers as guidance, how do they identify and prioritise the objectives pursued? Even when drafting instructions are in place, whose role is to 'illuminate the nature of the problem..., the purposes of the proposed legislation, the means by which those purposes are to be achieved, the impact of the proposals on existing circumstances and law'[54] the effort actually invested in determining objectives and their interrelation is neither clear not subject to scrutiny, as instructions are not public or traceable documents. Retracing the historical path of formation of purpose while a law is designed is difficult, if not impossible. Consequently, the purpose of a law often becomes obvious only after a draft and/or explanatory material are in place or even after a law is adopted. And it might be too late for its effective formulation. The objectives to be pursued need to be the starting point of every legislative effort.

The practice observed in some countries, where explanatory reports provide a comprehensive overview of the lawmaking choices associated with legislation is unquestionably a positive one, provided they do make the legislative objectives clear and do not fall into the trap of indiscriminately presenting information which seems relevant. While mapping the thinking process associated with legislative decision making is important, this practice needs however to respect the differentiation between justification and objective setting.

---

[54] Garth C. Thornton, *Legislative Drafting* (4th edn, Tottel 1996) at 130.

3.2. Specific, measurable and well-formulated objectives

The nebulous and fuzzy content and location of legislative purpose is a challenge for all actors in the life cycle of legislation. Effective lawmaking needs to move past this ambiguity towards purpose/objectives clauses that are operative provisions of the Act, expressed in clear, precise, and unambiguous terms[55] that reflect the full range of hierarchy of goals that a law pursues. Between extreme specificity and extensive generality, balanced statements setting meaningful goals are not easy to find. What should meaningful purpose clauses look like?

Purpose clauses need to indicate both the specific and the broader objectives pursued but also their hierarchy and interconnection in order to be a functional link with policy. To the extent possible they need to be specific, measurable, achievable, relevant and time-bound.[56] These qualities make them tangible, rather than abstract, and functional, rather than just symbolic. However, their most essential feature is to differentiate between the specific goals of legislation (what the law aims and *can* achieve) and broader objectives (leading to outcomes).

The meaningful formulation of objectives combines specific (descriptive or procedural) and broader (policy relevant) elements. In this way, specific elements of reform in the law are linked to their broader function. Mixed statements that balance legal objectives with broader policy objectives provide a more meaningful context for end users and effectiveness of legislation.

> *The purpose of this law is to lay down a general framework for combating discrimination on the grounds of ... with a view to putting into effect the principle of equal treatment.*

Secondly, legislation needs to list and provide a clear hierarchy of the objectives pursued in order to exhaust the means included in the law and serve the broader objectives.

Formulated in this way, objectives are clear, provide meaningful information to all actors and clear benchmarks against which the law can perform. They also link the mechanisms introduced by the law to monitoring results and evaluate them so as to ensure the connection between the elements of legislation and its cyclical nature.

---

[55] H. Xanthaki, 'An Enlightened Approach to Legislative Scrutiny: Focusing on Effectiveness' (2018) 9:3 European Journal of Risk Regulation 431–44.

[56] European Commission, Better Regulation Guidelines 2017, available at: https://ec.europa.eu/info/sites/info/files/better-regulation-guidelines.pdf (last accessed 8/12/2018).

Table 2.1   Hierarchy of legislative objectives

Specific objectives	Broader objectives (Outcomes)	Impact
Prohibit discrimination in specific areas of life (descriptive)	Promote equality of opportunities in the field of employment	Establish fairer working conditions
Establish procedures for reporting discrimination (descriptive) in order to provide effective remedies (mixed)	Facilitate and empower victims to claim their rights	Cultivate a culture of equality in the work place
Assist victims in reporting discrimination in order to increase reporting by 20% (mixed)		
Simplify reporting procedures and requirements (procedural)		

3.3.   Objectives as benchmarks

The main function of legislative purpose is to set a benchmark for what a law aims to achieve. To function as benchmarks, purpose statements need to allow the formulation of a meaningful question that can be answered after the law has been implemented. In the case of Swiss Federal Law on the elimination of inequalities affecting people with disabilities this would be: has the law prevented, reduced or eliminated inequalities for people with disabilities? In the example of the Employment Equity Act of Canada this would be: has the Act achieved equality in the workplace and corrected the conditions of disadvantage in employment experienced by women, Aboriginal peoples, persons with disabilities and members of visible minorities? In the example of the German General Act on Equal Treatment this would be: has the Act prevented or stopped discrimination on the grounds of race or ethnic origin, gender, religion or belief, disability, age or sexual orientation? Pragmatic and descriptive statements would lead to a different benchmark question. In the example of the Greek law 3769/09 on equal access to services the question would be: has the law laid down a framework for combating discrimination based on sex in access to and supply of goods and services? Finally, in the example of the French law 2006-340 on equal pay, the question would be: has the law suppressed the identified gaps in gender pay by the set deadline?

If purpose is narrow, the question will essentially be narrow. If the purpose is broad, the question will also be broad. Every different purpose provision sets a different benchmark for effectiveness, and this determines not only the text per se but also on the ways in which results, and consequently effectiveness, can be measured, appraised and understood: different purposes lead to different understandings of effectiveness.

Broad statements set meaningful benchmark questions. However, these ambitious questions go beyond the reach of legislation and although they set clear questions/benchmarks against which outcomes could be measured, the answers are prone to be disappointing not because the act is not well conceived, drafted, structured or implemented but because the question is too broad. Complex, multifactor and socially embedded phenomena like discrimination, can usually never be eliminated only through legislation.

Pragmatic purposes are of limited value because of their technical or procedural nature. Descriptive narrow statements like 'to render unlawful certain kinds of discrimination' or to lay down a framework for... lead to a narrow benchmark question that would be meaningless provided the law is enacted.

When it comes to mixed statements, the example provided above links the legal framework for combating discrimination to the broader objective of equal treatment, a fact that makes the benchmark question not purely procedural (is the framework put in place) but meaningful and substantive in relation to a broader purpose that can provide direction required in problem solving (does the framework as established promote or put into effect the principle of equal treatment?). In this example, the benchmark question is not limited to whether the law established a framework but to what extent this has put into effect the principle of equal treatment. Different questions and different answers are sought. Measurable and quantifiable objectives, to the extent that they are feasible, set even clearer and measurable benchmarks for effectiveness.

When properly formulated, purpose clauses are valuable for effective legislation. They provide a clear direction to the implementer and the interpreter and a clear benchmark for post legislative scrutiny, they close the gap between legislative intent and legislative effect and become the reference point for effectiveness.

3.4. Traceable objectives

Purpose needs to be easily traceable in legislation. If the user does not know where to look for it, or finds too much information that needs to be interpreted, more trouble than good is caused. Whether it is in the legislative text, in explanatory memoranda or reports or elsewhere, the choice of placement is a jurisdiction-specific choice. The first important issue is that purpose needs to find a clear and stable place in legislation where users will revert to when they need information. The second is that placement (and formulation) need to be consistent. Independently of whether it is inside or outside the legislative text, implementers and users need to be in the position to identify it without effort and without the need to interpret it.

Purpose provisions have obvious advantages in terms of visibility. Preambles are visible yet often declaratory, eloquent but vague. Extraneous materials are

Table 2.2 Matrix of objectives and related benchmark questions

Specific objectives	Benchmark questions	Broader objectives	Benchmark questions	Impact	Benchmark questions
Prohibit discrimination in specific areas of life	Is the law enacted? Is the prohibition in full force? Has necessary secondary legislation been enacted?	Promote equality of opportunities in the field of employment	Has equality of opportunity in employment improved?	Establish fairer working conditions	Are working conditions fairer compared to the start situation?
Establish procedures for reporting discrimination (descriptive) in order to provide effective remedies (mixed)	Have the procedures been established? Are they applied? Are they effective?	Reduce incidents of discriminatory behaviour on the grounds of gender by 20%	Has the benchmark been achieved?	Cultivate a culture of equality in the work place	Has workplace culture changed in a positive or negative way in response to the law?
Assist victims in reporting discrimination in order to increase reporting by 20% (mixed)	Has reporting increased? Why yes, why no? What barriers, what facilitators?				
Simplify reporting procedures and requirements	Has the target been achieved? Are procedures simpler, less costly and time consuming?				

less evident to non professional users yet have the advantage of allowing for more detail and analysis on the purposes of an Act. Multiple statements of purpose in different parts of the law or extraneous material are to be avoided, as they can cause confusion or manipulation. To conclude, while the exact placement is a jurisdiction-specific choice that requires flexibility, it also requires consistency.

4. CONCLUSIONS: PURPOSE AS A BENCHMARK FOR EFFECTIVENESS

Purpose in legislation has a dual function: to guide lawmaking, implementation and interpretation and to set a clear benchmark for results and its effectiveness. If lawmakers wish to actively pursue effectiveness in lawmaking, purpose needs to be a clear and objective concept that sets a meaningful benchmark for what the law aims to achieve. It needs to be specific and unambiguous, reflect the different types of goals and their hierarchy and be easily identifiable and consistent.

From the perspective of effectiveness, purpose in legislation is not a formality but a substantive part of the law that needs to be clear, objectively identifiable and traceable, and set a pertinent benchmark for what a law aims to achieve. The task of the lawmaker is to formulate a clear and meaningful purpose, that is unambiguous and easily identified, reflects the different levels at which legislation is expected to operate (results, outcomes, effects) and sets a clear and substantive benchmark for what the law aims to achieve.

3. The content of legislation

> La loi permet ou elle défend, elle ordonne, elle établit, elle corrige, elle punit ou elle récompense
>
> Jean-Étienne-Marie Portalis, Discours préliminaire sur le projet de code civil

1. LAWMAKING CHALLENGES WHEN DESIGNING THE CONTENT OF LEGISLATION

Every law comes with a solution and a set of new regulatory 'messages' that add, complement or change pre-existing ones. The legislative solution and its internal 'mechanics' determine how the law will achieve its expected results.

Designing the content of the law is the heart of lawmaking. This the autonomous sphere of legislative decision making, and lawmakers need to make decisions on the ways in which the law will intervene, the types of rules to be used, ways to incentivise compliance, enforcement and implementation procedures and mechanisms and communication including structure, grammar, language even typography. They must determine the mix or dosage of each element and articulate them in a coherent whole.

The importance of these elements is obvious: the choice of rules determines what rights are conferred, what obligations are imposed, what procedures or standards are regulated and how behaviours will be directed towards the desired goals; the choice of enforcement mechanism determines how the rules will be administered and implemented, how the subjects will be induced to comply, what consequences or motives are attached to them; last but not least, the way in which the 'message' of the law is expressed determines how the targeted audiences will be reached. These are the main 'tools' the lawmaker has at hand to design legislation. The way they are used (or misused) has an impact on the capacity of legislation to achieve results.

What challenges do lawmakers face when making decisions on the internal mechanics of the law? How can they choose the most appropriate rules? How can they anticipate which rules are more likely to bring the expected results? How can they select the most appropriate enforcement styles and mechanisms? How can language, structure and form be used to transmit clear messages? Not all laws are the same, not all audiences are the same. What is most likely to work best in each case?

1.1. Selecting substantive rules

Laws intervene in social reality in a number of ways: they prohibit, punish or repair, set standards, confer benefits, grant powers or combine these techniques in different ways.[1] Each technique directs behaviour towards the desired goals through distinct types of rights and obligations and differs in terms of compliance, enforcement and broader consequences.

For example, command and control rules impose or prohibit specific behaviours or standards and impose penalties and (criminal or civil) sanctions in case of breach.[2] Alternatives, like self-regulation or 'self-administered command and control',[3] rely on the development, enforcement and monitoring of rules by interested parties. Public benefits mobilise recourses and offer positive or negative incentives. Behaviours can also be 'manipulated' through obligations to disclose information, 'naming and shaming' techniques, market harnessing controls etc. The choice of 'technique' determines *how* legislation will intervene but also how behaviours will be guided towards the desired aims, how the target audiences are expected to comply and how rules will be enforced.

Legislating a social problem or phenomenon is a contextual exercise. Every society faces similar problems which might be addressed using the same or completely different (legislative) means. For example, the need to address inequalities and discrimination through legislation is common in many countries, yet the legislative solutions differ. Equality legislation in the UK endorses a reparative–individualistic approach where discrimination is a breach of civil rights, while in France it follows a repressive approach where discrimination is 'branded' as an offence. In other jurisdictions, choices might place emphasis on self-regulation or on mixing different techniques to respond better to different types of behaviours. *There is no a priori wrong or right solution.* Instead, the question is how do they fit the specific context and reality of the legal order and what they are there to achieve. But how can lawmakers make these choices?

A 'rational' or evidence-based response would suggest a structured process of analysis and decision making. The lawmaker should study the problem at hand, determine the objectives, compare the options available including their

---

[1] Robert Summers, 'The Technique Element in Law' (1971) 59 California Law Review 745.

[2] Robert Baldwin and Martin Cave, *Understanding Regulation. Theory, Strategy and Practice* (OUP 1999) at 34–5; R. White '"It's Not a Criminal Offence"—or Is It? Thornton's Analysis of "Penal Provisions" and the Drafting of "Civil Penalties"' (2011) 32:1 Statute Law Review 17–37.

[3] Baldwin and Cave (n 2) at 39–41; Julia Black, 'Constitutionalising Self-Regulation' (1996) 59 Modern Law Review 24.

advantages and disadvantages, costs and benefits, for example the choice of a civil rights vs a repressive approach to address discrimination. The two techniques differ in the way they control behaviour: the latter relies on deterrence, the fear of criminal sanctions, sends out strong and clear messages regarding the immorality of such practices and has a high impact on culture. Limitations on the other hand would need to take into account the fact that several discriminatory behaviours may not be perceived as 'serious' crimes that deserve severe punishment, while intention (which holds a central place in a repressive approach) is problematic with regard to indirect discrimination, where no perpetrator can be identified. Further, this choice involves a legalistic and inflexible enforcement machinery (prosecution) that is costly and inflexible but removes the burden of proof from the harmed individual. Reparation on the other hand places emphasis on redressing harm (rather than punishing) and relies on individual litigation. It is 'weaker' in terms of deterrence or 'broader' impacts and might lead people to believe that the law stretches no further.[4] Further, civil offences place a heavy burden on harmed persons in terms of cost, effort and proof. A mix of techniques on the other hand, could balance these advantages and disadvantages, offering more options to harmed individuals and escalating solutions depending on the importance and the impact of different behaviours. Each solution comes with distinct advantages and disadvantages that might be more or less effective in different contexts. But is that how rules are selected? And what are the factors that influence legislative decision making?

What scholarship suggests and legislative practice confirms is that lawmaking is far from an exercise where decisions are made using pure logic and argumentation. Legislative choices are not only contextual but also obey distinct rationalities and are influenced or even driven by several factors – external to the narrow technocratic decision making process. Apart from limitations like time, skills, resources[5] and obvious ones, like political influences and power, several others are in place. Taking the example of equality legislation, historical legacies, like the French revolution or Apartheid in South Africa and racism in the United States, constitutions and constitutional principles as 'frameworks for the implementation of policies' or as policy instruments[6] and theoretical constructions are powerful influencers of legislative choices. In France, the reaction to inequalities, and particularly racial inequalities was

---

[4] Sandra Fredman, *Discrimination Law* (OUP 2011) 279.

[5] Luc Wintgens, 'The Rational Legislator Revisited. Bounded Rationality and Legisprudence' in Luc Wintgens, A. Daniel Oliver-Lalana (eds) *The Rationality and Justification of Legislation. Essays in Legisprudence* (Springer 2013) at 15.

[6] Jeffrey Jowell, 'Is Equality a Constitutional Principle?' (1994) 47 Current Legal Problems 6.

largely shaped by theoretical constructions like the 'French model of integration',[7] the unifying function of citizenship and the French 'passion for equality'[8] rather than a detailed consideration of the advantages and disadvantages of specific rules. Europeanisation and the influence of supranational legislation is another powerful factor. In many European Union jurisdictions, equality laws were shaped under the strong influence of EU hard and soft law as Directives were often transposed in the legal order almost intact, with limited consideration of whether and to what extent they correspond to the specific context and how they might work in practice. From this perspective, legislative decision making is a complex and delicate exercise in balancing distinct influences.

Taking a closer look at specific legislative context, for example equality legislation, the factors at play become more specific. In the early days of English non-discrimination legislation, the choice of techniques and the formulation of rules on race discrimination were influenced by politically inspired, ambivalent approaches operating on a 'twin track approach' with immigration legislation that prohibited entry to citizens from former colonies on the grounds of colour.[9] Along the years, equality rules evolved to reflect trial and error from pre-existing legislation and became more responsive and adaptive to 'real' expressions of discrimination,[10] both behavioural and structural ones. English legislation, especially in the last decade, appears to be particularly 'sensitive' and reactive to the situation on the ground. In France on the other hand, the range of choices with regard to the content of legislation were restricted by theoretical concerns, symbolism and internal tensions in the legal order. The choice of repressive techniques was more the result of historical, symbolic, theoretical notions highlighting the unacceptability of such practices[11] rather than an objective consideration of the potential of the

---

[7] Patrick Simon, 'Discriminations: les contradictions françaises' (2006) 9 Les Grands Dossiers des Sciences Humaines 21.

[8] Jacqueline Costa-Lascoux, 'Les Échecs de l'Intégration, un Accroc au Contrat Social' (2004) 4:111 Pouvoirs 19, 24, 27.

[9] Karon Monaghan, *Equality Law* (Oxford University Press 2007) 3.

[10] Bob Hepple, *Equality. The New Legal Framework* (Hart Publishing 2011) 1, 7.

[11] Éric Pélisson, *Les Discriminations* (Transversale Débats Ellipses 2007) 18; Haut Conseil à l'Intégration, *Lutte contre les discriminations: faire respecter le principe d'égalité: rapport au Premier Ministre* (La Documentation Française 1998) 7; Didier Fassin, 'Une brève histoire des discriminations' in Eric Fassin and Jean-Louis Halpérin (eds), *Discriminations: pratiques, savoirs, politiques* (Collection Etudes et recherches, Documentation Française 2009) 49; Patrick Simon, 'Discriminations: les contradictions françaises' (2006) 9 Les Grands Dossiers des Sciences Humaines 21; Guy Carcassonne, 'The Principle of Equality in France' [1998] St. Louis-Warsaw Transatlantic Law Journal 159, 169; Louis Favoreu, 'The Principle of Equality in the Jurispudence of the Conseil Constitutionnel' (1992) 21 Capital University Law Review 165–97; Francois Luchaire, 'Un Janus Constitutionnel: l'égalité' (1986) 5 Revue du Droit Public et de

specific technique to address existing inequalities. Further, interventions of the Constitutional Court limited the options and the usability of positive measures and quotas in particular[12] as a way to address existing inequalities. The choice of techniques was influenced considerably by these tensions – not to mention European legislation – and sidetracked the consideration about the features of discriminatory behaviours and practices that needed to be regulated. Finally, in countries like Greece, where equality rules were 'imported' under the influence of European legislation, their content was copied to an important extent by supranational rules that were transplanted almost intact in the legal order, without any substantive consideration of the situation on the ground.

Within this context of bounded rationality, the challenge for lawmakers when shaping the content of legislation is not to find an 'optimal' solution to a problem. This might not be even remotely possible. *The realistic challenge is to 'balance' opposing dynamics at play in order to design a solution that fits within the existing context (historical, constitutional, theoretical) and has the potential to work (to be effective).* The question is no longer whether there is a right recipe as to how things should be done. Instead, the question is reformulated with regard to what is a good recipe for the specific context and how well it can work.

Legislative practice shows that subject to these choices legislation often intervenes randomly in social reality. Laws that set standards that cannot be respected, or express principles that cannot materialise or simply assume that theoretical models will work in real life essentially miss the thinking that will make them workable. This limits their capacity to bring results.

---

la science politique en France et a l'étranger 1229–75; Jean Rivero, 'Rapport sur les notions d'égalité et de discrimination en droit public français' in XIV Documents of the Henri Capitant Association of the Friends of French Legal Culture (Dalloz 1961–62) 343–60; Daniel Borillo, 'Les instruments juridiques français et européens dans la mise en place du principe d'égalité et de non-discrimination' (2002) 1 Revue française des affaires sociales 113.

[12] Gwénaële Calvès, 'Les Politiques Françaises de Discrimination Positive: Trois spécificités' (2004) 4:111 Pouvoirs 29; cf Gwénaële Calvès, 'La parité entre hommes et femmes dans l'accès aux fonctions électives. Faut-il réviser la constitution?' in CURRAPP, *Questions sensibles* (PUF 1998) 218 ff; Décision n° 82-146 DC du 18 novembre 1982; Décision n° 2001-455 DC du 12 janvier 2002; Décision n° 2001-445 DC du 19 juin 2001; Décision n° 2006-533 DC du 16 mars 2006.

1.2. Compliance and enforcement

Compliance is voluntary behaviour in accordance with the law.[13] It is indispensable for effectiveness but extremely tricky to predict and measure as it differs by agency, subject matter and type of rule. For example, commands and prohibitions can be measured by obedience, sanctions or power conferring rules can be measured by enforcement, rights and freedoms by rates of use, persuasive measures by the attention they receive by potential beneficiaries.[14] Legislation and regulation are drafted on the assumption that subjects will comply. However, scholarship and research prove that compliance is a socially constructed concept, whose processes are complex, dynamic, interactive and rely on variables like motives, threats and promises, organisational capacities, social and economic environments and institutions including the influence and values of the peer group but also costs.[15] Reality proves that compliance cannot be taken for granted and that it can challenge even the most sophisticated rules. People might not comply at all or comply creatively and the reasons behind that might be linked to various factors. Further, the traditional understanding of compliance motivations as 'deterrence messages' are only one part of the story. The difference between 'laggards' or 'reluctant' compliers, 'committed' ones, 'strategists' and 'true believers' might be in the combination of regulation-induced fear, social license pressure, commitment and imaginative cooperation models.[16] Different rules elicit different compliance motivations, patterns and costs. How can lawmakers actively predict how target populations are likely to react?

If people do not comply, enforcement mechanisms will induce them to do so. Enforcement is the 'process of compelling observance' with the law

---

[13] Lawrence Friedman, *Impact. How Law Affects Behavior* (Harvard University Press 2016) at 46.

[14] M. De Benedetto, 'Effective Law from a Regulatory and Administrative Law Perspective' (2018) 9:3 European Journal of Risk and Regulation 391; A. Flückiger, 'Le droit administrative en mutation: l'emergence d'un principe d'efficacite' (2001) Revue de droit administrative et fiscal 95; J. Carbonnier, 'Effectivité et ineffectivité de la règle de droit' (1957–58) L'Année sociologique 6–7.

[15] Ch Parker and V. Lehmann Nielsen, 'Introduction', in Ch Parker and V. Lehmann Nielsen (eds) *Explaining Compliance. Business Responses to Regulation* (Edward Elgar 2011) 5; L. Friedman, *The Legal System* (Russell Sage Foundation 1975) 62–3, 69.

[16] R. Kagan, N. Gunningham and D. Thornton, 'Fear, Duty and Regulatory Compliance: lessons from three research projects' in Ch Parker and V. Lehmann Nielsen (eds) *Explaining Compliance* (n 15) (Edward Elgar 2011) at 37–41, 52–4.

through formal and informal techniques.[17] Choices range from strict legalistic sanctioning approaches to flexible ones encouraging compliance through persuasive, accommodating, deterring or sanctioning, insistent or responsive enforcement styles.[18] Enforcement has a triple function: to 'communicate' norms by threatening monitoring and sanctions, 'remind' obligations and 'reassure' compliers that they are not fools to comply.[19] Responsive,[20] smart regulation[21] and enforcement[22] promote escalating compliance and enforcement structures to address complex issues and the needs of diverse audiences.

Compliance and enforcement are often seen as implementation issues associated with questions of measurement, costs and effectiveness. It is true that important aspects of both are revealed during the implementation process. However, decisions of enforcement and compliance are essentially lawmaking ones that respond to the challenge to identify the implementation mechanism of the law. If this is not done when laws are being designed it might be too late. How to do that? The most crucial step in choosing an implementation mechanism is to think about the subject. How to know whether people will comply? What motives are necessary? What sanctions, remedies or penalties? What kind of enforcement mechanism/s, mandates and procedures?

For one matter, the choice of compliance and enforcement mechanisms is determined to an important extent by the choice of substantive provisions. However, a number of specific questions emerge which require consistent answers. For example, what kind of sanctions, penalties or fines? Practice shows how wrong choices in these issues can make all the difference.

---

[17] Baldwin and Cave (n 2) 96–7; B. Hutter, *The reasonable arm of the Law? The Law enforcement procedures of Environmental Health Officers* (Clarendon Press 1988) 5; Steven Shavell, 'The Optimal Structure of Law Enforcement' (1993) 36:1 Journal of Law and Economics 255–87.

[18] Hutter, ibid at 132, 148, 150–51, 157; Neil Cunningham, 'Enforcement and Compliance Strategies' in R. Baldwin, M. Cave and M. Lodge, *The Oxford Handbook of Regulation* (OUP 2010) 121; Ian Ayres and John Braithwaite, *Responsive Regulation: Transcending the Deregulation Debate* (OUP 1992) 4–5; John Braithwaite, 'The Essence of Responsive Regulation' (2011) 44 University of British Columbia Law Review 475; L. McAllister, 'Dimensions of Enforcement Style: Factoring in Regulatory Autonomy and Capacity' (2010) 32:1 Law and Policy 61, 62.

[19] R. Kagan, N. Gunningham and D. Thornton, 'Fear, Duty and Regulatory Compliance: lessons from three research projects' in Ch Parker and V. Lehmann Nielsen (eds) *Explaining Compliance* (n 15) (Edward Elgar 2011) 37–41, 52.

[20] I. Ayres and J. Braithwaite, *Responsive Regulation: Transcending the Deregulation Debate* (Oxford University Press 1992).

[21] N. Gunningham and P. Grabosky, *Smart Regulation. Designing Environmental Policy* (Clarendon Press 1998).

[22] M. Faure and F. Blanc, 'Smart Enforcement. Theory and Practice' (2018) 20:4 European Journal of Law Reform 78–104.

Sanctions that are too strict might not be applied, weakening the deterring effect of a law. Penalties or fines whose cost lawbreakers are willing to internalise are equally ineffective. Behaviours which are not perceived by popular morality as 'real' crimes yet are punished, might send perverse messages as to the function of the law or create confusion and incomprehension. More sophisticated ways of addressing complex issues like escalating remedies or enforcement might be costly and difficult to implement by immature or poorly resourced administrations. Further, compliance and enforcement have cost implications. The cost of compliance and enforcement needs to be factored in proactively otherwise one is looking for crude surprises. People might comply despite high costs and might not comply despite low costs, if they consider the rules unjust, unreasonable or burdensome. Solutions are not ready made. Each law leads to distinct compliance patterns and requires unique solutions depending on the issue, and the audience.

Enforcement choices are also closely related to the choice of rules. For example, the reparative approach of English legislation relied on individualistic court-based enforcement (through courts and tribunals) while repressive rules inevitably involved the prosecution. Enforcement and implementation often prove problematic in practice. The aphorism 'it is a good law, but not implemented' is commonplace. Inevitably, when issues arise during implementation these are termed as implementation problems. But are they?

For example, the extra judicial mechanism set up in Greece to enforce equality legislation was complex, dispersed, fragmented and polycentric, lacking a logical structure. Four distinct bodies were involved with different mandates, exposure to the public and resources, while their competencies within the enforcement mechanism were confusing and artificially conceptualised. Complaints against public authorities were addressed to one body (the Ombudsman), complaints against natural or legal persons to another (the Equal Treatment Committee established at the Ministry of Justice), complaints in employment and occupation were addressed to a third one (the Labour Inspectorate) while complaints on the grounds of sex in the private sector were directed to the Consumers' Ombudsman. The impact of these choices was not insignificant: some discrimination grounds received more attention and visibility than others, some equality bodies did not receive a single complaint. In France, the equality enforcement mechanism involved on the one hand the 'all powerful' prosecution and on the other an Equality body with weak sanctioning powers[23] creating a gap between the behaviours actually prosecuted (and prosecution was not often mobilised) and those that were not. The lesson is that

---

[23] Ch. Pettiti and S. Scalbert, 'La loi du 30 décembre 2004 portant création de la Haute autorité de lutte contre les discrimination et pour l'égalité' [2005] 25–6 Mars

problems in the design of enforcement are often disguised as implementation concerns, thus placing the issue at the wrong level.

To conclude, compliance and enforcement problems are lawmaking issues with a significant impact on the effectiveness of legislation. Difficult as it may be to anticipate how people will behave, effective lawmaking requires a meticulous consideration of compliance and enforcement issues when rules are being designed.

1.3. Communicating the law

When Moses said 'thou shalt not steal' everyone knew what he meant.[24] Legislation is a special form of communication directed to specific purposes and audience.[25] Every law includes messages addressing lawmakers, the judiciary and society.[26] Effective communication involves the message but also the recipient. The growing awareness of the role of lawmakers as 'communicators' involves a corresponding interest towards the audiences addressed by legislation. For whom is legislation written? Judges and lawyers alone or the public at large? Lawmakers often think too little about this question following established patterns in expression and communication without consideration. *This simple question alters the perspective of lawmaking from an introvertive to an extrovertive, user-oriented, exercise.* Research conducted by the National Archives in the UK in 2012 showed that representative readers of legislation in the UK include both specialised and non-specialised audiences: in fact, the majority of readers were non-lawyers who used legislation for work, followed by members of the public seeking to enforce their rights and finally, lawyers.[27] In Germany, satisfaction surveys reported a particular dissatisfaction within citizens with the comprehensibility of forms and legislation.[28] Choices in communication have an important impact on the accessibility of the law.

Gazette du Palais 10; Conseil d'Etat, Rapport Public 2001: Les autorités administratives indépendantes (La Documentation Française 2001) 308.

[24] Lord Renton, 'Current Drafting Practices and Problems in the United Kingdom' (1990) 1 Stat LR 11–17, 17.

[25] A. Allot, *The Limits of Law* (Butterworths 1980) at 11; Constantin Stefanou, 'Drafting as a form of communication' in Luzius Mader/Marta Tavares de Almeida (eds), *Quality of Legislation. Principles and Instruments* (Nomos 2011) 308ff.

[26] Lawrence Friedman, *Law and Society. An Introduction* (Prentice-Hall 1977) viii, 112ff.

[27] Alison Bertlin, What works best for the reader? A study on drafting and presenting legislation, Loophole (2014) 2 at 25–49.

[28] D. Kuehnhenrich and S. Michalik, 'Are Citizens and Businesses (Dis)satisfied with the Public Administration in Germany?', Paper at the 34th IARIW General Conference Dresden, Germany, 21–27 August 2016, accessible at: https://bscw.bund

From the perspective of the lawmaker, communication is primarily sought through clear, precise, specific and unambiguous rules. Clear rules are easily perceived or understood, precise rules are exact in expression or detail and unambiguous rules avoid uncertain or inexact meaning.[29] However, none of these standards are objectively identifiable and legislation often encompasses different grades of certainty ranging from 'the language of the law' that aims at precision to 'the language of politics'[30] that favours vagueness and ambiguity and appeals to sentiment or opinion, to precisely measured terms, abstractions or terms involving appeals to judgement or degree.

Poor communication can unfold in a number of ways. Vague or 'elastic phrases'[31] are a common problem which might be the result of poor drafting or a deliberate choice to fudge hard issues, delay results, pacify parties with conflicting interests. The decision to leave terms indefinite allows adaptability to varying circumstances but has the 'double aspect of liberty and peril' as flexible terms would have to be judged with the criterion of 'the circumstances under which, the persons by whom, and the sense of responsibility with which, the law will be applied, and the consequences which an error will entail'.[32] A 'policy of wait and see' and 'social experimentation'[33] expressed in the delegation from the legislator to the courts of the task of defining the subject matter of law, might be a questionable or a legitimate choice depending on the circumstances. It needs however to be a conscious (rather than random) decision.

Another common problem is the inconsistency between related terms or concepts in the same or different laws. For example, provisions that regulate the same behaviour differently or inconsistently, sending confusing or conflicting messages. Definitions of prohibited conduct in Greek equality laws differed in expression and content enough to create confusion. Direct discrimination on the grounds of sex and discrimination in access to goods and services differed in one crucial point: the latter linked less favourable treatment to the

---

.de/pub/bscw.cgi/d41513289/Aufsatz%20Lebenslagenbefragung%20englisch.pdf?nonce=dc600a08f456d340cb6ef8071631625967f805ad (last accessed 8/12/2018); Stephan Neundorf, Beyond compliance costs: How do you experience the law? Perception surveys as a complementary tool for Better Regulation, accessible at: https://bscw.bund.de/pub/bscw.cgi/d33672063/160614%20survey%20life%20events.pdf?nonce=863f3d4ccc7f2fcb841656474684658f265d0208 (last accessed 10/12/2018).

[29] Helen Xanthaki, 'On Transferability of Legal Solutions' in Constantin Stefanou and Helen Xanthaki (eds) *Drafting Legislation. A Modern Approach* (Ashgate 2008) 9, 10.

[30] Ernst Freund, 'The Use of Indefinite Terms in Statutes' (1921) 30 Yale Law Journal 437.

[31] Friedman (n 13) at 33.

[32] Ibid.

[33] L. Fuller, *The Morality of Law* (revised edn, Yale University Press 1969) 65.

complainants' sex, while the former was broader and linked less favourable treatment to sex in general (not necessarily the complainants' sex). Indirect discrimination with regard to race and sex (including access to goods and services) required a *prima facie* neutral provision, while for all other grounds it required an *apparently* neutral provision.[34] Did these definitions willingly introduce different standards? Or were they simply the result of careless lawmaking and poor expression?

An important issue for communication are legislative styles, traditions and practice. Style matters and includes the wording (general use of language, definitions, terminology), structure, superstructure and legal-cultural identity of legislation.[35] For example, the choice of whether to use definitions or not, where to place them, or how to express the law are to an important extent questions of style. Legislative tradition and style play an important role for continuity and homogeneity, and choices aligned with the tradition and styles of legal systems are often assumed to facilitate the communication of content, while choices foreign to the legal system might surprise the readers and complicate communication. However, they can both aid and obstruct effective communication. Legalese, jargon, complex and intelligible syntax or language make the law inaccessible to many users, yet they persist. Style needs to evolve from a static factor to a flexible facilitator of communication and the subject of conscious decision making.

The main challenge is that communication is perceived narrowly and is too closely attached to style and tradition. Although language is the main medium for expressing and transmitting the message of the law, communication is in fact a broader issue that involves structure, titles, language, syntax and grammar, graphic illustrations, tables, examples, to name only a few. Lawmakers have to balance legislative complexity with the need for clarity, precision and simplicity in expression. The more complex the issue to be addressed, the more complex the rules, the messages, the concepts involved. Willingness to transmit clear messages might not always be sufficient on its own. The ongoing debate tends to localise the issue on plain language concerns. This comes with a number of brilliant ideas but also a limited focus on minuscule detail that overshadows the broader picture. The use of must or shall, the subject of ardent debate among commonwealth drafters, will not fundamentally change the way in which users of the law perceive the obligations inscribed there. The challenge is to move away from details towards the

---

[34] Art. 3b and 7 par. 1b Law 3304/2005; art. 2b Law 3769/2009; art. 2b Law 3896/2010.
[35] Wim Voermans, 'Styles of Legislation and their Effects' (2011) 32:1 Statute Law Review 38, 53 at 41.

challenge of how the important regulatory messages of the law will be communicated in the best possible way.

Effective legislative communication is a complex task, no doubt. No matter how sophisticated rules and enforcement mechanisms are, they might fail if the message is not communicated properly. Legislation often touches upon broad and controversial issues and transfers material from the social sphere to the domain of law. Lawmakers have in their communication toolkit language, structure, layout, even typography. How can these be used to pursue the effective communication of the message of the law?

2. EFFECTIVE LEGISLATIVE MECHANICS

Designing the content of the law involves making decisions on rules, implementation, (compliance and enforcement) and communication. Legislative practice offers a spectacular array of examples of poor choices or mistakes in the design of the content of the law: standards and requirements which are irrelevant to local circumstances or out of reach of target audiences, rules that do not take into account behaviours, customs and traditions, are complex, ambivalent, unrealistic in terms of financial and institutional capacity or confusing in messages and fail to motivate people to comply.

There are distinct pathologies behind these decisions: the insufficient understanding of the problem addressed, conceptual mistakes, the choice of inappropriate rules, inconsistency in the rules introduced, complexity of solutions, the fact that rules do not reflect existing structures and capacity, solutions that are difficult (or impossible) to implement, complex or inarticulate choices in design, structure or communication; insufficient or limited consideration of compliance; complex or unrealistic enforcement mechanisms and structures; inaccessible or conflated communication choices. The typology is far from exhaustive: inevitably it will expand with the number of examples analysed. The point is that choices in content are critical for results and effectiveness. If the selected rules (or their combination) are inappropriate to address the problem the design of the law is ineffective; if enforcement mechanisms are inappropriate implementation is ineffective; if the subjects of the law do not know how to comply, encounter difficulties in complying or interpreting rules, communication is ineffective. What can lawmakers do to proactively make effective decisions on the content of legislation?

2.1. A clear legislative strategy

Lawmaking is not science to apply the same rules and get the same results.[36] Far from it, lawmaking is contextual and represents a specific constellation of factors and influences at a specific point in time. The challenge for every law is to express (given the circumstances, resources, pressures and societal support) a solution that can work. The clearer the strategy of how the law plans to intervene, the clearer the hypothesis to be tested by reality. If this vision or hypothesis is missing, is devised ad hoc or is random, the law suffers from conceptual problems.

The case studies confirm the importance of this statement. English equality legislation, following a strenuous 40-year process of trial and error, reflects a straightforward strategy: discrimination is a breach of civil rights remedied by civil penalties and reparation. Equality legislation addresses both behavioural and structural forms of discrimination through prohibitions of specific behaviours and an obligation to promote equality through positive action in favour of disadvantaged individuals or groups. Enforcement is individualistic and strategic and operates through the courts and tribunals and a specialised enforcement body. Communication is overall consistent. The main 'formula' of the law is straightforward.

French equality legislation, on the other hand, is ambivalent in its approach. Legislative choices move between extremes, strict punishment (repressive rules) and 'soft' incentives (collective self regulation), linger between sanctioning or regulating and remain undecided between individualised, defensive, persuasive or preventive approaches while action extends at different levels without full engagement.[37] Sanctions are strict, rigid and rarely applied, while incentives are soft and ineffective and enforcement is non operational. The enforcement mechanism involves the prosecution and an independent body that is, however, too weak to counterbalance the prosecution.

Greek equality legislation, influenced by European equality legislation, comes with a sophisticated yet superficial formula. The legislative strategy is over-ambitious (a combination of command and control techniques, positive action, 'soft' techniques to promote equality and self-regulation) but insufficiently developed (penal provisions are specific, civil prohibitions are general and ambiguous, requirements for positive action are unclear, obligations for social dialogue are broad and vague). The enforcement apparatus is complex

---

[36] H. Xanthaki, *Drafting Legislation. Art and Technology of Rules for Regulation* (Hart Publishing 2014) at 7.

[37] Françoise Favennec-Héry, 'Non-discrimination, égalité, diversité, la France au milieu du gue' (2007) 1 Droit Social 3.

and largely ineffective (courts have only rarely been seized in more than ten years), extra-judicial adjudication remains a 'soft' remedy, and the apparatus is complex and confusing. Communication is not facilitated as the law either remains silent on the subject matter or provides such an abundance of definitions that leads to inevitable confusion. In short, the mix of techniques is superficial, their articulation is weak, they lack specification and depth.

Substantive provisions tell the people and the implementing mechanism what it is that they have to do. This message is articulated in the rules or sub rules established, the incentives, enforcement mechanisms and communication etc. and it needs to be very clear. For the message to be clear in legislation it needs to be clear in the mind of the lawmakers. The lesson from the case studies is that a clear strategy offers a clear hypothesis, a clear experiment, while over-ambitious or ambivalent strategies lead to challenges.

Responsive strategies encompass a broad range of regulatory solutions so that they can respond to 'plural configurations of support and opposition'.[38] They rely on a case by case mix of legislative techniques, and particularly punishment and persuasion, to address a specific problem effectively and a pyramidal structure of regulatory and enforcement strategies, that escalate as 'softer' means of intervention fail while compliance is streamlined at the less interventionist and less costly layers of the pyramids, through persuasion and self-regulation.[39] Such sophisticated solutions might look extremely good on paper but require a clear strategy and mechanics to be effective.

2.2. Clear mechanics

A clear legislative strategy expresses the vision of how the law plans to intervene. The strategy on its own is not enough, it requires clear mechanics. The selection of rules, compliance and enforcement mechanisms and communication are important when designing the content of legislation, but do not operate in isolation. Their internal alignment, coherence, consistency and balance are the *mechanics* of the specific solution. Selecting the ingredients is one task, arranging and balancing them in a way that the machine can function well is another.

The case studies highlighted several pathologies not only in the individual choices of content of legislation but also in their alignment and overall coherence that impede it from functioning well as a unity. Rules that point in different directions and are not well articulated; solutions that are not followed

---

[38] Ayres and Braithwaite (n 20) 4–5.
[39] John Braithwaite, 'The Essence of Responsive Regulation' (2011) 44 University of British Columbia Law Review 475.

through; enforcement choices that are either unrealistic or complex; choices that do not assist the communication of the messages of the law; all these do little to promote effectiveness.

The coherence, balance and proportionality between the legislative techniques chosen, the enforcement mechanisms and drafting choices was a factor that differentiated effective to non-effective choices. An articulate and consistent balance in these elements appeared to be conducive to effectiveness. On the contrary, imbalance between the techniques used or ambivalent and indecisive choices jeopardised effectiveness. Superficial approaches using techniques foreign to a legal system, disperse or ineffective enforcement mechanisms and confusing drafting choices limited a priori the prospects of effectiveness. In short, legislation with a balanced and coherent content appeared to have the capacity, at least theoretically, to bring about the desired results. Legislation with a weak, unbalanced or superficial conceptual structure appeared to have more chances to fail, partially or entirely.

The mechanics of the law need to be right: this means coherent, grounded, proportionate and clearly designed to serve the results of legislation. Each element reinforces the other and if this connection is weak, the law risks partial or entire failure.

Lawmaking as a balancing exercise requires consistent choices of rules and techniques, supported by an appropriate and feasible enforcement mechanism, clear choices for inducing compliance and a consistent approach to the communication of rules. Inconsistent choices might not be intentional yet they are almost always detrimental for effectiveness: gaps between the techniques used and the regulated behaviours in real life (too soft or too strict), internal legislative tensions (choices rendered void or remaining on paper), 'imported' choices, ambiguous approaches (nobody knows what is expected), complex enforcement mechanisms, and ambiguous communication raise problems of distinct texture. Ambivalence in the choices of the law (for example between individualised or defensive, persuasive or preventive approaches and legislative action in French legislation) do not serve its effectiveness. Maximalistic and pluralistic approaches that are not followed through or complex solutions that will make implementation difficult or impossible, threaten this consistency.

2.3. Choices informed by evidence but selected on the basis of effectiveness

Legislative decision making involves making choices on a number of complex issues. Unfortunately, there are no universal rules on how to legislate. The most important and practical step in choosing rules is to think about the subject and what we know about it. Transferred in the jargon of legislative studies, legislative decision making needs to be informed by evidence.

The power of data, evidence and empirical knowledge is that they can clarify and specify legal conditions and problems, help shape realistic goals and counterbalance intuition, impressionism and insight. Evidence-based lawmaking is incrementalist and seeks effective and customised solutions.[40] Legal rules and doctrines often resist empirical insights not only due to ignorance and laziness on the part of policymakers, officials or drafters but also due to ontological, epistemic, methodological, institutional, normative and moral barriers.[41] The kind of evidence that can be used in lawmaking (experiments, comparative knowledge, studies, expert studies, economic or mathematical models or statistics, stories etc), its reliability, epistemic limits and added value are still contested.[42] However, there is no doubt that it can enrich the esoteric doctrinal legal reasoning with awareness and data in problem solving.[43] From a practical perspective, what evidence (in the broad sense) offers to lawmakers is proof on how the law works, how rules impact individual behaviours and society but also pinpoint the limits of the instrumental use of law or question the design of proxies or formulas used in legislation (for example age proxies).[44] What it does not offer is a decision making criterion.

Evidence will neither necessarily produce effective legislation, nor is it invariably superior to intuition.[45] However, as problems become more intricate, the likelihood of 'guessing' the right answer decreases.[46] Empirical knowledge about rules can 'ground' legal solutions to reality, to what is possible, to anticipated impact and to potential contribution to broader goals.[47] It is a remedy against serendipity.

---

[40] S. Ranchordas, 'Consultation, Citizen Narratives and Evidence-Based Regulation' (2017) 1:2 European Journal of Law Reform Special Issue on Better Regulation 66–7.

[41] P. Cserne, 'Introduction: Legislation, Legal Episteme, and Empirical Knowledge' (2013) 1:3 The Theory and Practice of Legislation 387–93 at 387, 392.

[42] S.J. Kealy, A. Forney, 'The Reliability of Evidence in Evidence-Based Legislation' (2018) 1 European Journal of Law Reform 40–66 at 52.

[43] D. Nelken, 'Can Law Learn from Social Science?' (2001) 35:2–3 Israel Law Review 205–24; M. Derber, 'What the Lawyer can Learn from Social Science' (1963) 16:2 Journal of Legal Education 145–54 at 152.

[44] Cserne (n 41) at 388.

[45] J. Rachlinski, 'Evidence-Based Law' (2011) 96 Cornell Law Review 901–23, 910, 912.

[46] Edward L. Rubin, 'Legislative Methodology: Some Lessons from the Truth-in-Lending Act' (1991) 80 Geo. L.J. 301.

[47] Pauline Westerman, 'Breaking the Circle: Goal-legislation and the Need for Empirical Research' (2013) 1:3 The Theory and Practice of Legislation 395–414;

The enthusiasm around evidence-based lawmaking is not necessarily shared by lawmakers who, as practice shows, do not necessarily rely on it. Its main contribution is a structured way of thinking that can counterbalance or challenge intuitive choices, confirmation bias or naïve beliefs and minimise unconscious automatisms. Legislative decision making will always rely, to some extent, on experience, judgement, insight, intuition and political priorities. The critical question is when and how these choices can support rather than jeopardise the potential of the law to work. Further, evidence can be 'manipulated' or used 'on demand' to obscure or justify predefined choices rather than support objective choices. Evidence offers information but does not offer a decision making criterion.

Effectiveness is the only viable criterion for sound legislative choices. What does that mean for the choice of rules? It means that the consideration of options is not a dry juxtaposition of advantages and disadvantages, costs and benefits, but an effort to anticipate how these choices might work, hence their potential to be effective. Would it be impossible to anticipate that strict sanctions (for example imprisonment) might not work for offences that popular morality does not (yet) consider 'serious' crimes? Would it be impossible to anticipate that the difficulties in proving discrimination might cause a number of challenges to penalising behaviours? Would it be difficult to anticipate that a complex enforcement mechanism might confuse rather than encourage victims to report? No. What seems to be lacking in these decisions, and many others encountered on a daily basis in legislative practice, is the 'grounding' effect of considering these options from the perspective of effectiveness. Even if these choices were finally selected, seen from the perspective of effectiveness, they could be formulated in a better way.

Effectiveness is a *functional link* between the elements that determine the capacity of a law to be effective: objectives, content, context and results. It is hence the main *decision making criterion* for lawmaking and can help select legislative policy, serve as a criterion for pre- and post-legislative scrutiny, as a criterion on the '*whether*' and the '*how*' of legislation or as the main criterion for problem solving during the conceptualisation, design and drafting of drafting legislation, including the choice of compliance and implementation strategies.[48]

Stefan T. Trautmann, 'Empirical Knowledge in Legislation and Regulation: A Decision Making Perspective' (2013) 1 The Theory and Practice of Legislation 533–42.

[48] Maria Mousmouti, 'Introduction to the Symposium on Effective Law and Regulation' (2018) 9:3 European Journal of Risk Regulation 387–90.

2.4. Anticipating compliance

Compliance is a measure of effectiveness, yet so far, a marginal concern in lawmaking. At best, what is anticipated is how much compliance is expected to cost. Whether, why and how people will comply remains a mystery, until gloriously unveiled by reality. Yet compliance is not about mind games. It is about real people reacting to rules they consider necessary or unnecessary, reasonable or unreasonable, just or unjust. Getting into their shoes and walking around in them is the least a lawmaker can do.

How? There are no definite answers apart from a number of possibilities. Consultation and stakeholder involvement is a useful tool to detect the reaction of end users to planned rules. Asking the right questions can provide information and evidence on factors or elements that will facilitate or hinder compliance. If properly used, consultation can plan this important role. Other tools, like the Table of Eleven[49] developed by the Dutch Ministry of Justice maps eleven critical compliance factors lawmakers can consider: knowledge of rules, costs and benefits in terms of compliance expressed in time, money and effort, acceptance of rules, respect of the target group for authority, social control in terms of estimated risk of positive or negative sanctions on behaviour, risk of reporting, risk of inspection, risk of detection, perceived risk of inspection and detection of a contravention from a sample of end users and risk of sanction if a violation is detected. Considering typical cases is another simple yet useful technique to integrate the perspective of the end users in lawmaking.[50] Once a legislative option is designed, applying it in a case study involving a typical user could reveal important information. Mapping 'user-journeys' or getting user-feedback can play an important role in anticipating compliance – and saving money. Existing or new tools are useful for 'reverse engineering' with regard to how users will react to legislation.

Compliance costs are also an important learning depot. They provide information that can be useful in lawmaking. The information on ways of complying with legislation, costs and their origin, creative compliance patterns, 'congestion' points but also 'patterns' in lawmaking. German ministries

---

[49] Ministry of Justice, *The 'Table of Eleven' A versatile tool* (Version: November 2004), available at: http://www.sam.gov.lv/images/modules/items/PDF/item_618_NL_The_table_of_Eleven.pdf (last accessed 8/12/2018).

[50] Federal Chancellery, *Beyond compliance costs: How do you experience the law? Perception surveys as a complementary tool for Better Regulation* (2016), available at: https://bscw.bund.de/pub/bscw.cgi/d33672063/160614%20survey%20life%20events.pdf?nonce=863f3d4ccc7f2fcb841656474684658f265d0208 (last accessed 8/12/2018).

calculate compliance costs ex-ante and verify them following enactment.[51] This means that 'real' data is available on how costs evolve and where they are located. Compliance costs are often associated with specific provisions or formulations: the EU measurements show that in several areas a small number of obligations generates the majority of costs. In EU tax law three obligations represented more than 82% of the total administrative cost in that area of law. These obligations involved bookkeeping, submission of periodical returns and issuance of invoices, activities repeated in many areas beyond VAT legislation. The fact that specific 'patterns' are costly and burdensome is knowledge that can be exploited in other areas where such provisions are most certainly replicated. In short, measurements of compliance costs bring important lessons about 'patterns', bottlenecks and 'congestion' points in legislation. Avoiding the same mistakes sounds obvious but is not necessarily a reality.

Compliance shifts the focus from the doctrinal, introvertive and esoteric perspective of the lawmaker to an extrovertive, user-oriented, real world approach. Thinking about the users, early on, is an exercise that can make a difference in the design of effective legislation, in selecting appropriate rules and sending the right messages and giving the right motivation.

2.5. Consideration of enforcement and implementation

The enforcement and implementation of the law are complex issues. The 'implementation game' is a complex 'assembly' of mechanisms, funds and actors.[52] The challenge is not only how to select appropriate enforcement mechanisms but also to ensure that they will work. The case studies highlighted how challenges termed as 'implementation' problems might actually be problems in design, which fact places the discussion at the wrong level. Considering implementation as a law making issue and anticipating the impact of main choices and their capacity to work is the only viable strategy in effective lawmaking.

There are, roughly speaking, three alternative approaches in selecting implementation mechanisms.[53] First option: create a new mechanism, whether

---

[51] National Government, Nationaler Normenkontrollrat, Federal Statistical Office, *Guidelines on the Identification and Presentation of Compliance Costs in Legislative Proposals by the Federal Government*, (2012) available at: https://bscw.bund.de/pub/bscw.cgi/d56000782/Engl%20Leitfaden%20Erfuellungsaufwand%202012%20online.pdf?nonce=d6a0b7df93fc664480fad51f5974686378f0286f (last accessed 8/12/2018).

[52] E. Bardach, *The Implementation Game: what happens after a Bill becomes a Law* (MIT Press 1977) at 36–7.

[53] Edward L. Rubin, 'Legislative Methodology: Some Lessons from the Truth-in-Lending Act' (1991) 80 Geo. L.J. 233.

administrative or judicial. Second: restructure an existing one. Third, retain an existing mechanism and create a new set of substantive provisions. These decisions set a highly complex institutional dynamic into motion with major effects on the way the law will operate. Simplistic as they may sound they do reflect the main questions a lawmaker has to ask themself? Are new mechanisms necessary? Can existing ones do the job? What is required? How much will it cost? How to choose? Upon reflection of the parameters mentioned above the main decision making criterion is effectiveness and their efficiency. Realistic and straightforward solutions, even if not optimal, might be more effective than ambitious ones that remain on paper or have few chances to work in real life. Practice in several countries is to accompany draft legislation with a detailed table of the application measures required. An even more advanced practice is to design an implementation plan that determines what needs to be done, by whom and at what cost. This is highly recommendable to ensure that at least the most important implementation issues have been considered in sufficient detail in advance.

2.6. Clear messages for clear communication

Legislative communication is a concern that goes beyond language, clarity, precision and unambiguity and encompasses the need to clearly prioritise, structure and express the messages of the law in a way that they can be accessible and understood by the respective audiences.

The essence of effective legislative communication is to clearly identify the messages of the law and prioritise them in the best possible way. The 'main' or broad message of the law will be included in the title. Section headings and even title headings have to reflect the secondary messages and sub-messages. The overall structure has to make clear the interrelation between the distinct messages and move from the most to the less important and from the most general to the most specific. The language used is another element to be considered. Using visual aids, examples or tables, if this will help the end recipients understand remains to be decided. Even the existence or placement of definitions should be considered from the perspective of communication. Legislative style and tradition should be strictly obeyed only when it facilitates communication. When it comes to the provisions themselves, their level of specification and content needs to be determined by assessing what the particular recipients need to be told in order to achieve a desired result. This requires a clear thinking process and clear decisions. The lawmakers' toolkit is humble yet not deplorable.

Innovative approaches to communicate the law in a more accessible way should also be given serious thought. The layered approach[54] that suggests that legislation should be divided in parts and expressed in a way that can be communicated to different groups of users is an innovative approach. Although it seems to increase rather than eliminate complexity to the extent that the regulatory messages will be written three times, using different words, involving important issues in interpretation, it might work in some cases, or, might deserve to be tested. Even 'hard' legal issues like definitions might on some occasions or for some audiences benefit from a fresh approach, for example a narrative or a story telling approach.[55] Australian legislation includes a 'simplified outline' in the beginning of each Part giving a summary of the main interventions. Usability tests[56] of draft legislation (including text focused evaluation, readability, expert judgements evaluation, reader focused evaluation) are another way to test that it is sufficient, precise and understandable.

Legislative communication offers no one-size-fits-all solutions. Instead, every statute is unique and all available options need to be explored in concreto with regard to their capacity to add value in a specific case. Lawmakers need to make conscious use of all the tools at their avail but most importantly need to know and prioritise the messages.

2.7. Experimentation

Last but not least, the law cannot stand still. Noll considered all legislation as experimentation.[57] Legislation needs to evolve. In the context of lawmaking, experimentation means testing new provisions or techniques for a limited time, in a limited area, in order to inform long term choices and avoid large scale failures.[58] More than anything, it is a deliberate learning process that acknowl-

---

[54] Helen Xanthaki, *Drafting Legislation. Art and Technology of Rules for Regulation* (Hart Publishing 2014) at 76–9.

[55] Louise Finucane, 'Definitions – A Powerful Tool for Keeping and Effective Statute Book' (2017) 1 The Loophole 15–32.

[56] Duncan Berry, 'Techniques for Evaluating Draft Legislation' (1997) The Loophole at 31.

[57] Peter Noll, *Gesetzgebungslehre* (Reinbek 1973) at 76.

[58] Zachary J. Gubler, 'Experimental Rules', 55 B.C. L. Rev. 129 (2014). Articles 37-1 and 72 of the French Constitution and the Constitutional Law of 2003 (loi constitutionnelle relative à l'organisation décentralisée de la République, adoptée le 28 mars 2003) allows statutes and regulations to contain experimental provisions. Sofia Ranchordás, *Constitutional Sunsets and Experimental Legislation* (Edward Elgar 2014); R.A.J. Van Gestel, G. Van Dijck, 'Better Regulation through Experimental Legislation' (2011) 17:3 European Public Law 539; Edward L. Rubin, 'Legislative Methodology: Some Lessons from the Truth-in-Lending Act' (1991) 80 Geo. L.J. 233.

edges the need for reflection and change[59] and enables learning through observation, verification of hypotheses, evaluation of results. Concerns associated with experimental legislation related to equality before the law and legal certainty[60] are well founded yet it might still be necessary to test new techniques, especially in rapidly evolving areas or in areas where traditional approaches do not work.

Experimentation expands the artillery of lawmakers, tests new incentives for compliance or responsive ways to enforce. New experimental techniques, behavioural insights,[61] nudges, obligations to publish or disclose information, naming and shaming techniques are common examples. However, experimentation can also concern lawmaking per se. Whether it is the layered approach in communication, the narrative or story telling approach, the use of examples or case studies, the use of visual aids or even visualisations, inspired from the transformation of rules into signs as in the example of traffic codes, several experiments are worth exploring – in a controlled environment and with moderation – to discover their potential contribution in making law more effective. Human-centred development approaches,[62] tested within the Better Regulation Unit of the German Federal Chancellery are used to present the processes and functions required to draft laws and ordinances, as well as to ensure quality and improve standards.

Effective lawmaking is oriented towards results and is always open towards new ways to achieve these results.

3. CONCLUSIONS: THE IMPORTANCE OF LEGISLATIVE DESIGN

Examining the Truth-in-Lending Act passed by Congress in 1968 in the US, Rubin concluded that the failures of the Act in question were not political but

---

[59] F. Crouzatier-Durand, 'Réflexions sur le concept d'expérimentation législative. (à propos de la loi constitutionnelle du 28 mars 2003 relative à l'organisation décentralisée de la République)' Revue française de droit constitutionnel 2003/4 56 at 675–95.

[60] M.A. Heldeweg, 'Experimental legislation concerning technological and governance innovation – an analytical approach' (2015) 3:2 The Theory and Practice of Legislation 169–93; L. Barmes, 'Equality Law and Experimentation: the Positive Action Challenge' (2009) 68:3 Cambridge Law Journal, 623–54.

[61] N. Rangone, 'Making Law Effective: Behavioural Insights into Compliance' (2018) 9:3 European Journal of Risk Regulation 483.

[62] Caroline Paulick-Thiel, 'Summary of the expert findings on gathering, analysing and presenting information on organisational processes and structures in the context of national and international legislation' 2017, available at: https://bscw.bund.de/pub/bscw.cgi/d48976022/180111_SVB_CPT_EN_short.pdf?nonce=3e20b79a11f49326036ed4258546083708a568ca (last accessed 8/12/2018).

conceptual and methodological. It was not that the initial goals of the Act were ill-conceived or impossible to accomplish but rather that the lawmaker did not know how to accomplish them[63] because they lacked a method. The case studies examined in the previous chapters confirmed that legislation without a clear design (and strategy) might struggle to achieve its objectives. A clear process of legislative design is required for every law.

Legislative design is the process of making decisions on the fundamental elements of new legislation and fitting the pieces of the puzzle together. Design is not about microscopic detail but about the broader picture: the type of problem to be addressed and its features, the available options and techniques, anticipating compliance, testing the enforcement mechanism and the choices in communication. It is the process of incrementally moving from one decision to the other rather than attempting to do everything at once or nothing at all. Starting with the intended goal/s, the choice of substantive statutory provisions, the compliance and implementation mechanism and choices in communication. Legislative methodology guides the process, and becomes a habit that would allow coherent decision making. Effectiveness is the main decision making criterion in this process, in order to ensure feasibility and realism in the solution.

Legislative design needs to address the following aspects of a legislative solution

- Problem/situation addressed and aspects that can be addressed through legislation.
- Alternative ways to intervene. What types of rules can be used?
- Advantages and disadvantages. How will each technique intervene? What are the advantages? What are the disadvantages? Anticipated effect, cost, impact.
- How is compliance expected to evolve? What are the costs?
- How can enforcement assist compliance? Cost elements? Resources?
- What are the main messages? How can rules be best communicated?

Legislative design makes the transition from policy to lawmaking smooth. Where policy making ends, that is, in selecting a preferred option a number of legislative solutions arise. What penalties? What rules? What enforcement? Legislative design is not an evident step in lawmaking. In common law jurisdictions, drafting instructions include elements of legislative design, yet this role is not clear and is blinkered by the informality of the process. In civil law jurisdictions, design is in fact consolidated when a draft is in place. Yet design

---

[63] Edward L. Rubin, 'Legislative Methodology: Some Lessons from the Truth-in-Lending Act', 80 Geo. L.J. 233 (1991).

begins before the draft not because of it. The process of drafting often focuses on doctrinal or procedural issues and misses the broader picture. The result? Laws that intervene as the crow flies, assuming they can go straight from the status quo to the desired end result, and are often buffeted by reality. Design is a thinking process between policy making and legislative drafting that guarantees sufficient space to consider options, evidence, experience and shape the skeleton of the law. If this skeleton is weak, unbalanced or superficial, a law appears to have more chances to fail, partially or entirely.

Reality is never black or white and the dynamic process of shaping the content of the rules has to balance a number of factors, internal and external to the lawmaking process. Far from a laboratory exercise, the design of effective rules is a subtle exercise oriented to achieve a workable balance between politics, technique, evidence, compromise, intuition, tradition and experimentation. The main tools of the lawmaker come in the form of types of rules and techniques, methods to induce compliance, enforcement mechanisms and tools for communication, hence language, structure and form.

Effective lawmaking requires a clear process of legislative design, justified decisions on the basis of reality, evidence and their potential to work, internal consistency and coherence in the formula designed, openness to experimentation, and, most importantly, learns from experience rather than automatically repeat pre-existing legislative patterns.

4. Legislation and its context

1. WHY CONTEXT MATTERS

Every law is part of an 'operating system',[1] the legal system. Contemporary legal systems tend to acquire gigantic dimensions offering detailed solutions to millions of problems through rules of organisation, jurisdiction, procedure and substantive law.[2] The illustration below attempted to visualise the myriad interactions between distinct Acts coexisting in an imaginary statute book. This does not only give a flavour of how complex the system is but it also alludes to the kind of difficulties one might run into when looking for a nugget of legal information – that might be the answer to a specific legal problem – in this complex environment.[3] Some might argue that this is not a real lawmaking problem? Or is it? And if so, what can lawmakers actually do about it?

The legal system is saturated with legal messages, addressing the same or distinct audiences. Communication relates not only to the content of the law but also its superstructure: in other words, the way in which it will integrate the legal system and interact with it. Legislative messages transmitted through legislation have obvious or hidden interactions and can coexist harmoniously, 'compete', complement or simply 'sabotage' each other. Every new law adds new messages to this communication medium that compete with pre-existing ones for the attention and the allegiance of end-recipients.[4] The lawmaker, as the designer and the emitter of every new message, is obliged to make sure that this integrates the legal system smoothly and that it does not overlap or contradict other laws.

The relationship between legal messages is far from indifferent: it affects the effectiveness of the message itself, the direction in which behaviours are guided, the capacity of the end-recipient to locate and understand the message and the capacity of the implementer to trace it and interpret it in relation to other rules. For example, when one set of provisions directs a specific group

---

[1] L. Friedman, *The Legal System* (Russell Sage Foundation 1975) at 5.
[2] Ibid at 12.
[3] U. Lavery, 'The "Findability" of the Law' (1943) 27 Journal of the American Judicature Society 25.
[4] A. Allot, *The Limits of Law* (Butterworths 1980) at 121–2.

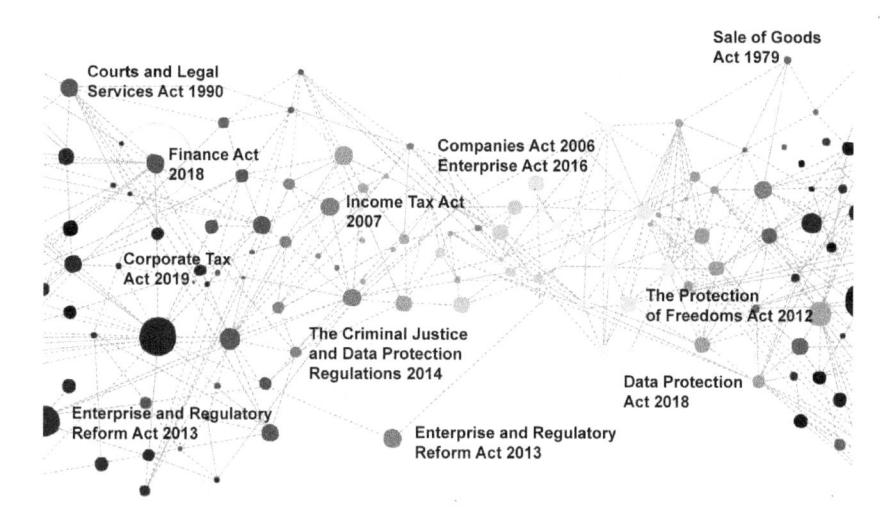

Figure 4.1   A visual depiction of an imaginary statute book

towards one behaviour while another offers motives to the exact opposite, there is an obvious problem in the coexistence of these messages and their coherence. From the perspective of the end-user, the challenge is firstly the possibility to easily identify messages relevant to them within a complex legal system (identify does not mean understand, it means locate) and secondly, to differentiate a message from competing ones and figure out their relationship. Does the new message change, override, alter or leave pre-existing or competing messages unaffected? How does it change the status quo?

The 'emitter' of the message on the other hand needs to ensure coherence in the message itself (the content of legislation was addressed in the previous chapter) but also in the way it integrates the legal order and interacts with it. Does a message repeal or override a previous one? Does it complement it? Does it change it? An idea, theory or message is coherent if it 'fits together, if its parts are mutually supportive, if it is intelligible, if it flows from or expresses a single unified viewpoint. An idea or theory is incoherent if it is unintelligible, inconsistent, ad hoc, fragmented, disjointed, or contains thoughts that are unrelated to and do not support one another'.[5] Beyond the evident appeal of the idea

---

[5]   K. Kress, 'Coherence' in D. Patterson (ed) *A Companion to Philosophy of Law and Legal Theory* (2nd edn Blackwell Publishing 2010) 521–38 at 521.

that the legal system is more than a random assemblage of unrelated and inconsistent rules, coherence is a precondition for legitimacy[6] and intelligibility.[7]

From the perspective of the lawmaker, the effort to sustain the coherence of the legal system and deliver a message that is accessible, intelligible and identifiable within a complex legal environment is not insignificant. The topic is extremely broad and can be explored from different angles. From a lawmaking perspective, however, it translates into three specific challenges: how to ensure that the message transmitted by a law is accessible and detectable? How to ensure that the message is coherent with other existing ones? Last but not least, how to ensure that the message is traceable and intelligible for the user in terms of the changes it brings? The next section will consider the basic choices that the lawmaker has with regard to the superstructure of the message, ways to integrate it in the legal system, make it identifiable and accessible, the important factors for a smooth coexistence between the new and pre-existing messages and the ways in which the choice of how to deliver the message affects the results of the law.

2. SUPERSTRUCTURE AND THE TRANSMISSION OF LEGISLATIVE MESSAGES

Delivering a message effectively depends on the emitter, the recipients, transmission methods, the clarity of the message, but also the interrelation with other messages, what Allot calls 'noise' or 'interference' from competing messages. Noise in emission might be an imperfectly formulated idea in the actual message, problems in expression or language or communication, while interference indicates the 'difficult' relationship with messages that affect or distort the one emitted. What choices do lawmakers have to deliver their message/s and what are the impacts of these choices? In other words, how can they 'package' the legislative message? Issues related to the expression of the message itself have been addressed in other parts of this study. This section will only deal with its superstructure and its interrelation with other messages.

---

[6] R. Alexy and A. Peczenik, 'The Concept of Coherence and Its Significance for Discursive Rationality' (1990) 3 Ratio Juris 130; L. Wintgens, 'Legisprudence as a New Theory of Legislation' in Luc Wintgens (ed) *The Theory and Practice of Legislation* (Routledge 2016) at 15.

[7] R. Grantham and D. Jensen, 'Coherence in the Age of Statutes' (2016) 42:2 Monash University Law Review 360–82.

2.1. The 'all-in-one' message

Regulating all aspects of an issue in a single piece of legislation seems an evident choice. This legislative choice attempts to exhaust an object, to the extent possible, and its content in a single instrument, labelled accordingly (through a suitable title) to 'mark' its unique space in the statute book. In this approach, the effort is to transmit the entire message at once. Complemented by effective choices of title, structure, parts, headings and sub-headings that organise and structure the material in a way to make it accessible and understandable it seems to be an ideal choice.

Advantages of this solution are multiple: at symbolic level, a single message facilitates conceptual consistency, logical structure of content and understanding. At legal level, it facilitates harmonised protection, uniformity of concepts and a consistent handling of cases. It has the additional advantage of internal coherence, which, being part of a single text, obeys a common logic and a consistent structure. At practical level, the message is easily traceable by end-recipients thus ensuring, at least to an initial level, accessibility (in the sense of treaceability). To conclude, this choice has strong advantages in terms of accessibility and conceptual coherence, while results and outcomes can be measured in relation to the specific act.

For example, the Equality Act 2010 unified and rationalised a disperse pre-existing body of discrimination messages into a single Act, organised under 'a single set of principles'.[8] This comprehensive Act now covers all related issues, including key concepts of equality, protected characteristics, prohibited conduct, services and public function, premises and areas of life including work, occupational pension schemes, equality of terms, education, associations, including measures concerning people with disabilities that were previously dispersed in a number of Acts and Regulations. Choosing to ratify a single Act, allows content to be organised in a logical way and ensures a comprehensive approach.

Equality Act 2010 (UK)
PART 1   **SOCIO-ECONOMIC INEQUALITIES**
1. Public sector duty regarding socio-economic inequalities
2. Power to amend section 1
3. Enforcement

---

[8] Bob Hepple, *Equality. The New Legal Framework* (Hart Publishing 2011) at 1, 7; Bob Hepple, 'Enforcing Equality Law: Two Steps Forward and Two Steps Backwards for Reflexive Regulation' (2011) 40:4 Industrial Law Journal 315; Simon Deakin, 'Editorial' (2011) 40:4 Industrial Law Journal 313.

PART 2 EQUALITY: KEY CONCEPTS
CHAPTER 1 PROTECTED CHARACTERISTICS
4. The protected characteristics
5. Age
6. Disability
7. Gender reassignment
8. Marriage and civil partnership
9. Race
10. Religion or belief
11. Sex
12. Sexual orientation
CHAPTER 2 PROHIBITED CONDUCT
Discrimination
13. Direct discrimination
14. Combined discrimination: dual characteristics
15. Discrimination arising from disability
16. Gender reassignment discrimination: cases of absence from work
17. Pregnancy and maternity discrimination: non-work cases
18. Pregnancy and maternity discrimination: work cases
19. Indirect discrimination
Adjustments for disabled persons
20. Duty to make adjustments
21. Failure to comply with duty
22. Regulations
Discrimination: supplementary
23. Comparison by reference to circumstances
24. Irrelevance of alleged discriminator's characteristics
25. References to particular strands of discrimination
Other prohibited conduct
26. Harassment
27. Victimisation
PART 3 SERVICES AND PUBLIC FUNCTIONS
Preliminary
28. Application of this Part
Provision of services, etc.
29. Provision of services, etc.
Supplementary
30. Ships and hovercraft
31. Interpretation and exceptions
PART 4 PREMISES
Preliminary
32. Application of this Part
Disposal and management
33. Disposals, etc.
34. Permission for disposal
35. Managements
Reasonable adjustments
36. Leasehold and commonhold premises and common parts

37. Adjustments to common parts in Scotland
Supplementary
38. Interpretation and exceptions
....

However, and although this does not entirely solve the problem of hidden interactions with other messages, reality shows that this is not always a feasible choice for a number of reasons: firstly, because the message might not be mature or ready to be transmitted in its entirety, secondly, because legislation often evolves incrementally, while time, pressure or the need to achieve compromise might lead to solutions that leave 'difficult' or confrontational issues for later.

2.2. 'Diffuse' messages

A second lawmaking choice is to adjust the legal message to different sectors or areas of law and 'diffuse' it in the legal system at different levels and layers. Reverting to equality legislation, this would translate into the following: rather than one general prohibition of discrimination, several sectoral prohibitions would exist: in employment laws, recruitment, education, healthcare, public life, etc. A typical example of this choice is equality legislation in France: provisions prohibiting discrimination are present in major areas of law, including penal law, labour law, social law, tax law, etc. Sectoral codes include special sections devoted to discrimination: a section 'discriminations' in the penal code, titles on 'discriminations', 'professional equality between women and men', 'harassment' in the labour code, the code on social action and families, the code of social security, the code of public health, general code of taxes, education code, etc.

Code penal (France)
Version consolidée au 12 septembre 2018
- Partie législative
  - Livre Ier: Dispositions générales
  ...
  - Livre II: Des crimes et délits contre les personnes
  ...
    - Titre II: Des atteintes à la personne humaine
    ...
      - Chapitre V: Des atteintes à la dignité de la personne
        - Section 1: Des discriminations. (Articles 225-1 à 225-4)
        - Section 1 bis: De la traite des êtres humains. (Articles 225-4-1 à 225-4-9)
        - Section 1 ter: De la dissimulation forcée du visage. (Article 225-4-10)

- Section 2: Du proxénétisme et des infractions qui en résultent. (Articles 225-5 à 225-12)
- Section 2 bis: Du recours à la prostitution. (Articles 225-12-1 à 225-12-4)

…..

Code du travail (France)
Version consolidée au 7 novembre 2018
- Chapitre préliminaire: Dialogue social. (Articles L1 à L3)
- Première partie: Les relations individuelles de travail
  - Livre Ier: Dispositions préliminaires
  ….
    - Titre III: Discriminations
      - Chapitre Ier: Champ d'application. (Articles L1131-1 à L1131-2)
      - Chapitre II: Principe de non-discrimination. (Articles L1132-1 à L1132-4)
      - Chapitre III: Différences de traitement autorisées. (Articles L1133-1 à L1133-6)
      - Chapitre IV: Actions en justice.
        - Section 1: Dispositions communes. (Articles L1134-1 à L1134-5)
        - Section 2: Dispositions spécifiques à l'action de groupe. (Articles L1134-6 à L1134-10)
    - Titre IV: Egalité professionnelle entre les femmes et les hommes
      - Chapitre Ier: Champ d'application. (Article L1141-1)
      - Chapitre II: Dispositions générales. (Articles L1142-1 à L1142-6)
      - Chapitre III: Plan et contrat pour l'égalité professionnelle
        - Section unique: Plan pour l'égalité professionnelle. (Articles L1143-1 à L1143-3)
      - Chapitre IV: Actions en justice. (Articles L1144-1 à L1144-3)
      - Chapitre V: Instances concourant à l'égalité professionnelle. (Article L1145-1)
      - Chapitre VI: Dispositions pénales. (Articles L1146-1 à L1146-3)
    - Titre V: Harcèlements
      - Chapitre Ier: Champ d'application. (Article L1151-1)
      - Chapitre II: Harcèlement moral. (Articles L1152-1 à L1152-6)
      - Chapitre III: Harcèlement sexuel. (Articles L1153-1 à L1153-6)
      - Chapitre IV: Actions en justice. (Articles L1154-1 à L1154-2)
      - Chapitre V: Dispositions pénales. (Articles L1155-1 à L1155-2)
    - Titre VI: Corruption
  - Livre II: Le contrat de travail
    - Titre Ier: Champ d'application
    …..

This approach 'diffuses' the legislative message horizontally (in different sectors and areas of law) and vertically (different levels of provisions). The obvious advantage is that the message is made more accessible to the specific audiences interested in a special area of law and can be adjusted to its intricacies. Rather than expecting the users, that is, workers, labour law lawyers, teachers, students and professionals in education or social security to adjust a general message to their circumstances, the lawmaker does this for them. This approach allows the message to become more focused and targeted and enhances accessibility by specific audiences.

Disadvantages of this approach relate to the fact that the 'sectoralisation' of the message makes it centrifugal, weakening the visibility of the broader or overall message; secondly, there is no unified and autonomous corpus of anti-discrimination legislation. Thirdly, it increases the need to coordinate and ensure coherence between the sectoral messages, not to mention the enforcement and administrative services involved in implementation. Another, less obvious implication of 'diffused' messages relates to the possibility to monitor or assess their results. Evaluating the performance of equality enactments dispersed in different codes, would either have to focus on specific groups of provisions (e.g. gender pay, disability pensions, reasonable accommodation, etc.), groups of provisions in areas of law (e.g. equality provisions in education or social security or tax law) or, in a more ambitious endeavour, in equality provisions across areas of law.

This choice can work well in jurisdictions that rely on codified law or for provisions that are relevant across areas of law. However, while bringing the message closer to its recipients and making it more accessible, this option increases the risk of coherence and consistency in the content and communication of the message.

2.3. 'Fragmented' messages

The third legislative choice is to 'break' the message into smaller ones and communicate them through distinct laws. In this case, the message is 'sliced' into fragments and packaged in separate Acts.

In the UK, before the unification of all equality legislation under the Equality Act 2010, legislation in force comprised an extended list of Acts and regulations linked to single protected grounds prohibiting racial discrimination, sex discrimination, discrimination on the grounds of disability, religion and belief, sexual orientation, age, imposed obligations for equal pay:

- Race Relations Act 1965 (RRA 1965) amended by Race Relations Act 1968 (RRA 1968) and Race Relations Act 1976 (RRA 1976) and Race Relations Act 2000 (RRA 2000);
- Equal Pay Act 1970 (EPA 1970);
- Sex Discrimination Act 1975 (SDA 1975);
- Disability Discrimination Act 1995 (DDA 1995);

- Employment Equality (Religion or Belief) Regulations 2003 (Religion Regulations 2003);
- Employment Equality (Sexual Orientation) Regulations 2003 (Sexual Orientation Regulations 2003);
- Employment Equality (Age) Regulations 2006 (Age Regulations 2003); Equality Act 2006 (EA 2006)

The criteria for fragmenting the message can vary and can be sectoral or thematic. The legislation previously organised the messages on the basis of the discrimination grounds protected (race, sex, disability, age, etc.). For example, in EU equality legislation the subject is divided between Directives using a thematic and sectoral approach:

- Council Directive 2000/43/EC of 29 June 2000 implementing the principle of equal treatment between persons irrespective of racial or ethnic origin;
- Council Directive 2000/78/EC of 27 November 2000 establishing a general framework for equal treatment in employment and occupation;
- Directive 2006/54/EC of the European Parliament and of the Council of 5 July 2006 on the implementation of the principle of equal opportunities and equal treatment of men and women in matters of employment and occupation (recast);
- Council Directive 2004/113/EC of 13 December 2004 implementing the principle of equal treatment between men and women in the access to and supply of goods and services.

Directive 2000/43 links the message to the protected ground of racial or ethnic origin, while Directive 2000/78, that prohibits discrimination on a number of other grounds, organises itself around the sector of employment. The two other Directives refer to sectors or areas of activity (employment and occupation and access to goods and services).

In gender equality, the Recast Directive (2006/54/EC) on equal opportunities and equal treatment of women and men in employment and occupation codified several pre-existing Directives with a more 'random' choice of themes:

- Implementation of the principle of equal treatment for men and women as regards access to employment, vocational training and promotion, and working conditions (Directive 76/207/EEC);
- Implementation of the principle of equal treatment for men and women in occupational social security schemes (Directive 86/378/EEC);
- Approximation of the laws of the Member States relating to the application of the principle of equal pay for men and women (Directive 75/117/EEC);

- The burden of proof in cases of discrimination based on sex (Directive 97/80/EC).

A number of other Directives are still in force on specific issues:

- Sex discrimination in access to and the supply of goods and services (Directive 2004/113/EC);
- Pregnancy Directive (Directive 92/85/EEC);
- Parental Leave Directive (Directive 2010/18/EU);
- Part-time Work Directive (Directive 97/81/EC).

The 'slicing' of the messages does not follow a common logic. Sometimes it applies to areas of life (employment), or to physical conditions (pregnancy), status (the status of being a parent) or on protected grounds. There is no evidence that the choice of approach in how to break down the separate messages has been a conscious one.

Arguments in favour of the fragmented approach highlight its positive impact on visibility and accessibility. In fact, the existence of separate acts can make the subject matter more visible to the affected parties and can be helpful for ownership, campaigning, education and advocacy purposes. In practice, disabled people or the LGBTI community found it easier to associate with what they considered to be 'their' Acts (the Disability Discrimination Act or the Sexual Orientation Regulations 2003). The Americans with Disabilities Act, one of the most well-known laws on the rights of people with disabilities, addresses directly a population of over 54 million Americans who have a disability and others who work or interact with them in different capacities. From their perspective, important (and to some extent autonomous) sub-messages of the law that are relevant to them, might be hidden or even lost in the wealth of other messages included in a comprehensive (and extensive) single Act. From a different perspective, fragmentation can be associated to the increasing specialisation of law,[9] and the need to convey more numerous and detailed messages.

On the negative side, fragmentation of messages, and consequently of rules and powers, increases the need for interaction and interdependencies, leaves space for information asymmetries,[10] while it might facilitate 'perverse' incentives[11] if not prepared with sufficient craft to ensure a perfect

---

[9] Patricia Popelier, 'Codification in a Civil Law Jurisdiction: A Northern European Perspective' (2017) 4 European Journal of Law Reform 253.
[10] Julia Black, 'Critical Reflections on Regulation' (2002) 27 Australian Journal of Legal Philosophy 1–35 at 3.
[11] Peter Grabosky, 'Counterproductive Regulation' (1995) 23 International Journal of the Sociology of Law 347–69 at 354.

alignment. Complex, fragmented and disperse frameworks can easily lead to inconsistencies in content of the law and result in complexity, gaps and poor coherence. Legislative practice offers ample examples where even differences in definitions in related or even the same legal concepts in different enactments caused confusion and required correction either through reform or through interpretation by the courts. Another aspect is that this is 'too much law' for end-recipients to understand, to comply with, to follow up with. To make matters more complex, legislation is constantly changing, thus requiring a sustained effort to keep up with changes, interpretation and case law. The more laws, the more changes and cases one needs to follow. Fragmentation appears to be inherently linked to complexity. The result is that it is difficult for end-recipients to locate and access rules, quick and fair dispute resolution might be jeopardised and compliance with legislation might be discouraged.

2.4. 'Patchwork' messages

A last option for transmitting legal messages is to assemble several of them, no matter how unrelated, in one law. This practice, known as 'omnibus', 'mosaic',[12] 'garbage', 'arrangement', 'Christmas tree',[13] chorizo[14] Bills or 'lois fourre-tout'[15] is observed in several jurisdictions. These Acts are a random list of provisions or amendments rather than a structured and organised content.

The only advantage of patchwork laws are in terms of efficiency, economy of parliamentary time, procedures and the possibility for rapid legislative responses. However, they raise serious concerns with regard to the complexity and incomprehensibility of the planned changes and the limited visibility and accessibility of the provisions under modification.[16] Indeed, the provisions included in such Bills are mostly intelligible if not integrated in their context, thus making the effort to understand and conceptualise the changes quite demanding, if not impossible. Further, the reader has no idea what to look for

---

[12] Patricia Popelier, 'Mosaics of Legal Provisions' (2006) VII:1/2 European Journal of Law Reform 47–52 at 47.

[13] Office of the Parliamentary Counsel Cabinet Office, *When Laws Become Too Complex* (2013) at 16, available at: https://assets.publishing.service.gov.uk/government/uplosystemads//uploads/attachment_data/file/187015/GoodLaw_report_8April_AP.pdf (last accessed 8/12/2018).

[14] P. García-Escudero Márquez, *Técnica legislativa y seguridad jurídica: ¿hacia el control constitucional de la calidad de las leyes?* (Cuadernos Civitas Thomson Reuters 2011) at 60.

[15] French Council of State, 'De la Sécurité Juridique' (1991) 43 Etudes & Documents 36–7.

[16] Popelier (n 12) 47–52.

in an omnibus Bill. Unless (or until) this is placed in its content, it might be very difficult to trace.

The first obvious difficulty is in locating change. An example of the problems of omnibus legislation is the Enterprise and Regulatory Reform Act 2013 (UK). The long title shows the diversity of subjects within it:

> *An Act to make provision about the UK Green Investment Bank; to make provision about employment law; to establish and make provision about the Competition and Markets Authority and to abolish the Competition Commission and the Office of Fair Trading; to amend the Competition Act 1998 and the Enterprise Act 2002; to make provision for the reduction of legislative burdens; to make provision about copyright and rights in performances; to make provision about payments to company directors; to make provision about redress schemes relating to lettings agency work and property management work; to make provision about the supply of customer data; to make provision for the protection of essential supplies in cases of insolvency; to make provision about certain bodies established by Royal Charter; to amend section 9(5) of the Equality Act 2010; and for connected purposes.*

Amidst several provisions, unrelated to each other, comes an amendment to the Equality Act 2010. The amendment made 'caste' an element of 'race' thus broadening the material scope of application of the law on a topic that has received attention and has been considered by the courts. Far from an insignificant amendment, this is hidden in a sea of messages – irrelevant to the topic – making it very difficult to trace. Will the message that something as important has actually changed reach the interested citizens and implementers on time?

The practice of such laws has triggered a reaction from the courts in a number of countries. The Supreme Court in Israel ruled them unconstitutional, although mainly for reasons of due legislative process rather than navigability.[17] The French Council of State considers that they encroach upon the citizen's right to legal certainty, while the Belgian Council of State criticises the legal uncertainty induced by them.[18] Cormacain suggests that the only time omnibus laws can be acceptable is when they repeal obsolete provisions which are no longer of practical utility (Statute Law Repeal Acts).[19] Even in this case, knowing that a provision has been repealed is important. The most important problem with omnibus laws, however, is when they introduce new rules.

The second problem is the difficulty in understanding what has changed in the law, especially if the amended provisions are not restated but only the

---

[17] Ittai Bar-Siman-Tov, 'The Dual Meaning of Evidence-based Judicial Review of Legislation' (2016) 4:2 The Theory and Practice of Legislation 107–33.

[18] Popelier (n 12) 47–51.

[19] Ronan Cormacain, 'Legislative Drafting and the Rule of Law' (PhD Thesis, University of London 2017) at 67.

changes are listed. In France, several changes to equality provisions were introduced through Acts introducing a series of amendments in areas of law ranging from public security, to public health, to employment, social security introduced, at different times and in different mixes, substantive provisions, extensions of material scope, new offences and sanctions, procedural or institutional changes.

> Loi n°2001-1066 du 16 novembre 2001 relative à la lutte contre les discriminations (France)
> *Article 1er*
> ....
> *II. L'article L. 122-35 du code du travail est ainsi modifié:*
>   *1o Au deuxième alinéa, après le mot: «moeurs,», sont insérés les mots: «de leur orientation sexuelle, de leur âge,»;*
>   *2o Au deuxième alinéa, après le mot: «confessions,», sont insérés les mots: «de leur apparence physique, de leur patronyme,».*
> *III. L'article 225-1 du code pénal est ainsi modifié:*
>   *1o Au premier alinéa:*
>   *a) Après le mot: «famille,», sont insérés les mots: «de leur apparence physique, de leur patronyme,»;*
>   *b) Après le mot: «moeurs,», sont insérés les mots: «de leur orientation sexuelle, de leur âge,»;*
>   *2o Au deuxième alinéa:*
>   *a) Après le mot: «famille,», sont insérés les mots: «de l'apparence physique, du patronyme,»;*
>   *b) Après le mot: «moeurs,», sont insérés les mots: « de l'orientation sexuelle, de l'âge,».*

In this example the problem is that the amendments are intelligible to the extent that they consist of isolated phrases cut out of context and without any logical sequence. In order for them to be understandable and for their impact to be obvious they would have to be integrated in the text and the amended provision would have to be restated.

A different type of amendment is when entire new sections are added to existing ones. In this case, the change itself is visible and understandable, but its traceability with regard to placement in its context remains an issue, especially if no official consolidations or codifications are in place. In the example below, the Amendment to the Race Relations Act extended its scope and added new prohibitions and competencies to the existing law.

Race Relations (Amendment) Act 2000 (UK)

> *Further extension of 1976 Act to police and other public authorities*
> *1. After section 19A of the Race Relations Act 1976 (in this Act referred to as "the 1976 Act") there is inserted—*

"Public authorities 19B.—(1) It is unlawful for a public authority in carrying out any functions of the authority to do any act authorities. which constitutes discrimination.
(2) In this section "public authority"—
 (a) includes any person certain of whose functions are functions of a public nature; but
 (b) does not include any person mentioned in subsection (3).
(3) The persons mentioned in this subsection are—
 (a) either House of Parliament;
 (b) a person exercising functions in connection with proceedings in Parliament;
 (c) the Security Service;
 ...."

Amendments to the Family Procedure Rules 2010 (UK)

3. For rule 2.1, substitute—
"*Application of these Rules*
2.1. Unless the context otherwise requires, these rules apply to family proceedings in—
 (a) the High Court; and
 (b) the family court."

Amendments to the Family Procedure Rules 2010
4. In rule 2.3(1)—
 (a) omit the definitions of—
  (i) "Allocation Order";
  (ii) "civil partnership proceedings county court";
  (iii) "court of trial";
  (iv) "designated county court";
  (v) "district judge";
  (vi) "district registry";
  (vii) "divorce county court"; and
  (viii) "Royal Courts of Justice";
 (b) in the definition of "court" for ", a county court or a magistrates' court" substitute "or the family court"; and
 (c) in the definition of "court officer" for the words after "means", including the words in parentheses at the end of the definition, substitute "a member of court staff".

5. In rule 2.5(1)—
 (a) for the words from ", any other enactment" to "1990," substitute "or any other enactment";
 (b) for paragraph (b) substitute—
 "(b) in relation to proceedings in the family court, by any judge.";
 (c) omit paragraph (c); and
 (d) for the words in parentheses at the end of paragraph (1) substitute—

> *"(Rules made under section 310 of the 1984 Act make provision for a justices' clerk to carry out certain functions of the family court or of a judge of the family court and for an assistant to a justices' clerk to carry out functions of a justices' clerk given under those rules, or by section 310(2) of the 1984 Act.)".*

In both cases but especially in the former, the problem of accessibility and intelligibility is solved once the amending provisions are incorporated in codified or consolidated legislation. But what if consolidated legislation is not available? What happens until a codification – usually a time-consuming enterprise – is completed? The problem also extends to the ex-ante accessibility and understandability of the rationale and content of the planned changes and the extent to which they can be considered by lawmakers.

2.5. Delivery options and their implications

The choice of 'package' affects the effectiveness of legislation in three main ways: in terms of accessibility of the message to the extent that it determines how easily end users will be able to detect and identify the message; in terms of coherence of the message with other common concepts, provisions, etc. And finally, in terms of the effectiveness of the message itself: how the results of legislation can be identified and measured.

The way new rules are articulated affects accessibility in a different way: the 'all in one message' offers a unified message which is traceable within one act; the 'diffuse approach' makes the message accessible in its specific context assuming it will be more approachable to those affected. The 'fragmented approach' communicates distinct messages through stand-alone acts. The 'patchwork' approach introduces several messages or changes at the time without any clear rationale as to their accessibility. Although there are obvious advantages in favour of the first option, the structure of the legal system, a specific area of law or specific circumstances might require a different approach.

Coherence is affected differently. The unified approach promotes coherence through a 'functional' codification of the subject matter; the 'diffuse' approach addresses coherence by placing the message in its 'rightful' position whether that is sectoral codified legislation or different sectoral laws. The fragmented approach and patchwork provisions do not offer a particular solution for coherence.

These choices, apart from leading to different levels of accessibility and coherence, essentially also lead to different conceptualisations of the results of the message/s. In the 'unified' approach, the results of the message can be appraised in relation to the theme-specific act and its results, a fact that makes its understanding and operationalisation tangible. In the 'diffuse' approach, these can be associated not to individual acts (which might include a number of new or amending provisions) but to either individual provisions or areas of law, for example, gender equality law, equal pay, disability law. In the 'fragmented' approach, results can be appraised with regard to specific pieces of legislation, allowing, however, only a fragmented and act-related view.

The observation of legislative practice leads to three interesting findings: firstly, the effort to legislate complex issues almost invariably leads to a body of complicated legislation consisting of multiple layers of protection and a big number of provisions. Secondly, the incremental development of legislation, a common feature in many jurisdictions, tends to lead to a piecemeal treatment of subject-matters. Thirdly, different legal traditions and legislative styles often lead to different models of organising and structuring legislation. Last but not least, there is little evidence that the superstructure of legislation is a conscious legislative choice. Instead, choices of structure appear to be, to an important extent, the result of distinct 'automatisms' associated with the structure of the legal order, legislative tradition and style, the transposition of supranational legislation or practical restrictions, like the lack of time and the need to introduce new provisions as soon as possible. How can the lawmaker respond to these challenges and transmit the legislative messages effectively?

3. DELIVERING THE MESSAGE EFFECTIVELY

Navigating the legal system can be a daunting exercise for all audiences, including the lawmaker. The option of 'throwing' new rules into the existing storehouse wishing for the best is not a recommended practice. Contextualisation is an important lawmaking task that only the lawmaker can conduct and one that has a number of implications.

3.1. Informed choices on superstructure

The superstructure of legislation needs to be a separate element in the decision making list of the lawmaker, especially with regard to how the legislative messages will be communicated (not in terms of content but in terms of package) and with regard to their connecting points with the broader context. Legislative practice suggests that the choice of whether to introduce a new Act, to amend an existing one or to consolidate or to bring existing material together in a codification is determined to an important extent on the grounds of concerns that do not necessarily consider the communication of the messages and their effectiveness. As already demonstrated this raises a number of concerns. The overarching structure of legislation needs to be a conscious choice in the lawmaking process and two issues need to be considered in particular: accessibility and coherence.

3.2. Accessibility

Legislation is expansive. New laws appear at great speed to add new provisions, amend pre-existing ones, broaden, narrow or alter the scope of existing legislation. This plethora of rules raises obvious concerns with regard to how end-users, implementing bodies and the courts can detect, hence, access the message and locate the new elements in the equation. Accessibility is a multilayered concept that covers both formal aspects such as promulgation and publication,[20] physical accessibility of legislative texts (in text or electronic format), but also the possibility to know the rules that are valid and applicable at a given moment. Under the perspective of homogeneity, even constitutions provisions require Bills to regulate a single issue and by prohibiting irrelevant provisions or amendments.[21]

Accessibility is promoted through drafting principles like availability, navigability and inclusivity.[22] Availability, whether in hard or electronic copies, encompasses six important aspects: availability of the law as enacted, as amended, at a point in time, in a particular geographical area, in context and its findability in terms of being locatable or navigable (it is possible for users to find their way around the statute and inclusivity refers to contain all relevant information).

One basic level of accessibility relates to physical accessibility of legislation. Portals like legislation.gov.uk and legifrance.fr, legislation.gov.au that allow free access of the public to legislation in force are important solutions for accessibility. Another level of accessibility is the availability of codified or consolidated versions of the law. Codification brings legislation in one text together under common principles and structure. Consolidation on the other hand is an informal compilation of legislation with no formal legal effect that allows access to legislation in its current form, including all its amendments. If online codified or consolidated versions of legislation are available, several of the challenges identified in the previous sections are resolved. If these options are not available, the lawmaker needs to give serious consideration on how the legislative messages will be transmitted.

A third level of accessibility deals with the traceability of the changes introduced by the law, especially in the case of amendments. The devil is in the detail and often amendments are a source of frustration for lawyers, citizens and judges alike. From a lawmaking perspective they are a cause of uncertainty due

---

[20] Karl Irresberger and Anna Jasiak, 'Publication' in: U. Karpen and H. Xanthaki, *Legislation in Europe* 165–85, 165–66.
[21] Art. 158 of the Constitution of Colombia.
[22] Cormacain (n 19) at 48–62.

Table 4.1   Example of accessible presentation of the amendments and consolidated version of amended articles

Code of Social Security	
Article 138-16 current	**Article 138-16 modified**
Le produit de la contribution et des remises mentionnées à l'article L. 138-13, dû au titre du taux (Lv), est affecté à la Caisse nationale de l'assurance maladie. Le produit de la contribution et des remises mentionnées au même article L. 138-13, dû au titre du taux (Lh), est affecté au Fonds pour le financement de l'innovation pharmaceutique mentionné à l'article L. 221-1-1.	Le produit des contributions et des remises mentionnées à l'article L. 138-13est affecté à la Caisse nationale de l'assurance maladie.

to the diversity of the task, its variability and difficulty.[23] From the perspective of the user, intelligibility and uncertainty are the major challenges. Whether in the form of express or implied amendments, direct or indirect amendments, apart from drafting challenges[24] raise a number of issues from the perspective of accessibility. A solution to this challenge is a horizontal requirement that any amending Act should reformulate the amended text and state it both in its initial and final form, rather than just state the isolated changes introduced (see table 4.1). The initial and amended text are juxtaposed, including the changes introduced and the reformulated text, so amendments become clearer.

Accessibility ensures that the end user can trace and access the text they are looking for. The lawmaker needs to make conscious choices on this point.

3.3.   Coherence

Coherence requires freedom from contradiction and alignment in a way that things 'make sense as a whole'.[25] 'Making sense' applies to the content of the law (and was addressed in a previous chapter) but also to other aspects of the legal system. Coherence has vertical and horizontal dimensions. Vertical coherence relates to conceptual consistency with other layers of provisions like constitutional or international rules. Horizontal consistency concerns the relationship and coexistence with other laws. *Adapted to lawmaking, this means*

---

[23] A. Lynch and P. Ziegler, 'The Amendment of Legislation' (1991) 12 Statute Law Society at 48, 50.
[24] H. Xanthaki, *Drafting Legislation. Art and Technology of Rules for Regulation* (Hart Publishing 2014) 223–41.
[25] Kress (n 5) at 521.

that every new law should integrate the legal system in a way that it does not produce obvious contradictions and overlaps with existing laws.

Anticipating coherence – or anticipating how the law will integrate its broader context – is not an easy task. On the contrary, it is a tedious and complex one. Thornton highlights two aspects of contextualisation that promote coherence in his five stages of legislative drafting: firstly, during the initial phase of placing the proposal in its policy context (understanding the proposal) and secondly when placing it in its legal context (analysing) before moving to more detail.[26] The first stage (understanding) aims to establish the position of the law in relation to policy or broader initiatives. The second stage (analysis) investigates in detail the legislative environment, hence the specific context within which the new law will be operating. This would essentially involve an analysis of existing law, interactions and points of contact with the law under preparation, as well as analysis of the main elements highlighted in the first phase as the content of the law. This legislative research report allows consideration and identification of all legislative issues relevant to the legislation in course of preparation and the initiation of a dialogue with policy makers on controversial points. Reports on legislation rarely go into much analytical depth on the points of contact or potential conflict of provisions. However, if this is not analysed early on it might cause important confusion.

3.4. Consider how the changes will be appraised

It has already been highlighted that the choices on superstructure impact the ways in which the effectiveness of the legislative message will be understood, monitored and measured. The ways in which the results of legislation can be measured differs substantially in each approach identified. In the 'single' message, results can be directly associated to the appraisal of the law. By looking at the effectiveness of a single act prohibiting discrimination, one can get at the same time a picture of how effective this piece of legislation is and on its broader impacts in the society in question. In the 'fragmented' message, results need to be associated to different pieces of legislation. This does not allow much macroscopic input to the extent that several pieces of legislation in the same area, for example, gender equality, equal pay or equality provisions in social security would make the association of impacts to specific provisions difficult or, to say the least, more complicated. It would however allow the effectiveness of the message to be associated to the individual Acts or to their entirety.

---

[26] Garth C. Thornton, *Legislative Drafting* (4th edn, Tottel 1996); Helen Xanthaki, *Thornton's Legislative Drafting* (5th edn, Bloomsbury Professional 2013).

4. CONCLUSION

The superstructure of legislation is an important anticipatory task in lawmaking. Communication does not concern only the content of the law but also its superstructure: the way it will interact with the legal system. It is an important lawmaking task to make choices that promote the accessibility of the legislative messages and their coherence with 'competing' messages in the legal system. Lawmakers have four main options for 'delivering' new message/s: as a single message, a diffused one, a fragmented pack of messages and a patchwork of messages. Effective lawmaking requires conscious choices that actively promote accessibility, coherence and the traceability and measurability of the results of legislation.

5. The implementation of the law: results, impact and effectiveness

1. LEGISLATION, RESULTS AND LAWMAKING

The 'implementation game' is a complex 'assembly' of mechanisms, funds and actors,[1] a game of actions and reactions.[2] What was, up to enactment, a conceptual exercise in law-making is thereafter expected to deliver results. The relation between the law as a 'vision', its 'working' in real life and its actual results closes the life cycle of legislation.

Legislation is a 'blind shot' if there is no knowledge about how it is implemented, what results are generated and how it operates in real life. Traditional legal thinking, with its emphasis on black letter law, leaves facts in the outskirts of legal studies and has been myopic towards the factual aspects of the implementation process.[3] Observing the 'real life' of the law is important from the perspective of democratic governance, legality and legal certainty, as an 'early warning system' against potential adverse effects on fundamental rights, a way to appraise the responsiveness of the law to the regulated problems and phenomena and to know whether rules are used, unused or misused. The necessity to look at the results of legislation and learn from them evolved in parallel with the rationalisation of lawmaking and the awareness of the fact that the obligation of the legislator to monitor and correct legislation does not end with enactment but extends to the entire lifecycle of the law[4] and requires the systematic collection of data and the evaluation of the effects of legislation.

---

[1] Eugene Bardach, *The Implementation Game: What happens after a Bill becomes a Law* (MIT Press 1977) at 36–7.

[2] J.-D. Delley, R. Derivaz, L. Mader, C.A. Morand and D. Schneider, *Le droit en action: étude de la mise en œuvre de la législation fédérale sur l'acquisition d'immeubles par des personnes domiciliées à l'étranger: rapport final au Fonds national* (CETEL, 1981) at 1.

[3] Lawrence M. Friedman, *The Legal System. A Social Science Perspective* (Russell Sage Foundation 1975) at 15.

[4] Alexandre Flückiger, 'L'obligation jurisprudentielle d'évaluation législative: une application du principe de précaution aux droits fondamentaux' in Andreas Auer, Alexandre Flückiger and Michel Hottelier, *Les droits de l'homme et la constitution:*

Processes to respond to the need to follow up and review legislation post enactment are evolving rapidly but remain relatively fragmented and unsystematic, especially compared to ex-ante ones. A statistical survey conducted by the UK National Audit Office in 2009 found that 46% of the regulations in the sample had not been subject to any form of follow-up evaluation and only 29% had been subjected to full post-implementation review.[5] And while the figures have improved, the overall position of ex post review or evaluation of legislation in jurisdictions around the world still points at significant gaps in the effort to systematically capture legislative results revealed by reality and learn from them. However, if retrospection is the only way to confirm, reinforce or correct the internal mechanics of legislation and its responsiveness to reality what is the role of the lawmaker in this respect?

2. CHALLENGES FOR LAWMAKERS

Legislation can produce different types of results that range from the settlement of individual disputes to broad legal or social change. The legal discipline, and lawmakers, are not particularly at ease with terms like results, outputs, outcomes, impacts and effects, concepts that go beyond doctrinal issues to include factual or empirical elements. However, the desired results will not magically appear. They need to be engineered, and it is the lawmaker who has to anticipate what legislation is expected to deliver and plan ahead with regard to how results will be captured, managed and used to improve and correct during the life of the law.

2.1. What kind of results does legislation produce?

Rules perform multiple functions and, depending on their nature, produce different types of results. Results are the exclusive and direct consequences of the law[6] and range from consequences on the actor, other persons, the social structure, culture and the civilisation, intended or unintended ones.

The discussion about results is inevitably linked to that around the objectives of the law. Chapter 2 identified two main types of objectives relevant for

---

études en l'honneur du Professeur Giorgio Malinverni (Schulthess 2007) 155–70 at 170.

[5] House of Lords, Merits of Statutory Instruments Committee, '8th Report of Session 2009 10. What happened next? A study of Post-Implementation Reviews of secondary legislation: Government response' (2010), available at: https://publications.parliament.uk/pa/ld200910/ldselect/ldmerit/43/43.pdf (last accessed 1/12/2018).

[6] Robert K. Merton, 'The Unanticipated Consequences of Purposive Social Action' (1936) 1:6 American Sociological Review 894–904 at 895.

legislation: specific and broader ones. How do they translate into results? And what kind of results do they produce?

Legislation generates a matrix of results at micro (individual), meso (cumulative) and macro levels that range from individual compliance and individual solutions to problems, to broader legal and social change. Three 'types' of results are relevant for legislation: direct results, outcomes and impacts (or effects).

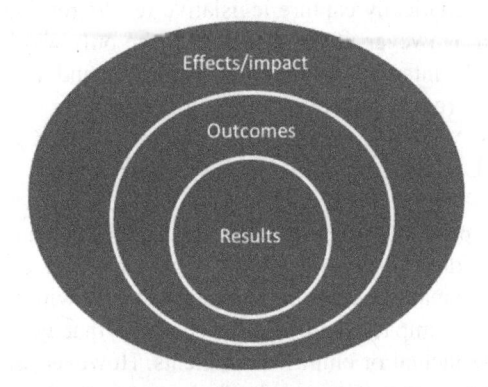

Figure 5.1   The results of legislation

All three types capture real altered situations achieved *through* the law. Where they differ is their scope and nature. Results are a direct consequence of the implementation of the law, and include outputs like judgments, permits, convictions or decisions settling disputes generated on the basis of the law but also immediate consequences attributable to the law, including compliance.

Outcomes are cumulative effects of direct results including broader legal, behavioural or societal change. The outcome of compliance with legislated quotas for the participation of women in decision making bodies is the more equitable representation of both genders in the corporate world. The outcome of tobacco banning legislation is a smoke free environment in public spaces. The outcome of legislation imposing the use of seatbelts is the increased safety of drivers and passengers and potentially also increased road safety.

Impact reflects the total effect of an Act on behaviour, positive and negative, independently of what the lawmaker had in mind.[7] It captures causal connections between law and human behaviour on an even broader scale, beyond

---

[7]   Lawrence Friedman, *Impact. How Law Affects Behavior* (Harvard University Press) at 45, 48.

direct results and outcomes. Effects reflect how legislation has affected its subjects within and beyond the scope of the law. Impact indicates not only whether people comply with legislation but whether and to what extent their behaviours have been affected or changed, positively or negatively. Impact reflects the macro functions of legislation and is the result of several factors including the content of the law, immediate social context, peer pressure, inner conscience and other psychological motives.[8]

The three concepts are closely interrelated and interact in a complex relationship which is unique for every law. For example, the results of a law aiming to 'lay down a general framework for combating discrimination on the grounds of … with a view to putting into effect the principle of equal treatment' would include recording the enacted provisions of what is allowed or prohibited, the procedures set in place for reporting violations, punishment or reparation, decisions or cases solving disputes, including the extent to which people comply with obligations or use their rights. Its outcome would be the improved protection for the disadvantaged groups or individuals targeted, while impact would record the existence of a more open and equitable society, the elimination of stigma, the diversification of labour markets but also adverse consequences like social tension or friction due to positive measures, etc. This unique matrix of results, outcomes and effects needs to be anticipated by the lawmaker and measured (in order to be verified, refuted or adjusted) when the law is implemented. What techniques can lawmakers use to capture results?

2.2. How can results be anticipated and measured?

Results are not generated magically or instantaneously. Implementation, as the process 'of achieving social change through law',[9] is a complex 'assembly' of mechanisms, funds and actors,[10] that requires strategic interactions, the adoption of regulation, the set up or mobilisation of enforcement mechanisms, the transfer of funds and resources, to name only a few of the processes that have to take place. During this maturation process, several 'incidents' can affect or even alter their course: changes in facts, diversion of resources, deflection of goals, resistance from stakeholders or actors are only few examples.[11] How can these situations be recorded and measured?

A first problem is the confusion in the definition of concepts like monitoring, review, post legislative scrutiny and evaluation. To mention one

---

[8] Ibid at 5.
[9] W. Clune III and R.E. Lindquist, 'What "implementation" isn't: toward a general framework for implementation research' (1981) Wisconsin Law Review at 1045.
[10] Bardach (n 1) 36–7.
[11] Ibid at 36–7; Clune and Lindquist (n 9) 1044ff.

characteristic example, European legislation in the period from 2014–17 used seven different expressions to describe related obligations in legislative texts. The terms report, review and report, review and evaluation report, evaluation and report, evaluation, review and evaluation and review[12] were used without a clear hierarchisation or delineation of their interrelationship. The lack of agreed definitions reflects a more general problem, as terms are used either indiscriminately or have jurisdiction-specific nuances.

For the purpose of this study, three distinct processes are identified: the monitoring, review and evaluation of legislation. Monitoring is the process of overseeing, following up the implementation of legislation. It includes the systematic collection of data on implementation and can produce implementation, application or other reports that describe the state of play and provide information on progress. Review on the other hand is an interim assessment of the 'working' of the act. Last but not least, evaluation is a one-off exercise that takes a broader perspective and appraises the Act comprehensively in relation to its objectives.

There are three important differences between monitoring, review and evaluation: firstly, the focus and timing of the exercise. Monitoring is a continuous process of data collection on the implementation of the law, while review and evaluation take place at specific moments in time. Secondly, in terms of scope, monitoring focuses on progress in implementation, review focuses on a periodic assessment of performance while evaluation looks at the act in a more holistic way. Thirdly, while monitoring and review record concepts relevant to 'rights in practice', evaluation aims to capture results as 'policy outcomes'. Last but not least, while the first two processes tend to be more esoteric and introvertive focusing on the inner working of the law, evaluation has a more political character and involves, more or less actively, also the Parliament. But once more what is the role of the lawmaker in all of this?

The lawmaker has to think about the law around its lifecycle. This means that they have to anticipate results but also to make clear decisions on when, where, how and by whom the three processes described above will take place. These will be examined separately in the next sections.

2.2.1. Monitoring

Legislating techniques for monitoring the implementation of legislation can include horizontal (administrative) follow up procedures that apply to all laws

---

[12] Ivana Kiendl Krišto and Vagia Poutouroudi, *Review Clauses in EU Legislation. A Rolling Check-List* (European Parliament, European Parliamentary Research Service 2018), available at: http://www.europarl.europa.eu/RegData/etudes/STUD/2018/621821/EPRS_STU(2018)621821_EN.pdf (last accessed 1/12/2018) at 16.

or specific legislative clauses. Horizontal monitoring procedures introduce general follow up procedures especially with regard to the timely adoption of secondary regulations. In France, an intergovernmental procedure was established in 2008 to monitor the application of legislation.[13] According to this, one minister is appointed responsible for each new law, a provisional implementation timetable is drawn up, a structure within each ministry conducts centralised follow up and reports to the Prime Minister. Progress is examined internally on a three-month basis and reports are submitted to the Parliament every six months.

Monitoring clauses in legislation usually establish reporting obligations requiring the preparation of annual or biannual implementation reports on all or specific aspects of legislation. For example:

Regulation 2016/400 (EU)
[...] the Commission shall submit an annual report [...] on the application and implementation of this Regulation and Title V of the Agreement and on compliance with the obligations laid down therein.

Directive 2015/1794 (EU)
The Commission [...] shall submit a report [...] on the implementation and application of Articles 4 and 5 by [...]

Gender Recognition Act 2015 (Ireland)
6. (1) The Minister shall keep a record, in the form that he or she considers appropriate, of a decision made by him or her under section 8, 11, 14, 15 or 16.
(2) The Minister shall, not later than 30 June in each year prepare a report on the performance of his or her functions under this Act in the immediately preceding year, or in the case of the period from the date this Act comes into operation to the next following 30 June, that period, and as soon as may be after the report has been prepared, shall cause copies of the report to be laid before each House of the Oireachtas.

2.3. Review

Review clauses in legislation or regulations require a specific body to review the operation of a law and publish the findings. The OECD identifies several types of review, with distinct advantages and disadvantages in terms of feasibility, content and cost: programmed reviews, post-implementation reviews and catch-all reviews; ad hoc reviews, 'principles-based' reviews, benchmark-

---

[13] Circulaire du 29 février 2008 relative à l'application des lois, available at : https://www.legifrance.gouv.fr/affichTexte.do?cidTexte=JORFTEXT000018217158 (last accessed 7/12/2018).

ing and 'in-depth' reviews, red-tape reduction targets, etc.[14] Reviews can be statutory (required by statutory texts) or non-statutory, required for example by Impact Assessments. The nature and type of reviews differ per jurisdiction but the main rationale behind it remains the same. In the UK, post-implementation reviews revisit the underlying assumptions of a law or regulation (mostly the latter), verify their validity and adequacy and assess whether it is working as expected or has unintended consequences.[15] They focus on three main questions: are the objectives that led to the introduction of the regulation still valid and relevant?, if yes, is regulation still the best way of achieving those objectives, compared to the possible alternatives?, and if regulation is still justified, can the existing regulation be improved? Post-implementation reviews often complement or revisit the assumptions of ex-ante reviews.

Review clauses can cover 'core' or 'non core' aspects of a law,[16] including a review of 'substantive' provisions or just implementation processes. They can cover all or some elements of legislation and different types of review can be provided, including 'internal' or independent reviews. For example:

Sanctions and Anti-Money Laundering Act 2018 (UK)
30 Review by appropriate Minister of regulations under section 1
(1) Subsection (2) applies where any regulations under section 1 are in force.
(2) The appropriate Minister who made the regulations must in each relevant period review whether the regulations are still appropriate for the purpose stated in them under section 1(3).
(3) If a purpose so stated in any regulations under section 1 is a purpose other than compliance with a UN obligation or other international obligation, any review of those regulations under this section must also include a consideration of—
  (a) whether carrying out that purpose would meet any one or more of the conditions in paragraphs (a) to (i) of section 1(2),
  (b) whether there are good reasons to pursue that purpose, and
  (c) whether the imposition of sanctions is a reasonable course of action for that purpose.
(4) In subsection (3)(c) "sanctions" means prohibitions and requirements of the kinds which are imposed by the regulations for the purpose in question (or both for that purpose and for another purpose of the regulations).

---

[14] OECD, 9th OECD Conference on Measuring Regulatory Performance. Key Findings and Conference Proceedings, available at: http://www.oecd.org/gov/regulatory-policy/Proceedings-9th-Conference-MRP.pdf (last accessed 8/12/2018).

[15] Department for Business, Energy, and Industrial Strategy (BEIS) Better Regulation Executive (BRE), 'Producing Post-Implementation Reviews (PIR) Principles of Best Practice' 2018, available at: https://assets.publishing.service.gov.uk/government/uploads/system/uploads/attachment_data/file/726992/producing-post-implementation-reviews-pir.pdf (last accessed 07/12/2018).

[16] Krišto and Poutouroudi (n 12) at 22.

(5) An appropriate Minister who has carried out a review under this section must lay before Parliament a report containing—
   (a) the conclusions of the review,
   (b) the reasons for those conclusions, and
   (c) a statement of any action that that Minister has taken or proposes to take in consequence of the review.
(6) Nothing in subsection (5) requires the report to contain anything the disclosure of which may, in the opinion of that Minister, damage national security or international relations.
(7) For the purposes of this section each of the following is a "relevant period" in relation to regulations under section 1—
   (a) the period of one year beginning with the date when the regulations are made;
   (b) each period of one year that begins with the date when a report under this section containing the conclusions of a review of the regulations is laid before Parliament
...
31 Independent review of regulations with counter-terrorism purpose
(1) The Secretary of State must appoint a person to review the operation of such asset-freeze provisions of relevant regulations made by the Secretary of State as the Secretary of State may from time to time refer to that person.
(2) The Treasury must appoint a person to review the operation of such asset-freeze provisions of relevant regulations made by the Treasury as the Treasury may from time to time refer to that person.
...
(4) In each calendar year, by 31 January—
   (a) the person appointed under subsection (1) must notify the Secretary of State of what (if any) reviews under that subsection that person intends to carry out in that year, and
   (b) the person appointed under subsection (2) must notify the Treasury of what (if any) reviews under that subsection that person intends to carry out in that year.
(5) Reviews of which notice is given under subsection (4) in a particular year—
   (a) may not relate to any provisions that have not been referred before the giving of the notice, and
   (b) must be completed during that year or as soon as reasonably practicable after the end of it.
(6) The person who conducts a review under this section must as soon as reasonably practicable after completing the review send a report on its outcome to—
   (a) the Secretary of State, if the review is under subsection (1), or
   (b) the Treasury, if the review is under subsection (2).
(7) On receiving a report under this section the Secretary of State or (as the case may be) the Treasury must lay a copy of it before Parliament.
...
32 Periodic reports on exercise of power to make regulations under section 1
(1) The Secretary of State must as soon as reasonably practicable after the end of each reporting period lay before Parliament a report which—
   (a) specifies the regulations under section 1, if any, that were made in that reporting period,
   (b) identifies which, if any, of those regulations—

    (i) *stated a relevant human rights purpose, or*
    (ii) *amended or revoked regulations stating such a purpose,*
  (c) *specifies any recommendations which in that reporting period were made by a Parliamentary Committee in connection with a relevant independent review, and*
  (d) *includes a copy of any response to those recommendations which was made by the government to that Committee in that reporting period.*
...
(3) For the purposes of this section the following are reporting periods—
  (a) *the period of 12 months beginning with the day on which this Act is passed ("the first reporting period"), and*
  (b) *each period of 12 months that ends with an anniversary of the date when the first reporting period ends.*
(4) For the purposes of this section—
......

Review provisions specify the point in time when a review is to take place and often prescribe also its content and procedure.

Legal Services Regulation Act 2015 (Ireland)
Review of the Act
6. *(1) The Authority shall —*
  (a) *not later than 18 months after the establishment day, and not later than the end of each subsequent 3 year period, commence a review of the operation of this Act, and*
  (b) *not later than 12 months after the commencement of a review under paragraph (a), make a report to each House of the Oireachtas of its findings and conclusions, including such recommendations (if any) to the Minister resulting from that review as it considers appropriate.*

(2) Recommendations under subsection (1)(b) shall include such recommendations (if any) for amendments to this Act (including amendments to Part 7), the Solicitors Acts 1954 to 2015 or any instrument made under those Acts, as the Authority considers appropriate arising from its findings and conclusions.

(3) In conducting a review under this section, the Authority shall consult with the Competition and Consumer Protection Commission, professional bodies and such other persons as the Authority considers appropriate for such purpose.

Regulation of Lobbying Act 2015 (Ireland)
Review of Act
(1) The Minister shall— (a) before the end of each relevant period, commence a review of the operation of this Act, and (b) not more than 6 months after the end of each relevant period, make a report to each House of the Oireachtas of the findings resulting from the review and of the conclusions drawn from the findings.
(2) ... —
(3) A report made under subsection (1) shall include any such recommendations for amendments of this Act, or any instrument made under it, as appear to the

> *Minister to be appropriate in consequence of the findings resulting from the review.*
>
> *(4) In conducting a review the Minister shall— (a) consult the Commission, (b) take into account any relevant report of a committee appointed by either House of the Oireachtas or jointly by both Houses, and (c) consult such persons carrying on lobbying activities and such bodies representing them, and such other persons, as the Minister considers appropriate.*

Review obligations can establish or require specific diagnostic or reporting mechanisms and can be more or less sophisticated to reflect the intricacies of each Act. Sophisticated review clauses can combine a review of actual costs, benefits and achievements ensuing from implementation. For example, the Equality Act review obligations differ per sections of the Act.[17] The duty to consider socioeconomic inequalities when taking strategic decisions is monitored through arrangements already in place (Comprehensive Area Assessment for local authorities and their partners), compliance is assessed on the basis of that data and the degree of achievement of effects is assessed through long-term monitoring of local and national statistics on education, health and employment. For age discrimination in the provision of goods, facilities, services and public functions, review details were to be established following further consultation on draft secondary legislation. The gender pay gap review is streamlined through reporting from the Equality Commission, monitoring of reporting costs and measuring benefits. Other provisions, like indirect disability discrimination or gender reassignment are reviewed in accordance with the general clause. This sophisticated and complex arrangement addresses all important aspects of legislation at a thorough level but is complex, resource intensive and burdensome.

Reviews are concluded with reports, which might or might not be submitted to Parliament.

Overall, there are no 'typical' review clauses. They vary in terms of requirements, formulation, level of complexity and detail. They can introduce regular monitoring and reporting requirements, including provision of data, to broader reviews and evaluations of Acts; they can be regular, annual, interim, mid-term or final reports; they can range from simple to complex review provisions; call for single or repetitive reviews; be general or specific covering an entire Act, or only one or a set of articles of an Act.[18] This variety makes them a flexible instrument that can be adjusted to the specificities of each law.

---

[17] Government Equalities Office (GEO), 'Equality Act Impact Assessment. Final Version' (Royal Assent) (TSO 2010) 9, 32 ff.

[18] Krišto and Poutouroudi (n 12) at 22.

2.3.1. Sunsetting

Sunset clauses are 'statutory provisions providing that a particular law will expire automatically on a particular date unless it is re-authorised by the legislature.[19] Expiration is usually subject to a review that ascertains whether the measure should be renewed, amended or allowed to expire. The use of sunsets is becoming more and more evident in legislative practice during the last decades. In the United States, the practice of sunset reviews can range from comprehensive (where all statutory agencies undergo a sunset review on a preset schedule), regulatory (where only licensing and regulatory boards undergo sunset reviews), selective (where only selected agencies and regulatory boards are reviewed) or discretionary (the legislature chooses which agencies and statutes to review).[20] The Legislation Act 2003 of Australia (Part 4, Chapter 3) includes a horizontal sunset clause for all legislative instruments based on the date of their introduction.

> *50* Sunsetting
> *(1) This subsection repeals a legislative instrument on the first 1 April or 1 October falling on or after the tenth anniversary of registration of the instrument, unless the instrument was registered on 1 January 2005.*
> *(2) This subsection repeals a legislative instrument on the day worked out using the table if the instrument was registered on 1 January 2005.*

However, it is more common to have sunset provisions in specific Acts or regulations. For example:

> *Citation, Commencement, and Expiry*
> *(1) These Regulations may be cited as the [ ] Regulations 2011.*
> *(2) They come into force on 2011.*
> *(3) They cease to have effect on at the end of the period of seven years beginning with the day on which these Regulations come into force.*

Sunsets emerged with the rationale to reduce spending, increase the level of government services,[21] reduce red tape, deliver clearer laws, maintain the

---

[19] Antonios Kouroutakis, *The Constitutional Value of Sunset Clauses: An Historical and Normative Analysis* (Routledge 2016) 3.

[20] Brian Baugus and Feler Bose, 'Sunset Legislation in the States: Balancing the Legislature and the Executive' (Mercatus Research, Mercatus Center at George Mason University, 2015).

[21] Jonathan Waller, 'The Expenditure Effects of Sunset Laws in State Governments' (All Dissertations 2009) 381.

alignment of legislation with policy[22] and monitor regulatory burden.[23] Despite their advantages, sunset clauses raise serious concerns about legal certainty[24] and can be the subject of political manoeuvring[25] or bargaining between the executive and the legislature.[26] To this aim the lawmaker needs to use them cautiously and in a targeted way.

2.3.2. Evaluation

Evaluation or post legislative scrutiny is broader compared to monitoring and review. It is based on the idea that results and effects of legislation can be studied and used for correcting and improving it[27] and is concerned with the relations between normative contents and social reality. It is an effort to analyse and assess the effects of legislation in a clear, systematic and objective way[28] and generate information on 'the potential or actual causal relationships between legislative action and observable social attitude, behaviour or circumstance'.[29] Evaluation is an accountability and learning process[30] that appraises activities and outcomes to enable governments to effectively enforce legislation[31] and improve its quality.[32] It examines the necessity, cost-efficiency

---

[22] Australian Government, Guide to Managing Sunsetting of Legislative Instruments, 2016, available at: https://www.ag.gov.au/LegalSystem/AdministrativeLaw/Documents/guide-to-managing-sunsetting-of-legislative-instruments-december-2016.pdf (last accessed 1/12/2018). See also the Report on the Operation of the Sunsetting Provisions in the Legislation Act 2003 at: https://www.ag.gov.au/LegalSystem/AdministrativeLaw/Pages/Review-of-the-sunsetting-framework-under-the-legislation-act-2003.aspx (last accessed 1/12/2018).

[23] HM Government, Sunsetting Guidance, 2011, available at: http://data.parliament.uk/DepositedPapers/Files/DEP2011-0504/DEP2011-0504.pdf (last accessed 7/12/2018).

[24] Sofia Ranchordás, 'Sunset Clauses and Experimental Regulations: Blessing or Curse for Legal Certainty?' (2015) 36:1 Statute Law Review 28–45.

[25] Manoj Viswanathan, 'Sunset Provisions in the Tax Code: A Critical Evaluation and Prescriptions for the Future' (2007) 82 N.Y.U. L. Rev. 656 at 658.

[26] Baugus and Bose (n 20) at 19.

[27] Heinz Schäffer, 'Evaluation and Assessment of Legal Effects Procedures: Towards a More Rational and Responsible Lawmaking Process' (2001) 22 Statute Law Review 132.

[28] Luzius Mader, 'Evaluating the Effects: A Contribution to the Quality of Legislation' (2001) 22:2 Statute Law Review 119, 126 at 123.

[29] Ibid, 123.

[30] S. Smismans, 'The Politicization of ex post Policy Evaluation in the EU' (2017) 19:1–2 European Journal of Law Reform 74–96 at 74.

[31] Nicoletta Stame, 'Governance, Democracy and Evaluation' (2006) 12:7 Evaluation 7.

[32] P. Stephenson, 'Why Better Regulation Demands Better Scrutiny of Results, The European Parliament's Use of Performance Audits by the European Court of Auditors in ex post Impact Assessment' (2017) 1–2 European Journal of Law Reform 97–120.

and feasibility of options. In terms of process it is a systematic collection and analysis of information that permits a critical appraisal. Ex post evaluation attempts a comprehensive assessment of what legislation has attained and is gaining important momentum.

Conceptually, evaluation is more complex compared to monitoring and review. The logic 'what gets measured, gets changed' is appealing, yet challenging when associated with legislation for two main reasons: firstly, the methodological and practical difficulties linked to attributing effects to legislation and establishing causal links between rules and real life phenomena.[33] Statutes are complex instruments regulating one or several matters, with multiple aims, a vast number of subjects and – usually – no boundaries in time. Evaluation methodologies cannot always identify in a convincing way a legal text as the cause of outputs, impacts and results[34] and isolate influences within a context of complex societal and economic relations.[35] Secondly, the interdisciplinary nature of evaluation between the law and social science poses additional substantive and methodological challenges that limit the potential of evaluations to illuminate the effects of policies and yield insights into how effectively they achieve their aims.[36] Last but not least, evaluation mainly views legislation as an instrument of social engineering and change. This 'instrumentalist' perception views legislation as the result of a rational process, thus (partly) ignoring its complexity; undermines the fact that legislation might not be the result of need for regulation but of political constraints or pressure and it might serve a multiplicity of other functions (symbolic, educational, etc).[37] Thus, evaluation might be in the position to capture only limited aspects of legislation and to attribute causalities that do not exist.

Another specific challenge is methodology. Evaluation balances between subjectivism and objectivity. On the one hand, it is more than 'impressionistic, intuitive political analysis' but it is also far from pure science.[38] In fact, it is a systematic appraisal of legislation through the use of 'juridical and social-scientific' standards[39] and uses a wide range of methodologies, techniques and tools. Their limitations are methodological and practical: eval-

---

[33] Werner Bussmann, 'Evaluation of Legislation: Skating on Thin Ice' (2010) 16:3 Evaluation 280.
[34] Ibid at 284.
[35] Schäffer, 'Evaluation' (n 27) 1.
[36] Charles Tremper, Sue Thomas and Alexander Wagenaar, 'Measuring Law for Evaluation Research' (2010) 34(3) Evaluation Review 242–66.
[37] Mader (n 28) 130–131.
[38] Ibid at 123.
[39] K. van Aeken, 'From Vision to Reality: Ex post evaluation of legislation' (2011) 5:1 Legisprudence 50.

uations often cannot provide absolute certainty about causal connections while they are time-consuming and costly. The suitability and appropriateness of evaluation methodologies for different types of statutes[40] is an important question. Depending on the kind of law, different methods will be used. For statutes that regulate behaviours without specifying concrete outcomes (social ordering) goal-oriented evaluation appears adequate, hybrid statutes that combine social ordering with social problem solving require 'combined' approaches, descriptive strategies provide data and information but might leave several possibilities for improving legislation unexploited, experimental strategies are less appropriate, while a strategy of plausible arguments[41] could respond to the complexities of the evaluation of statutes.

At practical level, evaluation is either a horizontal requirement or is triggered by 'evaluation clauses' or provisions requiring mandatory evaluation of the impact of public policies or legislation.[42] A review of the implementation of evaluation clauses in Switzerland, one of the pioneers of legislative evaluation worldwide, reveals a number of problems linked to their operation. Firstly, the inconsistent and often imprecise phrasing of these clauses that leads to ambiguities during implementation, and the ambiguity in their overall function to assess effectiveness, efficacy, cost efficiency, control or monitoring.[43] In fact, due to the similarities and overlaps between the two processes, the challenges analysed in relation to review clauses are also relevant for evaluation. A typical example of an evaluation clause would read:

Regulation 2015/1017 (EU)
[...] the Commission shall submit to the European Parliament and the Council a report containing an independent evaluation of the application of this regulation.

Article 17 Evaluation and review
1. By 31 December 2019, the Commission shall evaluate the initial functioning of the EFSD, its management and its effective contribution to the purpose and objectives of this Regulation. The Commission shall submit its evaluation report to the European Parliament and to the Council, containing an independent

---

[40] Bussmann (n 33) 285–6; Peter Ziegler, 'Information Collection: Techniques for the Evaluation of the Legislative Process' (1988) 160 Statute Law Review 160–85; A. Flückiger, 'L'évaluation législative ou comment mesurer l'efficacité des lois' (2007) XLV:138 Revue Européenne des Sciences Sociales 85.

[41] Bussmann (n 33) 286–8.

[42] Damien Wirths, 'Procedural Institutionalization of the Evaluation Through Legal Basis: A New Typology of Evaluation Clauses in Switzerland' (2017) 38:1 Statute Law Review 23 39.

[43] Swiss Federal Audit Office, Review of the Implementation of Evaluation Clauses in the Federal Administration, available at: https://www.efk.admin.ch/images/stories/efk_dokumente/publikationen/andere_berichte/Andere%20Berichte%20(38)/10361ZF_e.pdf (accessed 1/12/2018).

> external evaluation of the application of this Regulation, and accompanied by a reasoned proposal to amend this Regulation, as appropriate, in particular with a view to extending the initial investment period referred to in Article 8(2). That evaluation report shall be accompanied by an opinion of the Court of Auditors.
> 2. By 31 December 2019 and every three years thereafter, the Commission shall evaluate the use and the functioning of the EFSD Guarantee Fund. The Commission shall submit its evaluation report to the European Parliament and to the Council. That evaluation report shall be accompanied by an opinion of the Court of Auditors.
>
> *Art. 78 Ex post evaluation*
> In 2024, an ex post evaluation report shall be prepared by the Member States for each of their rural development programmes. That report shall be submitted to the Commission by 31 December 2024.
>
> *Art. 79 Syntheses of evaluations*
> Syntheses at Union level of the ex ante and ex post evaluation reports shall be undertaken under the responsibility of the Commission. The syntheses of the evaluation reports shall be completed at the latest by 31 December of the year following the submission of the relevant evaluations.

Ex post evaluation is gaining importance in theory and practice. For one matter, it is a function that can be found in Constitutions[44] and is increasingly institutionalised,[45] it has a visibly more prominent place in regulatory reform agendas and programmes, while it is becoming a field of interaction between Governments and Parliaments. In essence however, it is the functional role of Parliaments in evaluation, and its comprehensive approach towards legislation that places evaluation at a different level in relation to other forms of review.

2.4. Horizontal questions: when, how and who will record and measure results?

For the lawmaker who thinks across the life cycle of legislation, monitoring, review and evaluation are important aspects of the design and drafting of an Act and there are a number of questions they need to address or take into account.

The first lawmaking question relates to when should a law be evaluated. Monitoring, review and evaluation can take place at different points in time depending on the logic and the needs of each Act. An average period for review of evaluation ranges between 2–5 years following enactment. In

---

[44] Article 170 of the Swiss Constitution; Art 24 of the French Constitution.
[45] Sénat, L'évaluation de la législation, available at : https://www.senat.fr/lc/lc7/lc7_mono.html (last accessed 1/12/2018).

Germany, compliance costs are evaluated by the Federal Statistical Office after two years from enactment. In Australia, sunsetting occurs automatically ten years following enactment. The time when a law will have produced results and effects to an extent that their partial or overall assessment is meaningful varies significantly and needs to be considered specifically. While it might be meaningful for some laws to be reviewed or evaluated even two years following enactment, others might not produce visible outcomes for five or even 10 years. The timing of monitoring, review and evaluation depends on the type of Act and its specificities.

A second question relates to who should monitor, review or evaluate legislation. Usually, monitoring and review are conducted by the authority in charge of implementation, which is reasonable given the fact that they have the most direct access to implementation data. Evaluations on the other hand (and often reviews when they resemble evaluations) can be assigned to specialised, independent or external bodies or be conducted by the administration and scrutinised in terms of substance by the Parliament. For example, the task of monitoring implementation and assessing the effectiveness of equality legislation in the UK is assigned to the Equality Commission, while in other countries, state bodies might be responsible for its evaluation. The functions assigned in relation to monitoring, review and evaluation can be limited to the collection of events data to a much broader mandate to monitor the application and the effectiveness of the law, identify changes in society, outcomes, determine reference indicators for progress, and periodically monitor progress towards identified outcomes.[46]

In relation to the role of different actors, there is an emerging discussion around the role of Parliaments in the monitoring, review and especially the evaluation of legislation. Parliaments are claiming a more active role in ex ante and ex post evaluation activities[47] visible through the establishment of specialised structures and an increased involvement in such activities. For example, the French National Assembly established a specialised Committee for the Evaluation and Control of Public Policies to respond to the mandate to assess public policies assigned to it by the Constitution. In Switzerland, the Federal Assembly[48] and its organs can evaluate the effectiveness of measures by requesting impact assessments to be carried out; examining the impact assessments and instructing impact assessments to be carried out themselves. The European Parliament established a specialised Directorate enabling it to

---

[46] EA 2006 s 3, 11, 12.
[47] Senat, 'Law Evaluation and Better Regulation: The Role for Parliaments' (2013), available at: http://www.senat.fr/evenement/colloque/evaluation_et_qualite_de_la_legislation.html (accessed 1/12/2018).
[48] Federal Act on the Federal Assembly, Art 27.

conduct its own evaluations of Commission impact assessments and justify proposals made by the Parliament. The House of Commons and the House of Lords in the UK engage in scrutiny either on their own initiative or triggered by a Government Memorandum. Further, in most cases where reviews are conducted, the outputs of this exercise are sent to Parliament for political deliberation. Is this part of oversight of the Executive? Is it part of the legislative mandate of the Parliament? Or is it an aspect of regulatory management? This emerging discussion still has several issues to address. So far, the role of Parliaments in scrutiny ranges from passive scrutinisers who simply assess ex-post scrutinies of the government (German Bundestag), to informal ones (Italian Senate), to formal and institutionalised ones where procedures are in place (Switzerland, France and Sweden) as well as hybrid (European Parliament).[49] The interaction between the Government and the Parliament in evaluations both in terms of legislative management and terms of oversight is fascinating and still open.

A third question relates to the method and the criteria against which legislation will be reviewed, monitored or evaluated. Although generic methodologies can be in place, specific ones might be required. For example, the Equality Measurement Framework[50] was a specific tool developed to allow the collection of evidence that would measure progress and social outcomes from the perspective of equality and human rights and provide a baseline to inform policy priorities in equality law in the UK. This Framework would compile objective evidence to guide further action, provide a transparent account of the actual situation, set a baseline for further decisions and provide benchmarks for measuring the impact of actions.[51]

The French Law 2006-340 on pay equality (art. 5) defined a specific mechanism to evaluate progress: annual appraisals of the negotiations on pay differences by the national commission for collective negotiation, a medium term evaluation of the application of the law by the Supreme Council of professional equality, an appraisal from a national conference on the basis of this report and an evaluation report six years after the promulgation of the law.

---

[49] Elena Griglio, 'Post-Legislative Scrutiny as a Form of Executive Oversight' (2019) 21:2 European Journal of Law Reform 118–136.

[50] Equality and Human Rights Commission (EHRC), 'Measurement Framework for Equality and Human Rights' 2017, available at: https://www.equalityhumanrights.com/en/publication-download/measurement-framework-equality-and-human-rights (last accessed 07/12/2018).

[51] EHRC, 'How fair is Britain? Equality, Human Rights and Good Relations in 2010. The First Triennial Review' (EHRC 2011) 12–16; EHRC, Is Britain Fairer? The state of equality and human rights 2015; EHRC, Is Britain Fairer? The state of equality and human rights 2018.

Based on the mid-term evaluation, the Government could impose, if necessary, salary-based contributions for non-compliant enterprises. A Decree established specific methodological tools for the follow-up of the application of the law, including a review of negotiations and related agreements, a scoreboard based on information provided by the enterprises, indicators on the workforce; total annual earnings reported to social security, gross salaries, bonuses and benefits in kind; average number of hours of different types of training; promotions and recruitments by type of contract.[52] Designing new methods for every new law is costly and unfeasible, but where required, this might be necessary.

The review of legislative practice highlights the relevance of results in proactive lawmaking; the importance of monitoring, review and evaluation as aspects of legislative design; and finally, the nature and scope of questions that need to be addressed from a lawmaking perspective. How can lawmakers best address these concerns?

3. RESULTS IN EFFECTIVE LAWMAKING

Anticipating results is essential for proactive lawmaking. Determining what is to be expected as a result of legislation and having a clear strategy on how to monitor, review and evaluate it is an essential requirement for a lawmaker that thinks across the life cycle of the law.

3.1. Clearly defined results

The objectives and the anticipated results of legislation are shaped at a moment in time when many aspects of the future life of a law are unknown or uncertain. Yet anticipation of results and outcomes makes the transition from objectives to 'real' results smoother and easier to capture.

Specific + broader objectives ➡ Anticipated results + outcomes ➡ 'Real' results, outcomes + effects

Figure 5.2   Matrix of results across the life cycle of the law

---

[52] Décret n° 2006-1501 du 29 novembre 2006 relatif aux outils méthodologiques de suivi de l'application de la loi du 23 mars 2006 relative à l'égalité salariale entre les femmes et les hommes.

Table 5.1   Example of objectives and anticipated results

Specific objectives	Anticipated results
Prohibit discrimination in specific areas of life (descriptive)	Lawfully enacted, regulations adopted within 6 months
Establish procedures for reporting discrimination (descriptive) in order to provide effective remedies (mixed)	5 procedures provided in the law fully enacted and operational within 3 months; remedies operational within 6 months
Assist victims in reporting discrimination in order to increase reporting by 20% (mixed)	Specific assistance measures enacted and operational (funds transferred, institutional mandates extended, personnel transferred, etc.) within 6 months; reporting increased by 20% in comparison to 2015
Simplify reporting procedures and requirements (procedural)	Reporting procedures less costly and speedier compared to 2015

To facilitate their operationalisation along the life cycle of the law objectives should be linked to anticipated results that identify specific and measurable elements that will need to be captured through monitoring, review and evaluation.

Where possible, linking anticipated results to measurable targets and benchmarks would be a practice worth testing in practice. For example, the quantified target set by UK Climate Change Act that '*net UK carbon account for the year 2050 is at least 80% lower than the 1990 baseline*' makes expected results visible and measurable and sets a threshold for holding the competent authorities accountable. This can help concentrate implementation efforts on long-term goals and function as a way to induce commitment to the achievement of the specific goal.

3.2.   Anticipating implementation

Implementation is a complex, demanding and multifactor process. Even though it is not rocket science, implementation deficits due to non calculation or miscalculation of costs, requirements, resources or impacts are one of the most common concerns about legislation in many contexts. Implementation plans drafted together with the Bill are a practical solution to anticipate the most important requirements that will have to take place in order to avoid surprises, and inaction. Although an assessment of costs and impact of legislation on national or local budgets are required in many countries together with a Bill, calculations are superficial and unreliable. An implementation plan can assist when the implementation of an Act is complex and involves multiple actors. In France, the UK and many other jurisdictions, Bills are accompanied by a list of the main secondary regulations that will be required for full enactment. This also helps pave the way for monitoring, review and evaluation of legislation. A more complex implementation plan can include the required actions beyond regulations, transfer of funds, transfer or recruitment of staff, etc. For each action, competent actors can be identified including indicative timelines. Once an Act is adopted, implementation plans will have to be elaborated in greater detail and can include compliance checks, reporting requirements, inspections, among others. However, during lawmaking, at least the basic aspects of implementation need to be anticipated in as much detail as possible.

3.3. A clear monitoring, review and evaluation framework

Monitoring, review and evaluation are interconnected yet distinct functions. Monitoring refers to follow up, review is a periodical assessment of application and/or performance while evaluation and post legislative scrutiny entail a holistic appraisal of a law. Every law requires a clear monitoring, review and evaluation plan that reflects its intricacies and 'personality' and can generate sufficient information and data to enable periodic assessments of implementation but also its efficacy, effectiveness and efficiency. A smart mix of clauses depending on the scope and specificities of an Act (and taking into account the burden involved in conducting all these tasks) is the recipe for triggering effective monitoring, reviews and evaluation. The placement of these clauses in legislation, in impact assessments of regulation is a jurisdiction specific choice that remains open. A matrix of evaluation provisions escalating from monitoring, to review and evaluation need to be established for each Act.

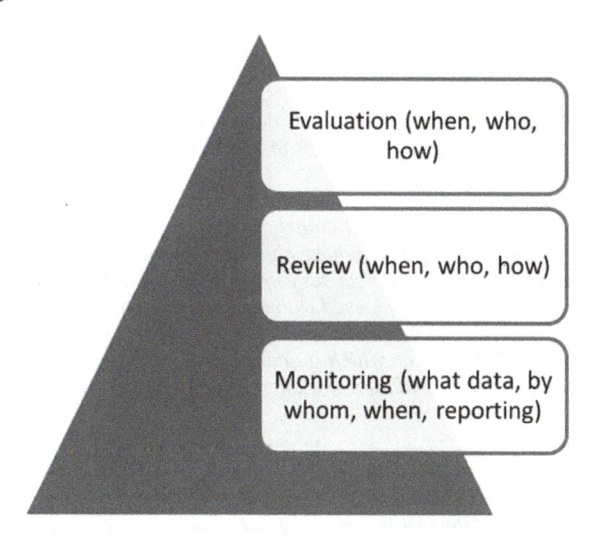

Figure 5.3   *Monitoring, review and evaluation matrix*

Each exercise should have a clear focus and complement the other two. But on which criterion should this decision be made? For monitoring and review the main decision making criterion is which actor is better placed to collect and process the required data at the less cost. For evaluation, the criterion is which actor has the relevant mandate or overarching perspective. The evaluation, review and monitoring framework can go into more detail by listing specific indicators on how specific elements of an Act will be monitored. This can include even the sets of data required, for example events-based data, standards-based data, survey-based data, expert evaluations, quantitative indicators, subjective data, qualitative data or comprehensive methodologies. An example is presented in table 5.2.

3.4. Clear and specific monitoring, review and evaluation clauses

Legislative practice shows that the mere existence of monitoring, review and evaluation clauses is only half a solution: if not specific and clear with regard to what and how needs to be reviewed or monitored they might become a bureaucratic and formal exercise.

Such clauses need to be clear and focused on necessary and substantive information. They need to reflect the specificities of an Act with a particular focus on points that are uncertain in lawmaking. As a minimum they need to determine who, when, how and against what criteria these exercises will be conducted and what the output will be. For example:

Monitoring
(1) The Secretary of State must publish every year a report on the implementation of .....
Review
(1) The Secretary of State must (a) carry out a review of [regulations ... to ...], (b) set out the conclusions of the review in a report, and (c) publish the report.
(2) The review report must
   (a) set out the objectives intended to be achieved by the regulatory system established by [those regulations],
   (b) assess the extent to which those objectives are achieved, and
   (c) assess whether those objectives remain appropriate and, if so, the extent to which they could be achieved with a system that imposes less regulation.
(3) The first review must be published before the end of the period of five years beginning with the day on which [regulations ... to ...] come into force
(4) Reports under this regulation are afterwards to be published at intervals not exceeding five years.
Evaluation
(1) Ten years following the enactment of regulations, the Secretary of State must appoint an independent expert to carry out an evaluation of the regulations.
(2) The evaluation report must

Table 5.2 Analytical monitoring, review and evaluation framework

Type of review	Who?	When?	How?	What	Indicator	Frequency
Monitoring of implementation	Ministry X	Bi annually	Internal	The entire Act	Number of cases in which the Act is applied	Once per year
					Number of citizens and businesses affected by application	At least for every evaluation
Review	Ministry X	Every five years	Internal	The entire Act, specific emphasis on S 1, 8, 10	Number of cases in which XXX is used	Once per year
					Number of applications/procedures/ documents produced	Once per year
					Number of instances where item not be used and reasons why	Once per year
					Usefulness of information contained in the portal	At least for every evaluation
Evaluation	Independent expert	After seven years	External	Entire Act and specific provisions subject to review	Number of cases where clause x is applied	Once per year
					Number of judgments passed	Once per year
					Case law at national level pointing to uncertainties (e.g. lack of clarity on certain concepts)	At least for every evaluation
					Estimates on the length of proceedings and reasons for undue delays	At least for every evaluation

>   (a) set out the objectives intended to be achieved by the regulatory system established by [those regulations],
>   (b) assess the extent to which the intended objectives are achieved,
>   (c) identify wanted and unwanted consequences and impacts and make recommendations for improving the regulation
>
> (3) The evaluation report will be submitted to the Parliament.

Monitoring and evaluation clauses in legislation need to be exercises in constraint. They are resource intensive exercises and need to serve the overall balance of the Act, not overshadow it. A balance between what is necessary and the burden it imposes on the administration is an important factor the lawmaker needs to keep in mind. Monitoring and evaluation are resource-intensive exercises and need to be used with prudence and caution and to be factored in the plans for the evaluation of legislation.

3.4.1. Learning from results

Evidence, knowledge and experience are important for sharpening the lawmakers' perception on legislation, reducing, within rational limits, ambiguity and distrust and acquiring knowledge on the relevance, appropriateness, effectiveness, cost-efficiency and coherence of action. Knowledge around results is an important learning mechanism.

In practice, monitoring, review and evaluation are rather weak in terms of impact and especially in their function as learning mechanisms. While the existence of evaluation clauses in legislation increases the chances of ex post review, in EU legislation these are often ignored and other factors, like the need to enforce legislation towards the member states and evaluation capacity,[53] determine their occurrence. In the UK, the limited evidence available on how post legislative scrutiny is conducted shows not only that the selection criteria are open and relatively random (interest from industry, a memorandum, best use of expertise of the members of parliament, etc.) but also that recommendations have limited strength and a loose follow up.[54] At EU level, only a small percentage (16%) of evaluations are used for accountability purposes, as there is a poor follow up through questions. They appear more useful, however, for forward-looking agenda-setting purposes.[55] The national use of evaluations

---

[53] S. van Voorst, E. Mastenbroek, 'Enforcement Tool or Strategic Instrument? The initiation of ex-post legislative evaluations by the European Commission' (2017) 18:4 European Union Politics 640–57.

[54] Tom Caygill, 'A Tale of Two Houses?', (2019) 21:2 European Journal of Law Reform 87–101.

[55] P. Zwaan, S. van Voorst and E. Mastenbroek, 'Ex post legislative evaluation in the European Union: questioning the usage of evaluations as instruments for accountability' (2016) 82:4 International Review of Administrative Sciences 674–93.

suggests a strong interest-led nature[56] or their use as an instrument to oppose or collect information rather than as a source of learning through actual findings.[57] Even in Switzerland, where evaluation is an embedded practice, evaluation findings and recommendations are rarely used in decision-making, and when they are, it is often as a means of legitimation. Evaluation activities are strongly related to 'power games' and ways to gain power and influence within the administration[58] rather than a learning mechanism. Another source of learning about legislation is judicial review. Lawmakers have a lot to learn from case law. Judicial problem solving highlights gaps, ambiguity, clashes and can provide useful lessons on how to legislate better. The use of the judicial review findings as a different type of scrutiny needs to be strengthened.

These findings suggest that at the moment, the knowledge around the results of legislation is predominantly seen as a political asset. However, at least in the closed circle of lawmakers, learning from the results and failures of legislation is their most important strategic added value and probably the only concrete way to improve lawmaking. More effort needs to be invested in learning from evaluation.

4. CONCLUSIONS

Results are produced during the 'real' life of the law. Three 'types' of results are relevant for legislation: direct results, outcomes and impacts or effects. Every law generates a unique matrix of results, outcomes and effects that need to be anticipated by the lawmaker so that they can design an appropriate monitoring, review and evaluation system. Lawmakers need to decide what, when, by whom and how legislation or regulations will be monitored, reviewed or evaluated. Effective lawmaking requires clearly defined results and where possible measurable targets, a smart mix of monitoring, review and evaluation clauses integrated in legislation, a conscious learning from the results of monitoring and evaluation and a validation of the knowledge to be gained by judicial work.

---

[56] F. Varone, P. Bundi and R. Gava, 'Policy Evaluation in Parliament: interest groups as catalysts' (2018) International Review of Administrative Sciences.

[57] P. Bundi, 'Parliamentarians' strategies for policy evaluations' (2018) 69 Evaluation and Program Planning 130–38.

[58] Katerina Stolyarenko, 'Case-Study #1: National Evaluation Policy in Switzerland (Parliamentary Forum for Development Evaluation 2017) 17, available at: https://www.seval.ch/app/uploads/2017/07/case_study_Switzerland_kstolyarenko.pdf (last accessed 1/12/2018).

6. Which tools for effective lawmaking?

There is nothing a government hates more than to be well-informed; for it makes the process of arriving at decisions much more complicated and difficult.

John Maynard Keynes

1. INTRODUCTION

The effort to rationalise lawmaking holds a central position in the discussion around legislation in the last decades. At theoretical level, rational lawmaking focuses on the importance of anticipation, informed decision making and retrospection. At operational level, regulatory reform initiatives developed on both sides of the Atlantic, with distinct logic and priorities, to enhance the rationality and accountability of discretionary decision making of regulatory agencies[1] or to produce transparent, accessible and clear legislation.[2] What these programmes contributed was a politically neutral framework to improve the 'inner workings' of the bureaucratic engine of policy making.[3] This was attempted through regulatory policies, institutions and a set of tools to support evidence-based decision making.[4] These tools included Impact Assessment, examining alternatives to regulation, consultation, simplification, and measures targeting the 'regulatory stock' such as codification and consolidation. Overall, regulatory management processes[5] were expected to lead to a 'framework in which regulations and regulatory regimes are efficient in terms of cost,

---

[1] T.T. Smith, 'Regulatory Reform in the USA and Europe' (1996) 8:2 Journal of Environmental Law 257–82 at 258.

[2] European Commission. Growth, Competitiveness, and Employment. The challenges and ways forward into the 21st century, COM (93) 700 final. Brussels: 05.12.1993.

[3] K. Wegrich, 'Which Results? Better Regulation and Institutional Politics' (2015) 6:3 European Journal of Risk Regulation 369–71.

[4] OECD, 'Building Capacity for Regulatory Quality: Stocktaking Paper' (2004) GOV/PGC 11, 2.

[5] Patricia Popelier, 'Management of Legislation' in U. Karpen and H. Xanthaki, *Legislation in Europe. A Comprehensive Guide for Scholars and Practitioners* (Hart Publishing 2017) 53ff.

effective in terms of having a clear regulatory and policy purpose, transparent and accountable'.[6]

The reform agendas came with a strong claim to neutralise and improve decision making processes through evidence, transparency and participation based on the assumption that decisions informed by evidence will be better decisions. Two main tools are particularly used in the proactive aspects of policy and lawmaking: Impact Assessments, that provide a structured decision making process, and consultation, that provides a framework for collecting information and ensuring participation. Simplification intervenes ad hoc to improve compliance, remove barriers in implementation and improve coherence and consistency. Codification also intervenes ad hoc and is aimed mostly at improving coherence and accessibility of the stock of legislation or regulation.

The use of Impact Assessments and consultation in jurisdictions around the world is expansive. Although there is little empirical evidence to associate the results of their use with improved quality of legislation, it is considered the main tool that policy – and lawmakers – have at their avail to rationalise decision making processes. A closer look at Impact Assessments and consultation as lawmaking tools raises a number of questions. To what extent are they useful to the practical aspects of lawmaking? Do they address or reflect the thinking process and questions emerging when designing and drafting legislation? Or are new approaches necessary?

2. ON TOOLKITS, TOOLS AND LAWMAKING

The importance of legislation in contemporary states is as obvious as sunrise and sunset for the day cycle and in this challenging and important task, lawmakers have little to guide them. Constitutions confine themselves to the legislative process, parliamentary regulation sets the framework for debating and adopting legislation, scholarly debate contributes with abstract standards, like legal certainty and proportionality, with little practical value.

Binding rules are rare but nonetheless, three kinds of 'tools' can be encountered that claim to play this role: a first group includes recommendations and guiding principles, like the ones developed by OECD in 1995, 2005 and 2012[7] which refer to broad principles that need to be observed when legislating, like efficiency, effectiveness, clarity, simplicity, precision, concision, consistency

---

[6] OECD, Stocktaking Paper (n 4) 11.
[7] OECD, Recommendation of the Council on Improving the Quality of Government Regulation (1995) C(95)21/FINAL; OECD, 'Guiding Principles for Regulatory Quality and Performance' (2005); OECD, 'Recommendation of the Council on Regulatory Policy and Governance' (2012).

etc. A second set of tools includes guidance, checklists or templates for conducting Impact Assessments, consultations or burden reduction exercises. The OECD checklist, the first of its kind, is the most general and lists 10 questions to guide the decision making process, on the problem to be solved, justification, appropriateness, legal basis, costs and benefits, distribution of effects, clarity, consistency, comprehensibility, accessibility, etc.[8] In the European Union, the Better Regulation Guidelines[9] provide guidance on 'the essentials' for regulating better: forward planning and political validation, stakeholder consultation, evaluation/fitness checks, impact assessment, quality control and implementation support and monitoring. The Guidelines are complemented by a 'Toolbox' and detailed guidance to assist practitioners in applying the individual 'tools'. The toolbox is to be used 'selectively and with common sense'.[10] Detailed guidance or templates can be encountered in abundance at national level for general or specialised Impact Assessments,[11] for example, equality or privacy impact assessments, among others. The same stands for consultation principles[12] and codes of practice.[13]

A third set of tools includes manuals and practical guides with an explicit focus on the drafting of legislation. Examples include the Joint Practical Guide for the drafting of Community Legislation in the European Union,[14] the Guide for Making Legislation of the Cabinet Office in the UK,[15] the Guide de

---

[8] OECD, Recommendation (1995) ibid.

[9] European Commission, Better Regulation Guidelines, (2017), accessible at: https://ec.europa.eu/info/sites/info/files/better-regulation-guidelines.pdf (last accessed 07/12/2018).

[10] European Commission, Better Regulation 'Toolbox' (2015), accessible at: http://ec.europa.eu/smart-regulation/guidelines/docs/br_toolbox_en.pdf (last accessed 07/12/2018).

[11] Better Regulation Executive, 'Impact Assessment Toolkit. A guide to undertaking an Impact Assessment (IA) and completing the IA Template', 2011.

[12] Cabinet Office, Consultation Principles, 2018, available at: https://assets.publishing.service.gov.uk/government/uploads/system/uploads/attachment_data/file/691383/Consultation_Principles__1_.pdf (last accessed 07/12/2018).

[13] HM Government, Code of Practice on Consultation (2008), available at: https://assets.publishing.service.gov.uk/government/uploads/system/uploads/attachment_data/file/100807/file47158.pdf (last accessed 07/12/2018).

[14] European Communities, *Joint Practical Guide of the European Parliament, the Council and the Commission for Persons involved in the Drafting of Legislation within the Community Institutions* (Office for Official Publications of the European Communities 2003).

[15] Cabinet Office, Guide to Making Legislation, 2017 available at: https://assets.publishing.service.gov.uk/government/uploads/system/uploads/attachment_data/file/645652/Guide_to_Making_Legislation_Jul_2017.pdf (last accessed 7/12/2018).

Legistique in France,[16] the Guide to Making Federal Acts and Regulations of the Canadian Government[17] and several others. These are focused on standardising practice with regard to structure, use of language, form, and cross referencing among several other issues.

There is important variety in the information provided in these tools, especially in their degree of generality or specificity. Documents referring to principles are too broad, templates are too specific while drafting manuals tend to be very prescriptive and detailed. These tools are used more and more, yet their usefulness is not uncontroversial. For one matter, the 'toolkit' approach is over-simplistic in its assumption of instrumentality. When it comes, in particular, to drafting manuals and guides, these are considered useful for ensuring consistent standards and homogeneity in the drafting of legislative texts but their rigidity, static nature, detailed character and instructive rather than educative approach[18] limit their adaptability and flexibility. Drafting tools can never be exhaustive or applied mechanically, while they quickly become outdated. And although their usefulness is acknowledged and maximised if combined with organisational and procedural measures, training, use of computer-based technologies and other means to improve the drafting process, they are considered a partial response to the need for improving quality.[19]

The question remains, however, to what extent these tools are suitable to provide meaningful guidance to lawmakers rather than restrict their choices or thinking? If lawmaking is a dynamic process that requires 'looseness, flexibility, innovation and change'[20] the only meaningful purpose for any type of 'tool', guidance, checklist or manual is to support the thinking process leading to conscious and informed decisions. Any instrumental and purely formalistic use of 'tools', whether templates, manuals or others, is in fundamental tension with the open and flexible nature of lawmaking. On the other hand, tools with

---

[16] Premier Ministre, Secrétariat Général du Gouvernement, Conseil d'État, Guide de légistique (3e édition La Documentation française 2017), available at: https://www.legifrance.gouv.fr/Droit-francais/Guide-de-legistique2 (last accessed 07/12/2018).

[17] Government of Canada, Guide to Making Federal Acts and Regulations (2nd edn 2001), accessible at: https://www.canada.ca/en/privy-council/services/publications/guide-making-federal-acts-regulations.html (last accessed 07/12/2018).

[18] Helen Xanthaki, 'Drafting Manuals and Quality in Legislation: Positive Contribution towards Certainty in the Law or Impediment to the Necessity for Dynamism of Rules' (2010) IV:2 Legisprudence 119, at 127; Eric Millard, 'Les limites des guides de legistique: l'exemple du droit français' in Alexandre Flückiger and Christine Guy-Ecabert (eds) 'Guider les Parlements et les Gouvernements pour mieux légiférer – Le rôle des guides de legistique' (Schulthess 2008).

[19] William Robinson, 'Manuals for Drafting European Union Legislation' (2010) IV:2 Legisprudence 152.

[20] Xanthaki, 'Drafting Manuals' (n 18) at 124.

a flexible nature that prompt lawmakers to think have a lot of potential to perform this function. The extent to which the existing toolkit achieves this has not been examined in sufficient depth and in its empirical dimensions. What can be noted however is an important gap in the scope of existing tools: these range from broad, abstract questions to very specific (drafting) ones with little in-between to capture the questions that emerge when facing the challenge of formulating the content of rules.

3. A CLOSER LOOK AT THE CONTEMPORARY LAWMAKING TOOLKIT FROM THE PERSPECTIVE OF EFFECTIVE LAWMAKING

3.1. Impact assessment

Impact assessment is the 'crown jewel' of evidence-based policy making. It is a structured method of 'connecting the dots' between a problem and its features, options for addressing it and their potential impacts on beneficiaries, the economy, the environment, etc. and making a decision informed by existing evidence and information.

IAs have multiple functions: they are a control mechanism for the regulatory powers of lawmakers, a procedural device to align trade-offs in lawmaking[21] but also a tool to ensure coherence in policy design, transparency, communication and information.[22] Its primary added value, however, lies in the enhancement of the evidence base and transparency, especially the analysis of the situation and alternative options,[23] taming 'bureaucratic drift', ensuring accountability but also policy learning and symbolic politics.[24] IAs are used nowadays extensively in the preparation of primary and secondary legislation and their usefulness appears to be taken for granted. But is that so? Do law-

---

[21] A. Meuwese and S. van Voorst, 'Regulatory impact assessment in legal studies' in C. Dunlop and C. Radaelli (eds) *Handbook of Regulatory Impact Assessment* (Edward Elgar Publishing 2016) 22, 24.

[22] P. Andrews, 'Are Market Failure Analysis and Impact Assessment Useful?' in Stephen Weatherill (ed) *Better Regulation* (Hart Publishing 2007) 49ff cf; Alberto Allemanno, 'A Meeting of Minds on Impact Assessment' (2011) 17:3 European Public Law 495.

[23] OECD, 'Regulatory Policies in OECD Countries: From Interventionism to Regulatory Governance' (OECD Publishing 2002) 47; OECD, 'Building an Institutional Framework for Regulatory Impact Analysis (RIA): Guidance for Policy Makers' (OECD Publishing 2008) 24–5.

[24] Claire Dunlop and Claudio Radaelli, 'The politics and economics of regulatory impact assessment' in Claire Dunlop and Claudio Radaelli (eds) *Handbook of Regulatory Impact Assessment* (Edward Elgar Publishing 2016) 8–14.

makers use Impact Assessments? Do they even read them? What kind of value do Impact Assessments bring to the design and drafting of legislation? The answers to this question are inevitably empirical. Anecdotally however, drafters and experts involved in drafting legislation, have confessed that they rarely, if ever, read Impact Assessments, because they are neither relevant nor useful for their task. Do Impact Assessments fail to address the specific challenges that lawmakers struggle with?

The main strength of Impact Assessments is that they have, in principle, a clear thinking process[25]: they define and analyse a problem, examine the need to address it, set the objectives to be achieved, examine alternative options and assess their impacts (the triad of economic, social and environmental impacts is a classic, but variations include impacts on the budget, competition, SMEs, privacy, gender, children, equality, poverty, among many others), costs and benefits, compare and select the preferred option.

In the EU these functions are codified into seven questions: what is the problem and why is it a problem? Why should the EU act? What should be achieved? What are the various options to achieve the objectives? What are their economic, social and environmental impacts and who will be affected? How do the different options compare (effectiveness, efficiency and coherence)? How will monitoring and subsequent retrospective evaluation be organised? An Impact Assessment in the UK considers four main questions: What is the problem under consideration? Why is government intervention necessary? What policy options have been considered, including any alternatives to regulation? What is the cost of the preferred option?[26] In Germany, the assessment of intended unintended impacts[27] covers financial implications, impacts on the public budgetary income and expenditure (gross), on the budgets of the Länder and local authorities, compliance costs to the public, industry, and public administration, among others. In France, impact assessment focuses on the state of the law and a diagnostic of the current situation; objectives; options beyond legislating; impact of the planned provisions; consultations organ-

---

[25] Cf Stephan Naundorf and Claudio Radaelli, 'Regulatory Evaluation Ex Ante and Ex Post: Best Practice, Guidance and Methods', in U. Karpen and H. Xanthaki, *Legislation in Europe. A Comprehensive Guide for Scholars and Practitioners* (Hart Publishing 2017) at 187–211.

[26] Department for Business, Innovation and Skills, Impact Assessment Guidance (2010), available at: https://webarchive.nationalarchives.gov.uk/+/http:/www.web.bis.gov.uk/assets/biscore/better-regulation/docs/10-898-impact-assessment-guidance.pdf (last accessed 07/12/2018).

[27] Joint Rules of Procedure of the Federal Ministries (GGO) 2011 available at: https://bscw.bund.de/pub/bscw.cgi/d52920962/120119%20GGO_neu_engl.pdf?nonce=03349cf7faa309dce38778bbd9215cf97cb14c6e (last accessed 07/12/2018).

ised and implementation modalities of the proposed measures.[28] In Canada, Regulatory Impact Analysis focuses on identifying and assessing public policy issues, setting objectives and expected outcomes, selecting the appropriate mix of instruments, assessing legal implications, compliance with international obligations, analysing the benefits and costs of regulation, recommending an option and looking at coordination, cooperation, implementation, compliance and enforcement and evaluation and review.[29]

In principle, these questions make a lot of sense in any context. The definition of the problem explores the policy and legislative framework and context, objectives are identified and a clear solution is selected. Where Impact Assessments fail is firstly in transitioning from the selection of policy to legislative options, secondly in the lack of analytical detail on the legislative aspects of the selected option and thirdly their emphasis on costs that often obscures other critical points of analysis.

Despite their chameleonic nature, the main dilemma behind Impact Assessments appears to be 'to regulate or not to regulate'? IAs serve to an important extent, and justifiably so, a 'deregulation perspective'. Even though 'technocratic' and participatory perspectives are present, at least in EU Impact Assessments,[30] an important part of the effort is directed towards justifying why regulating is necessary or not. What is to be regulated comes as a secondary concern and Impact Assessments do not go much further than selecting a policy (rather than legislative) option. Even when regulating this approach is evident. An Impact Assessment on cooperation between the courts of the EU Member States in the taking of evidence in civil or commercial matters[31] opted for a 'policy package' that included a number of legislative and non-legislative measures: a default channel for electronic communication and document

---

[28] Secrétariat général du Gouvernement, Mode d'Emploi: Comment renseigner l'étude d'impact d'un projet de loi?, 2017, available at: https://www.legifrance.gouv.fr/Droit-francais/Evaluation-prealable-des-projets-de-normes/Etudes-d-impact-des-lois/Methodologie (last accessed 07/12/2018).

[29] Government of Canada, Cabinet Directive on Regulatory Management, 2012, available at: https://www.canada.ca/en/treasury-board-secretariat/services/federal-regulatory-management/guidelines-tools/cabinet-directive-regulatory-management.html (last accessed 07/12/2018).

[30] A.C.M. Meuwese, 'Regulatory Review of European Commission Impact Assessments. What Kind for Which Better Regulation Scenario?' (2017) 19:1 European Journal of Law Reform 16–33.

[31] European Commission, Executive Summary of the Impact Assessment, Accompanying the document Proposal for a Regulation of the European Parliament and of the Council amending Council Regulation (EC) No 1206/2001 of 28 May 2001 on cooperation between the courts of the Member States in the taking of evidence in civil or commercial matters, SWD/2018/284 final.

exchange; modern means of taking evidence as the default approach; removing legal barriers to the acceptance of electronic (digital) evidence; increasing legal certainty by additional means of cross-border evidence-taking; tackling divergent interpretations of the term 'court'; communicating the uniform standards provided by the Regulation; best practices for courts; and making court and other legal professionals more aware of the direct channel for taking evidence under the Regulation.

But even when purely regulatory options are considered, their analysis rarely goes into much depth. For example, an IA on nuclear standards in the UK identified two options: a first one framed as 'adopt domestic standards of nuclear safeguards of broad equivalence to those adopted by Euratom' and a second one to fulfil nuclear safeguards, without replicating Euratom's standards.[32] However, from the decision to select either option to an actual Bill a number of more specific issues need to be considered: the detailed standards and their impact, their nature, their specificity, changes to existing norms, etc. More than a genuine lawmaking tool, an IA resembles policy instructions where the framework and the context for developing and drafting the legislative text is set. *Where IAs stop (the preferred option) actual lawmaking begins.*

Further, Impact Assessments are too much oriented towards the quantification of costs and benefits to the extent that they might obscure other concerns, long term interests and uncertain variables.[33] Legislation might often need to go beyond cost and benefits to protect moral values and commitments that might be impossible to capture in cost-benefit analysis but that do matter and might generate losses[34] if lawmakers fail to take them into account. Although IAs have expanded to integrate substantive concerns on fundamental rights, competitiveness, or gender issues, to name only a few, quantification often overshadows them especially given the difficulties in quantifying moral or other hazards or benefits[35] while there is no clear criterion for the selection. How are these prioritised? What happens if the most cost beneficial option has important adverse effects on fundamental rights or minority issues that cannot be quantified?

A disclaimer: generalisations are impossible as much depends on the way in which Impact Assessments are used in practice and practice differs not

---

[32] BEIS, Euratom Nuclear Safeguards IA No: BEIS032(F)-17-ESNM, available at: https://publications.parliament.uk/pa/bills/cbill/2017-2019/0109/Nuclear%20Safeguards%20Impact%20Assessment.pdf (last accessed 07/12/2018).

[33] Wim Voermans, 'To Measure is to Know: the Quantification of Regulation' (2015) 3:1 The Theory and Practice of Legislation 91–111.

[34] Eric A. Posner and Cass R. Sunstein, 'Moral Commitments in Cost-Benefit Analysis' (2017) Coase-Sandor Working Paper Series in Law and Economics 802.

[35] Ibid.

only between jurisdictions but also between laws in the same jurisdictions. Impact Assessments are indeed used (or misused) in different ways that cover the whole spectrum from refabricated, to perfunctory or thought provoking analysis or simply for symbolic reasons.[36] Examples from several countries highlight that the concept of better regulation is often poorly integrated into national processes and the actual management of the IA of policies and draft legislation is far from satisfactory,[37] which means that an assessment with an even remote claim to validity would have to be very specific.

So what do Impact Assessments bring into lawmaking? A lot of valuable information and analysis on the problem and the need to legislate, the identification of legislative provisions that need to be fixed or corrected or the general spirit of the new instruments to be introduced; they are particularly helpful in objective setting as a context for the objectives of legislative action; they contribute quantified information on where costs lie; they touch upon compliance and delivery; the affected audiences and their features. Another positive contribution is their proactive emphasis on delivery, enforcement and implementation. In other words, they set the framework and the context for developing and drafting the legislative text and set the main parameters of legislative design.

To come back to the initial questions, Impact Assessments remain policy rather than lawmaking tools. They inform lawmaking but are far from the level of detail and analysis that would be meaningful for lawmakers. Where IAs finish, actual lawmaking starts and its substantive questions are still to be answered. It comes as no surprise that drafters find little use for them.

3.2. Consultation

Consultation is the two-way relationship between citizens and governments on information and feedback.[38] As a tool of openness, transparency and participation it has played an important role in the effort to improve governance and the quality of the regulatory environment.[39] Participation of stakeholders and interested parties in the formulation of policies and legislation promotes

---

[36] Claire Dunlop and Claudio Radaelli, 'The politics and economics of regulatory impact assessment' in Claire Dunlop and Claudio Radaelli (eds) *Handbook of Regulatory Impact Assessment* (Edward Elgar Publishing 2016) 8–14.

[37] Scot Jacobs, 'Towards a simpler and practical approach' in Dunlop and Radaelli (eds) *Handbook* ibid at 78–90.

[38] OECD, 'Citizens as Partners. Information, Consultation and Public Participation in Policy-Making' (OECD Publishing 2001) 22.

[39] Anne Meuwese, 'Embedding Consultation Procedures: Law or Institutionalization?' (2011) 17:3 European Public Law 531, 534.

good governance, enables socio-political interaction, encourages partnerships and joint solutions and increases the efficiency and legitimacy of decisions.[40] Especially as part of the legislative process, it can inform and improve transparency, enhance legitimacy, test the feasibility of proposed solutions, engage in fact finding and improve the implementation and practicability of legislation.[41]

In practice, consultation is a flexible tool that can be used in different directions. It can be used in policy or lawmaking or both, but much depends on the kind of questions consultations will ask. In most contexts, existing guidance on consultation offers mostly a procedural framework for conducting it, like information on how to make it 'targeted', when to publish, time limits to be respected, acknowledgement of feedback, etc.[42] In the UK, consultation principles[43] stress the need for clarity and concision, clear purpose and information, a fixed and reasonable duration, etc. They do not highlight the issues on which consultation can be useful, for example consensus-building, correcting faulty assumptions, testing the acceptance of distinct choice of substantive rules or standards, exploring critical aspects of compliance, enforcement, communication and implementation. In this sense, the substantive focus of consultation is left open.

In practice, consultation often comes without a clear vision of what it entails, static methods and questions and often conflicting objectives.[44] The use of consultation remains mostly instrumental and focuses vaguely on 'listening better' or 'hearing more stakeholders' rather than asking the right questions in order to get useful answers. More specific criticisms include selection biases, little focus beyond organised interest groups towards those most affected by an initiative[45] and limited use of techniques that can provide meaningful or more

---

[40] D. Obradovic and J. Alonso Vizcaino, 'Good Governance Requirements concerning the Participation of Interest Groups in EU Consultations' (2006) 43 Common Market Law Review 1050.

[41] F. Uhlmann and Ch. Konrath, 'Participation' in U. Karpen and H. Xanthaki (eds) *Legislation in Europe. A Comprehensive Guide for Scholars and Practitioners* (Hart Publishing 2017) 76–81.

[42] European Commission, Chapter VII Guidelines on Stakeholder Consultation, available at: https://ec.europa.eu/info/sites/info/files/better-regulation-guidelines-stakeholder-consultation.pdf (last accessed 07/12/2018).

[43] Cabinet Office, Consultation Principles, 2018, available at : https://assets.publishing.service.gov.uk/government/uploads/system/uploads/attachment_data/file/691383/Consultation_Principles__1_.pdf (last accessed 07/12/2018).

[44] F. Blanc and G. Ottimofiore, Consultation in Claire Dunlop and Claudio Radaelli (eds) *Handbook of Regulatory Impact Assessment* (Edward Elgar Publishing 2016) 155–76, 155–7.

[45] A. Alemanno, 'How Much Better Is Better Regulation? Assessing the Impact of the Better Regulation Package on the European Union – A Research Agenda' (2015) 3 European Journal of Risk Regulation 344–56.

in-depth information.⁴⁶ The lack of clear orientation on the specific aspects of lawmaking it can actually clarify (compliance, communication, implementation) make consultation an untargeted endeavour that can produce random outcomes. In short, consultation has a lot of potential to inform specific lawmaking questions, if properly used in this direction.

3.3. So, does the toolkit contribute to lawmaking?

Impact Assessment and consultations were readily promoted from *policy to lawmaking tools*, without the necessary maturation process and adaptations to reflect the differences between the two processes. The law needs politics to be enforced and politics use law to diversify access to power, yet the function of the law is to ensure certainty of expectation.⁴⁷ The two differ substantively, essentially in scope: policy is oriented towards broader social problems, values and goals while legislation is confined to the narrower scope of what can be done through the law (establish prohibitions, procedures, rights and obligations). Policy thinks big, legislation thinks specific. Policy might set a goal to reduce inequality, legislation can only provide a legislative framework for it, including rules, prohibitions, procedures, etc. Although the rationale of both Impact Assessment (problem, objectives, options, costs and benefits) and consultation is very meaningful for both, the questions to be asked, the focus and the level of detail of the analysis would differ substantially.

Overall, there are three problems with Impact Assessments and consultation as lawmaking tools. Firstly, both tools integrate multiple rationales without a clear prioritisation or balance. Efficacy, efficiency, rationality, legitimacy, transparency, or participation might not always look in the same direction or lead to the same decisions. None of the tools prioritises these concerns, although efficiency appears in practice to be of particular weight. Making sense of complex analysis without a clear orientation is not easy. The larger the number of criteria, the more complex the analysis, the more benchmarks, the harder to 'pass' or 'fail' with clarity and clear focus.⁴⁸ The ambitious effort to integrate several concerns appears to lead to a lack of focus that minimises their potential for targeted contributions.

---

⁴⁶ S. Ranchordás, 'Consultations, Citizen Narratives and Evidence-based Regulation: The Strange Case of the Consultation on the Collaborative Economy' (2017) 19:1–2 European Journal of Law Reform 52–73.

⁴⁷ N. Luhman, *Law as a Social System* (tran. Klaus Ziegert Oxford University Press 2004) 162–3.

⁴⁸ C. Hood, R. Baldwin, H. Rothstein, 'Assessing the Dangerous Dogs Act: When does a regulatory law fail?' (2000) Public Law 282–305.

This broad focus helps in legislative design but not in the detailed craft of actual lawmaking. There are different levels of deliberation with regard to a legislative text. Broad questions on strategy and design and specific ones associated with the details of choice of rules, compliance motives, structure, etc. Legislative design is the process of making strategic decisions on the fundamental features of new legislation and the legislative strategy, in other words, the policy side of lawmaking, the 'conception' of a rule, while legislative drafting is the actual 'birth' of a rule. Impact Assessments and consultations can be useful in legislative design with a clearer focus in this direction. And although practice will always differ, both between jurisdictions but also between laws in the same jurisdictions, and good quality assessments coexist with perfunctory ones, while meaningful consultations will coexist with futile ones, the design of the tools is critical with regard to their overall function.

Last but not least, the toolkit serves the lawmaking values of efficacy, effectiveness and efficiency in different ways and to a different extent. Efficacy, that looks at whether legislation can contribute to broader policy objectives is served by the rationale of Impact Assessments. Efficiency, that studies which option achieves the most benefits with the least cost is by far the ruling value. The entire toolkit is governed by an explicit cost-benefit rationale, that catalogues costs and benefits and makes decisions primarily on this criterion. Effectiveness on the other hand, which examines which options have the best potential to achieve the desired results, appears to be lost somewhere between the two. It is an underlying concern but its importance appears to decrease in the light of the other functions.[49] This might be reasonable with regard to a broader exploration of options. But what about the selected option? If the entire exercise led to the option that best serves policy objectives with justified costs, it is then where effectiveness becomes important and really needs to come into play. The solution should have the capacity to work. A clear focus on effectiveness, especially considering the selected option appears to be missing.

4. ADDING 'EFFECTIVENESS LENSES' TO EXISTING TOOLS: THE EFFECTIVENESS TEST

The previous sections established that Impact Assessments and consultation are useful in legislative decision making but lack the detail that would make them 'proper' lawmaking tools. They are primarily oriented towards efficacy

---

[49] Dirk H. van der Meulen, 'The Use of Impact Assessments and the Quality of Legislation' (2013) 1:2 Theory and Practice of Legislation 305–25.

(the achievement of broad policy goals) and efficiency, while effectiveness is an underlying rather than prevalent concern.

However, if effective legislation is the result of complex mechanics in the conceptualisation, design and drafting of the law, it requires a consistent effort especially when a law is designed and drafted. *Effectiveness cannot materialise unless explicitly anticipated.* It is obvious by now that many of the challenges identified in the previous chapters result from errors in design and from insufficient consideration of their operational dimensions. Laws will have the potential to be more effective, if effectiveness is a clear concern in legislative decision making.

This means that effectiveness requires a focused thinking process, which is not present at the moment in impact assessments and consultations. From another perspective, the fragmentation of existing scrutiny exercises does not allow a holistic view of conceptual effectiveness, legislative concepts, communication, expression, presentation and monitoring.[50] In other words, effective lawmaking requires a method. After the preferred policy option is selected there are a number of critical decisions remain to be made. Which requirements will best achieve the basic goal? How should these requirements be framed and expressed? What kind of motives are necessary? What kind of incentives? Who should oversee implementation? What enforcement strategy should be used? Existing tools provide only partial answers to these questions.

Impact assessments define the framework within which the lawmaker will have to work and provide useful information and analysis but without going into the detailed lawmaking issues linked to the 'mechanics' of the law. On the other hand, drafting guidance, manuals or checklists which primarily address legislative drafters are too detailed and prescriptive. Actual lawmaking that deals with formulating the content and form of the law lies between the two and has no tools to guide it. More focus on the effectiveness of legislation is appropriate to fill the gap between them.

4.1. The effectiveness test

The 'effectiveness test'[51] is a conceptual tool to make lawmakers aware of relevant issues, engage them in a thinking process that will assist them in con-

---

[50] Helen Xanthaki, 'An Enlightened Approach to Legislative Scrutiny: Focusing on Effectiveness' (2018) 9:3 European Journal of Risk Regulation 431–44.

[51] For earlier versions of the effectiveness test see M. Mousmouti, 'Operationalising Quality of Legislation through the Effectiveness Test' (2012) 6:2 Legisprudence 201; Maria Mousmouti, 'Making Legislative Effectiveness an Operational Concept: Unfolding the Effectiveness Test as a Conceptual Tool for Lawmaking' (2018) 9:3 European Journal of Risk Regulation 445–64.

trolling and identifying – early on – potential critical points for their drafts. It is a logical exercise to support legislative decision making that can strengthen the operational aspects of an effective law, namely purpose, content, superstructure and results, and guide lawmakers, as the 'designers' of effective legislation, towards conscious decisions on critical points for their drafts. The effectiveness test is an 'exercise', a thinking process that can be used flexibly by lawmakers. It consists of a set of questions around the operational elements of effectiveness that can be useful if addressed in a consistent manner.

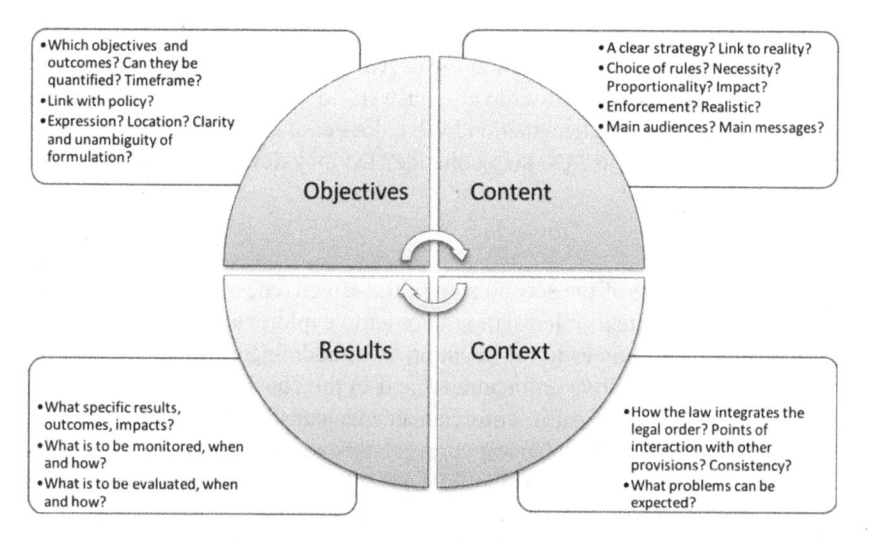

Figure 6.1   The effectiveness test

4.2.   The structure and elements of the 'effectiveness test'

The effectiveness test consists of five sets of questions around the elements of effectiveness that are meant to guide and assist the thinking process when making decisions on the content of legislation. The questions are neither rigid nor exhaustive and are only meant to be thought provoking and prompt the lawmaker to consider these elements. They do not define answers but require the actor to consider what decisions are made and why.

4.2.1.   Purpose

The main objective of the first step of the effectiveness test is to explore the purpose in relation to the underlying problem, policy and the objectives of the law and ensure that it provides a meaningful link and benchmark for what the law aims to achieve. The main questions are: What problem does the law address and what aspects of it can the law address? In this context, what are the specific and broader objectives of the law? How do they interrelate? Can they be quantified? Is there a timeframe?

How do objectives project into expected results, outcomes and effects? Can these be quantified? What is the relation between them and the objectives of the relevant policy/ies? How are objectives expressed? Are they easy to find, clear and unambiguous? Do they set a clear and meaningful benchmark for what the law aims to achieve? What is this benchmark? Does it provide a meaningful direction for the implementer and interpreter (judge)?

When looking at purpose retrospectively, the purpose and objectives will be juxtaposed with results to ascertain the degree of coincidence or achievement. Relevant questions are: How do the answers to the questions above differ taking into account implemetnation? What does case law show? Do objectives correspond with results? Do they coincide? Do they deviate? To what extent? And why?

4.2.2. Content

The main objective of the second step of the effectiveness test is to scrutinise the substantive content of legislation in order to explore: a) the responsiveness of the legislative choices to the situation to be addressed; b) the potential for compliance and effective enforcement; and c) the consistency and alignment between the choice of rules, enforcement mechanisms and communication. If applied critically this step can prevent the adoption of rules which are incongruent with reality, can highlight potential barriers to compliance and enforcement and challenges in construction and can help make the content of legislation realistic, proportional, responsive to the reality and conducive to results.

The main questions to be addressed in lawmaking are: What are the legislative choices through which the law intervenes? How are they relevant to the problem addressed? Do these reflect the reality on the ground (target audiences, resources, institutions, etc.) and the available information and evidence? Are they proportionate and appropriate in relation to the defined objectives? How are they expected to impact the problem as it currently stands? What implementation/enforcement mechanisms/strategies are used? Are they realistic? Do they take into account current/existing institutional capacity and resources? What are the main audiences of the law? How are they expected to comply with the law? What kind of motives or incentives are used? Is their use supported by existing information and evidence?

What are the main regulatory messages of the law? Are they structured and organised in a way to be clear and intelligible? Are more general messages prioritised in relation to more specific ones? Are the messages expressed and communicated to the target audiences in a straightforward way making clear what is expected?

Retrospectively, this step would examine to what extent the assumptions expressed during lawmaking have been verified throughout the enforcement and implementation of the law, what worked well, what did not work well etc.

4.2.3. Context

The purpose of the third step of the effectiveness test is to look at the law in relation to the broader legal environment with which it will interact and identify points of coherence or conflict. Questions to be addressed during lawmaking are: how will the law integrate the legal order (as a new message, a message diffused to existing laws through amendments or sectoral provisions, as parallel laws)? Why is this solution chosen? What potential problems can it create? Does the law introduce new concepts or new definitions to existing concepts? What are the potential points of conflict with existing provisions? Does the law provide a clear solution to identified conflicts or inconsistencies? Are the changes introduced easy to identify and understand? What problems can be expected?

Retrospectively, the questions to be asked are: How did the law interact with other provisions and laws? Were there overlaps, gaps or inconsistencies? What problems arose? To what extent were these predictable? How can these be solved?

4.2.4. Results

The fourth step of the test scrutinises a number of issues: firstly, whether expected results are clear, whether sufficient mechanisms are in place (or introduced in the law) to ensure proper monitoring of implementation and whether sufficient information and data will be available for the identification, review and evaluation of results; and secondly to identify the actual results achieved and their relation to the initial objectives of legislation. During lawmaking, emphasis lies on making sure that sufficient mechanisms (horizontal or specific) are in place to ensure that results will be consistently monitored and measured and that sufficient data will be collected to allow information about results.

The main questions to be addressed (in lawmaking) are: what are the specific results, outcomes and impacts to be expected? How will the implementation of the law be monitored? How and when will the law be reviewed and evaluated? How will results be measured? What information is required to monitor implementation? What data and information are required to evaluate the law? Who will collect this data/information and under which processes?

During the evaluation phase, emphasis is on actual results and juxtaposing them with the initial objectives. The main questions to be addressed are:

According to the data collected, were the objectives and expected results achieved? What were the broader impacts of the law? Are these positive or negative, expected or unexpected? Are there clear causal relationships between the law and its results or effects? Are these associated to the choices related to the content, context or purpose of legislation? Have the intended objectives been achieved? If yes, what worked well and why? Has the law failed partially or entirely? Why? What did not work and why? Were failures a question of conceptual design, communication or implementation? Were the assumptions of the law in terms of legislative choices, enforcement, etc., confirmed?

4.2.5. Overarching questions

The elements of effectiveness do not operate in isolation but interact. The aim of this last set of questions is to look at the internal coherence and alignment of the elements of effectiveness within the law and examine the extent to which they interact optimally and are proportionate. Relevant questions are: Does the law reflect a clear regulatory strategy? Does it intervene in a clear way? Are purpose, content and expected results well aligned and proportional? Are the mechanics of the law appropriate to support its effectiveness and implementation?

4.3. 'Testing' the effectiveness test: three case studies

The effectiveness test is not a theoretical tool. On the contrary, it is meant to operationalise the elements of effectiveness in a way to identify and anticipate weak points. Three case studies are presented below to critically examine the extent to which the test can provide meaningful information.

Case Study 1: Equality legislation in England

Equality legislation in England consists of a single act, the Equality Act 2010, that was the result of the unification of pre-existing fragmented approaches. The Equality Act only indirectly informs on its substantive purpose and where so (through long titles, explanatory notes and guidance) it provides procedural rather than substantive information. The benchmark for what the legislative text aims to achieve remains rather obscure. The substantive content of the law is consistently articulated, using few but complementary techniques structured around a logic of 'negative' prohibitions and 'positive' actions. Compliance is promoted through persuasive and escalating remedies and through a clear mandate of the Equality Commission. The design of the enforcement mechanism has a clear logic and structure consisting of individualistic court-based enforcement and strategic action which is the mandate of the Equality Commission. The communication of the law is faithful to the prescriptive tradition and style of the legal order. A selective and non-exhaustive use of definitions is chosen and although several controversial concepts are left unaddressed, while more evident terms are defined, these appear to be conscious choices on matters resolved by the legislator and those left to the courts. Overall, the substantive content of legislation and choices of form and expression are articulate and consistent. A systematic and multi-level review process is in place to monitor and appraise the underlying assumptions of the law, 'social' evolutions, the 'working' of the law in practice and policy results. Clear benchmarks against which provisions will be appraised partly cover for its indefinite aims. Overall, English equality legislation demonstrates a clear strategy and mechanics as a result of consistent and articulate choices.

Case Study 2: Equality legislation in France
French non-discrimination legislation evolved under the irreconcilable rationales of colour-blindness, that emanates from the universalistic principle of equality in the French Constitution, and group-specific approaches in European legislation. Equality law is 'diffused' across the legal system in sectoral codes, constitutional, primary and secondary legislation and stand-alone acts. This makes it fragmented, polycentric and centrifugal. Purpose is eloquently discussed in reports on motives accompanying draft Bills while constitutional provisions play an important role in providing direction and unifying the fragmented approaches. The substantive content of non-discrimination legislation combines repressive techniques, (more limited) civil or administrative law techniques and self-regulation (through collective bargaining). Positive action is a controversial concept that exemplifies the tension between the universalistic conception of equality and measures defined on the basis of group or individual characteristics. Positive measures 'à la française' are only exceptional, specific and temporary. The enforcement mechanism includes the prosecution, the labour courts and mediation through an equality body, the Defenseur des Droits, with limited sanctioning powers and main emphasis on mediation. Strategic enforcement is weak. Legislative expression follows the traditions and styles of the legal order and does not seem to pose problems. The application of legislation and its results are monitored and evaluated in an uneven way. Monitoring of enactment is consistent but overall evaluation is selective. Individual laws include different monitoring clauses, diagnostic tools and instruments, obligations for data collection and reporting but are asymmetric and evaluation is not pursued in a way to offer a comprehensive picture. Follow-up and evaluation varies considerably among different texts, while it is vague with regard to codified legislation. As a result, the amount and the quality of information available on the application and the results of the law are highly variable and uneven.

The overall picture of the effectiveness of French non-discrimination legislation is one of ambivalence: a complex structure, ambitious objectives, ambivalent choices to promote them and with difficulties in implementation and uneven data on results. 'Weaknesses' in the individual elements of effectiveness are intensified by their poor articulation: purposes are eloquent (often too eloquent) but too abstract, substantive content cannot or does not go all the way to meet these objectives, while results data is selective and uneven. Superstructure does not facilitate coherence. The tensions and imbalances between the purpose, the legislative techniques, the enforcement mechanisms and the realities of the problem pose important challenges to the potential of the law to be effective.

Case Study 3: Equality legislation in Greece
Non-discrimination legislation in Greece in its majority consists of stand-alone Acts transposing different European Directives. Equality legislation includes explicit statements of purpose inside and outside the legislative texts as a result of a mot à mot transposition of the relevant provisions of the Directives. Although well formulated, their link to the constitutional provisions on equality and the rich case law is weak.

In terms of content, legislation follows closely the ambitious legislative choices of the Directives. A combination of legislative techniques is used, including penal prohibitions, civil prohibitions, administrative provisions, requirements for positive action and obligations for social dialogue. This rich mix of techniques is poorly articulated through provisions that are either too general and ambiguous or unclear and vague. The enforcement mechanism includes the courts and four distinct equality bodies with different mandates, scope and means of intervention, resulting in an unbalanced enforcement of different grounds. In terms of expression, there is a poor alignment between concepts and behaviours regulated in distinct instruments. Last, the monitoring and evaluation of results is prescriptive rather than substantive. Monitoring of the law by the equality bodies is fragmented and allows only a limited, ad hoc and casuistic view of the application of legislation, while general evaluation of legislation has not materialised.

Overall, Greek equality legislation, from the perspective of effectiveness, is full of contradictions. Its 'imported' strategy, although sophisticated, has superficial mechanics that are inconsistent. Legislative choices are insufficiently elaborated, disconnected from the legal tradition, substantive content is ambitious but superficial, enforcement is over-complex and fragmented and results inconsistently monitored. Apart from the weaknesses in the individual elements, the most important 'error' in this case study is the lack of consistency in the choices made: the purpose, content, enforcement, expression and monitoring of the law are uncoordinated and detached from reality.

4.4. Usefulness, relevance, advantages and limitations

The effectiveness test appears to have the potential to highlight the strategy, conceptual design and mechanics of legislation. By looking at the four elements of effectiveness and their alignment and interconnection these three elements become clear, including strengths, weaknesses and points on which effort is required for improvement. Secondly, the test makes sense in different contexts. Third, it can spot shortcomings in the individual elements of legislation and discrepancies between them. It does not provide a direction for action but instead marks the need for action. Where does the problem lie? Is it in the conceptual design? Is it in mechanism introduced? Is it in the implementation? The test can highlight the lack of a clear aim, and allow for decisions to be made bearing that in mind. When it comes to content, the test looks into the mechanics of the 'preferred option' and scrutinises from the perspective of their capacity to work. Are the chosen rules appropriate? Is compliance anticipated? What does experience teach us? How can enforcement be best structured? How can language, structure and other tools available to the drafter be used in the best possible way to send out the message to the specific audiences? When it comes to context, the effectiveness test provides insight on accessibility, overall coherence and potential points of conflict. Last but not least, when it comes to results, the test helps the lawmaker formulate clear anticipated results and make decisions on when and how to monitor implementation and evaluate.

The advantage of this conceptual tool is that it can help detect inconsistencies in the rationale of legislation and improve them or at least make conscious choices about them. It allows a diagnosis of the weaknesses in the conceptualisation and design of legislation, from the proactive position of the lawmaker, to prevent, as much as possible, regulatory failures. It allows identification at an early stage of the failures in design (whether rules are inappropriate to address the problem tackled or are too broad or too narrow in relation to the stated purpose), implementation (whether the enforcement strategy or mechanism is inappropriate or implementation is inadequate) and drafting (whether the subjects of the law do not know how to comply with it or encounter difficulties in complying because the rules are not accessible, coherent or clear, or are complicated and imprecise). Through the effectiveness test, weaknesses can be identified and addressed.

An additional advantage is that the effectiveness test is a neutral tool. It does not promote specific legislative choices but looks at the content and the consistency of the features of legislative texts and judges them from the perspective of design – and effectiveness. It does not measure perfection or quality in abstract terms but instead assists lawmakers to grasp the whole picture, anticipate failures, highlight the weak points in terms of design and orient the required effort there and promote – to the extent possible – sound, aligned and consistent mechanics in the law that have the potential to deliver the desired results.

A weak point is that the test, if applied in a formal manner, can prove meaningless. If understood as a formality, or as a checklist it can be rendered pointless. Like much of the effort invested in lawmaking, its power lies in the thinking process behind the questions rather than the answers.

The effectiveness test does not override the existing tools to promote quality in decision making. Instead, it complements the existing quality toolkit and especially impact assessments with effectiveness-focused lenses. It can be used during the drafting of legislation or after the impact assessments are finalised to shape the details of the legislative solution.

5. CONCLUSIONS

If drafting is the actual 'birth' of a rule (as opposed to the 'conception' of a rule) and a practical process of making legislative decisions backed by evidence and supported by anticipation, analysis and creativity, it is a dynamic process. If this is accepted, effective lawmaking is the result of complex mechanics in the conceptualisation, design, drafting, enforcement and implementation of the law. Existing tools provide the context, the starting point, the analysis, the evidence basis, information *but lack the depth* required by lawmakers and an emphasis on effectiveness as the essential feature of the selected option. The 'effectiveness test' is a practical exercise that examines the strategy, design and mechanics of the law from the perspective of effectiveness and highlights where its strengths and weaknesses lie and where effort needs to be directed.

7. Legislative failure

> 'I have not failed. I've just found 10,000 ways that won't work.'
> Thomas A. Edison

1. FAILURE AND LEGISLATION

A google search using the terms 'failed legislation' or 'legislative failure' brings up a large and highly diverse number of results ranging from analyses on the function of legislatures and the separation of powers, analysis of bills that failed to be adopted, failures of the rule of law, interest group papers promoting specific agendas, expert opinions, actors advocating for legislative improvement, media pieces reacting to tragic public events, etc. A more diligent researcher will spot, with considerable difficulty within this bric-a-brac of information, only few systematic studies producing evidence-based arguments on the success or failure of policies or legislation.

Lawmaking is a flourishing industry invested with high hopes. Failure is a popular topic, but one often addressed in a shallow way. The reasons why appraisal of failure tends to be controversial – or avoided – are firstly, the inherent difficulty in being objective about it, especially since it does not come in fixed forms and might differ not only within and across societies but also across areas of law[1]; secondly the inevitable political dimensions that intrude or frame the discussion and thirdly, the undisputable fact that different actors perceive issues quite differently.[2]

However, understanding and studying failure, as the flipside of effectiveness, is the only way to understand pathologies in legislation and what causes them, correct them, prevent further failure and improve the lawmaking method. In the same way that knowledge advanced through negative findings,[3] so can legislation.

---

[1] D. Galligan, 'Legal Failure: Law and Social Norms in Post-Communist Europe' in D. Galligan and M. Kurkchiyan, *Law and Informal Practices: The Post-Communist Experience* (Oxford Scholarship Online 2012) at 2.

[2] C. Hood, R. Baldwin and H. Rothstein, 'Assessing the Dangerous Dogs Act: When does a regulatory law fail?' (2000) (Summer) Public Law 282–305.

[3] Peter Grabosky, 'Counterproductive Regulation' (1995) 23 International Journal of the Sociology of Law 347–69, 364.

1.1. Understanding failure

Taking a closer look at the concept of failure raises a number of questions: what counts as failure? How can it be objectively recognised and explained? By whom? Failure is in itself a 'heavy' term. Scholars have used more nuanced expressions to refer to legislative misgivings. Merton talked about 'unanticipated consequences', Fuller about 'miscarriages' of the legal system, Grabosky about 'counterproductive regulation'. More dramatic expressions include 'disasters', 'fiascos' or 'catastrophes'. Independent of the terms used, however, the concept of failure invariably has two interrelated aspects: firstly, the mismatch between legislative intent and the results produced and secondly the extent of harmful effects of legislation. It can range from a failure to reach all or some of legislations' intended results, to legislation backfiring entirely or even causing significant harm. But to what extent is failure a lawmaking issue?

Scholars studying government processes have focused on the political process as the single explanation why legislation fails.[4] Yet the reasons behind legislative failure are much more complex. Merton identified three main reasons behind the 'unanticipated consequences of purposive action': ignorance, inadequate knowledge and incomplete analysis; errors in projecting a problem to the future, selecting or executing action; and capture, in terms of immediacy to interest and values which may require or prohibit specific conduct.[5] Taking a broader approach, Fuller identifies eight distinct routes to disaster: failure to achieve rules, to publicise or make them available, abuses of retroactivity, failure to make rules understandable, contradictions, rules that require conduct beyond the powers of the affected party; frequent changes; and lack of congruence between rules and their administration.[6] Grabosky focuses on lack of theoretical understanding and bad science expressed as overgeneralisations, failure to understand causal processes upon which interventions are planned; bad planning and failure to learn, implementation failures especially due to inadequacy of resources, lack of coordination or oversight failure and bad politics.[7] Galligan highlights the lack of congruence between law and social norms.[8] Rubin identified conceptual failures and the lack of method of

---

[4] E. Rubin, 'Review: The Conceptual Explanation for Legislative Failure' (2005) 30:3 Law & Social Inquiry 583–606; E.L. Rubin, 'Legislative Methodology: Some Lessons from the Truth-in-Lending Act' (1991) 80 Geo. L.J. 233.

[5] R.K. Merton, 'The Unanticipated Consequences of Purposive Social Action' (1936) 1:6 American Sociological Review 894–904.

[6] L. Fuller, *The Morality of Law* (revised edn, Yale University Press 1964) at 39.

[7] Grabosky (n 3) at 356–61.

[8] Galligan (n 1) at 2.

statutory design.⁹ Political and administrative science adds the lack of legitimacy and adaptability of organisational capability,¹⁰ including the organisational environment within which failure occurs.¹¹ With regard to command and control regulation, five types of failure are identified: instrument failure when the instruments used are inappropriate and unsophisticated; information and knowledge failure, when regulators have insufficient knowledge to identify the causes of problems, design and identify appropriate solutions; implementation and motivation failure when those regulated are insufficiently inclined to comply, and capture when regulators fail to act in the public interest.¹²

This overview makes a number of points clear: firstly, that the analysis of failure needs to take into account multiple factors to avoid being simplistic or superficial; secondly that it can be as broad and diverse as the viewpoints examined or integrated in it with a potential to extend even social or cultural aspects. Thirdly, that the analysis of failure can have a micro or macro focus, looking at the legal system in general, groups or areas of law or specific Acts; fourth, that the patterns of failure are by definition an empirical question; and last but not least, that failure takes a unique shape and form in respect to each Act or regulation examined. Scholarship suggests however that some extent of generalisation is possible for the sake of analysis and further learning. From this perspective, can failure be systematised in a way to facilitate lawmakers to analyse it? In other words, is a typology of failure possible?

1.2. A typology of legislative failure

Obviously, there is no comprehensive catalogue of the intellectual curiosities that can be observed in legislation. The list will expand with every new law examined. However, despite the individual intricacies, scholarship highlights three main groups of factors associated with legislative failure: those linked to the conceptual design of the legislative solution (underlying assumptions, rationale, social norms, lack of method), its communication (accessibility, understandability, overlaps and contradictions, instability) and its delivery and implementation (poor administration, lack of resources, institutional environment, legitimacy, new facts). This set of factors leads to three 'types'

---

⁹ Rubin, 'Review: The Conceptual Explanation for Legislative Failure' (2005) 30:3 Law & Social Inquiry 583–606.

¹⁰ M. Lodge, 'The Wrong Type of Regulation? Regulatory Failure and the Railways' (2002) 22.3 Britain and Germany Journal of Public Policy 271–97.

¹¹ M. Lodge and K. Wegrich, *Managing Regulation. Regulatory Analysis, Politics and Policy* (Palgrave McMillan 2012) 29–46; Lodge, ibid at 293–4.

¹² J. Black, 'Critical Reflection on Regulation' (2002) 27:3 Australian Journal of Legal Philosophy 1–39.

of legislative failure which capture the perspective of the lawmaker and the parameters that fall within their control: failure in legislative design, in drafting and communication and in implementation.

This classification does not claim to be universal or generally applicable. Its humble aim is none other than the intention to organise the main factors behind legislative failure in order to study, understand, and analyse it in a way to direct the required effort at the right level. But let's take a closer look at the three types of failure.

1.2.1. Failure in legislative design

Failures in legislative design capture 'conceptual' errors in the regulatory strategy, the rationale and the mechanics of the law. This is quite broad in scope and scans errors in the analysis of the problem, objective setting, the techniques and intervention mechanisms chosen to address it, the choice of compliance and enforcement strategies, hence all conceptual aspects of the law. It highlights errors in the thinking behind the law, the choices of the law, and the expectations about what the law can achieve.

An example of conceptual failure is the US Clean Air Act 1970. The Act was designed to address a number of problems, one of which was the control of noxious emissions from point pollution sources. The objectives being justified and achievable, the basic choices available to lawmakers were between technology-based and risk-based standards. The first choice addressed pollution at the source and required the source owner to employ the best available pollution control technology. These standards were stringent but demanded only the use of economically feasible technology. On the other hand, risk-based standards demanded the elimination of pollution shown to cause harm by the source owner and a complete resolution of the problem regardless of technological feasibility. Lawmakers opted for risk-based standards, a choice that proved to be definitive mistake as it proved impossible to prove and enforce.[13] The Act's failure was in its conceptual design because it ignored the more effective approach of requiring use of the best available technology.[14] This interesting example shows the value of this type of analysis. By identifying the nature, source and causes of failure the required effort can be directed at the right level.

Obvious conceptual errors can include 'law-which-is-not-law', laws expressing impossible aspirations,[15] rules requiring conduct beyond the powers

---

[13] Rubin, 'Review' (n 4) 583–606.
[14] Ibid; Rubin, 'Legislative Methodology' (n 4) 233.
[15] N.J. Jamieson, 'The Pathology of Legislation' (1984) 2 Statute Law Review 87–101.

of the affected party, absurd, perverse or insincere rules that include deceptive mechanisms to induce compliance.[16] In their majority, however, they include less blatant or subtle errors in choosing rules or techniques that do not have the potential to work, enforcement mechanisms that are too complex, too costly or do not reflect existing resources or capacity, rules that are difficult (or impossible) for people to comply with. The choice of standards that are impossible to enforce are a conceptual problem. So is the complex design of an enforcement mechanism.

'Promissory', declaratory, aspirational or rhetorical laws that reflect political commitments, confirm rather than state the law, embody hope or emphasise preference over certain behaviours[17] require a careful assessment. Although if carelessly used they might be problematic from the perspective of design, symbolic and educational functions are important for legislation on a number of occasions, and might be necessary and expedient in a specific context. So rather than a list of pathogenies, examining failure is highly contextual and needs to take into account all specific circumstances. In particular, it would need to examine questions associated with the objectives, the choice of mechanism, solution or techniques, the design of the compliance and enforcement mechanisms.

1.2.2. Failure in drafting and communication

Failure in drafting focuses on errors in the communication of the law, in the broad sense. It addresses all aspects of communication of the messages of the law including accessibility, superstructure, language, structure, ambiguity but also the formulation of the provisions themselves. The effort is to examine if communication went wrong, and if yes, then to determine which aspect of it has been problematic and why. If the legislative message was ignored or misinterpreted, was it because of lack of clarity or ambiguity? Was it because contradictory rules are in place? Was it because rules changed too often?

Ambiguous and overlapping or poorly coordinated provisions are a common example of failure in the broader aspects of legislative communication that relate to the interaction of rules with other elements of the legal order. For example, in Kenya, a number of planning provisions introduce different rules: the Physical Planning Act 1996 authorises the director for physical planning to develop local physical development plans, the Constitution of 2010 allocates the function of land planning to the national government and

---

[16] Michael D. Gilbert, 'Insincere Rules' (2015) 101 Virginia Law Review 2185–223.

[17] D. Feldman, 'Legislation Which Bears No Law' (2016) 37:3 Statute Law Review 212–24 at 214.

coordination of planning to the counties, while the Urban Areas and Cities Act of 2011 requires municipalities to have an integrated development plan.[18] The contradictions between these provisions, the parallel procedures introduced, the unclear hierarchisation and relation between the different types of plans highlight that the problem, or part of it, lies in the conflicting legislative messages sent out through legislation. Other problems that would fall under this type of failure would include problems in drafting, ambiguity, complexity, incompleteness of provisions, inconsistencies between Acts or within one Act, badly interconnected definitions, inconsistent scope of application, unclear provisions affecting the scope of application, etc.

Failure in communication and drafting captures a number of factors associated with the structure and superstructure, accessibility, clarity, unambiguity, lack of contradiction both in the message and the language of the law.

1.2.3. Failure in implementation

Legislative failure often becomes visible during the implementation of legislation. Errors in implementation, however, capture cases where the promises of the law are not implemented, not because of faulty design but because resources have not been mobilised, actors have not taken the necessary action, target audiences were not motivated to comply or reality uncovered unexpected aspects of the problem. In short, implementation errors include failures in the administration and application of the law, unwanted effects, changes in facts that render the solutions inappropriate but it does not capture the design of the implementation and enforcement mechanism that would qualify as a conceptual issue.

Reality offers innumerable examples where implementers fail to respond to the promises made in legislation. From lack of synchronicity of legislative requirements, to the non-enactment of secondary regulation, practical barriers in implementation, inadequate infrastructure or resources, the type of implementation problems that come up are very diverse. For example, a valid 'right of use and enjoyment' of land in Mozambique presupposes, according to Urban regulations, the issuance of an urban plan. However, urban plans have not materialised and as a consequence a large number of low-income households are trapped into informal arrangements. The sequencing that lawmakers planned was not respected resulting in an implementation problem.

The assessment of implementation problems requires caution. In the UK, 'shocking failure' in housing legislation was reported in the media, because

---

[18] M. Mousmouti and G. Crispi, 'Good Legislation as a Means of Ensuring Voice, Accountability, and the Delivery of Results in Urban Development' (2014) 6 World Bank Legal Review 257.

the UK government's rogue landlord database, a key tool for local councils to target unfit landlords, remained unpopulated six months after the system started.[19] Was that a failure in implementation because the necessary action had been delayed or not taken? Was more time necessary because of the administrative procedures to be followed? Was it simply an exaggeration by the media as the invisible implementation processes were progressing (but were not yet finalised) far from the public eye? A number of questions would have to be answered before identifying whether this or many other examples would actually qualify as problems in the implementation of the law.

Implementation errors in principle include cases where governments do not keep the promises enshrined in laws, do not enact regulations, do not follow required processes, inadequate infrastructure and services are made available, etc. This is only a scarce list of 'implementation gaps'. These are not only problems of immature and poorly resourced jurisdictions but of administrations worldwide.

Implementation intersects with the design and the communication of the law, so it is easy to term anything as an implementation problem. Yet this is not always true. For example, implementation failures of European law at the level of member states are often associated with imperfect transposition or enforcement action from the part of the member states. From another perspective, however, this imperfect action is largely due to the ambiguity, complexity and incompleteness of the EU provisions themselves, inconsistencies between Acts or within one Act, badly interconnected definitions, inconsistent scope of application, unclear provisions[20] that inevitably lead to implementation problems, while the root cause lies elsewhere.

1.2.4. Combinations

Failure rarely comes in pure form. Complex laws addressing complex issues might suffer from interrelated failures. Poor design (limited mechanisms), poor drafting in the form of numerous, complex and ambiguous rules and poor implementation (part of the law remains unenforced) often go hand in hand to shape a complex failure pattern.

Identifying the root causes of failure, especially when this is due to several factors is essential for determining the right solution. The UK Mental Capacity Act 2005 was enacted with the ambition to establish a ground-breaking framework to empower and protect vulnerable people incapable of making deci-

---

[19] https://www.theguardian.com/business/2018/oct/23/governments-rogue-landlord-list-empty-after-six-months.

[20] M. Whelanová, 'Quo Vadis, Europa? Loopholes in the EU Law and Difficulties in the Implementation Process' (2016) 2 European Journal of Law Reform 179–208.

sions. A scrutiny of the Act in 2014 concluded that the law had failed in terms of understanding and implementation. Failure was localised on misperceptions on the application of core principles, lack of commitment, poor compliance and a gap between theory and practice. Gaps in both the design of the law and its application, including social and demographic change resulted in rights on 'paper' that were not followed through in practice.[21] In other words, specific errors in design, drafting and implementation were identified.

An analysis of failure is a complex and challenging task. An analysis of the infamous Dangerous Dogs Act[22] highlights the difficulty and the complexities of locating the sources of failure. Is it limits of knowledge about the 'nature' and the risk factors of the problem addressed? Difficulties inherent in designing a 'targeted' regime? Difficulties in addressing ambiguities in definitions? Challenges in anticipating compliance? Or a combination of factors? There is a fine line between assessing regulatory craft and judging underlying policies, especially under the influence of unpopularity, while assessors are no less liable to capture or be immune to pressures, than those they appraise.[23] The lesson is that this intricate and demanding exercise requires skills, knowledge, a deep understanding of the lawmaking process, but also a sense of perspective that allows them to grasp the broader picture. Who is better placed for such an exercise? And when should this take place?

1.3. The timing and actors of a diagnosis of failure

This last comment brings up the fact that the diagnosis of failure often comes too early, too late or from sources like the media, opposition politicians or interest groups. Are these reliable sources? Are these assessments a sufficient basis on which to act? Who is in the position to determine whether a law has been a failure or not? When? And how?

If the diagnosis of failure is necessary to place the problem – and the required corrective action – at the right level, the timing and the actors to be involved in this process are critical. Exaggerated accounts of failure may come with hidden agendas to promote specific interests. Popular discontent, no matter how genuine, might be the result of different triggers with a loose connection to the law. Appearances are often deceptive. From the perspective of lawmaking, none of the above provide a safe foundation for action. Legislation

---

[21] E. Cave, 'Determining Capacity to Make Medical Treatment Decisions: Problems Implementing the Mental Capacity Act 2005' (2015) 36:1 Statute Law Review 86–106.

[22] C. Hood, R. Baldwin and H. Rothstein, 'Assessing the Dangerous Dogs Act: When does a regulatory law fail?' (2000) Public Law 282–305.

[23] D. McBarnet and C. Whelan, 'The Elusive Spirit of the Law: Formalist and the Struggle for Legal Control' (1991) 54 MLR 848.

requires time to mature, produce results and effects and show its true colours. Apart from circumstances where immediate action is required, as in the case of disasters or blatant errors, the optimal timing for an appraisal of failure comes after legislation has been evaluated and failure has been positively diagnosed.

The evaluation of legislation, or post legislative scrutiny, is the point in time when a broader appraisal of legislation is attempted in order to identify the degree of attainment of objectives, the results actually produced, intended and unintended effects but also changed underlying conditions. Intermediate 'check points' for failure are the points when legislation is subjected to review but a detailed analysis should come only after a law has been evaluated and failure has been positively diagnosed. It is only then that one needs to understand what went wrong and whether this was due to the choice of wrong mechanism, poor drafting or implementation. Identifying the error is the first step to an effective solution.

As to the main actors of this appraisal, this is a tricky question. An assessment of failure needs to be impartial and go into sufficient depth to capture different aspects of the design and the operation of the law. Any actor with a link to the design or implementation of the law would be excluded as inherently biased. The actors in charge of evaluation are a defensible option. However, an independent viewpoint would reinforce the objectivity of the assessment of the causes of failure. External actors, academics, independent scientific institutes, or experts could meaningfully lead this diagnostic.

2. RESPONDING TO FAILURE

How do legal systems respond to legislation that has been diagnosed as failed, absurd, counter-productive, ineffective? What 'reactive' or response mechanisms are in place? And further, are these responses sufficient?

2.1. Amendments: a panacea or a curse?

If failure is a 'crack' in legislation, amendments are the most common way to 'repair' them. Amendments are the most common activity of drafters and parliamentarians and an important part of contemporary lawmaking. In fact, given the point that lawmaking rarely takes place in a vacuum, a significant part of new legislation is in fact amending legislation.[24]

Amendments are the most immediate 'self-correcting mechanism' of legal systems to perceived or diagnosed legislative failure. Amendments might

---

[24] Helen Xanthaki, *Drafting Legislation. Art and Technology of Rules for Regulation* (Hart Publishing 2014) at 223.

'correct' obvious or blatant errors in legislation, ranging from typos, numbering, to errors in the working of a rule or intervene in the content, scope or rationale of legislation, changing key concepts, introducing new techniques or mechanisms, altering the scope of application. Amendments can be explicit, implied, direct or indirect[25] and the source of uncertainty[26] if perceived to cause more harm than good. Amendments often balance between being a blessing, solving the problem they are meant to fix, or a curse that leads to more trouble and more amendments.

As a response mechanism to failure, amendments raise a number of challenges. Firstly, they are often drafted without proper consideration of their anticipated impacts. What might be labelled as a 'minor' amendment may in fact affect the entire design and rationale of an Act not to mention other ones. If an Act has been designed to work as a system, changing one part of it might affect the whole or require a series of adjustments. This is particularly true with amendments that intervene in the logic, scope and content of legislation. Changing substantive provisions or introducing new 'mechanisms' without having anticipated how these will affect the law as a whole raises a number of issues and often leads to a number of other amendments to correct the errors caused.

Secondly, amendments, especially frequent ones, are a source of legislative instability. The proportion of amendments in the total legislative output of parliaments and the rate of amendments are common indicators of legislative instability. For example, in Poland, in the period from 1997–2004 amendment laws amounted to 58–59% of the annual output. Out of 184 statutory laws adopted and amended between 2001 and 2004, 50% were amended once, 20% twice and 30% three or more times. Some laws were amended twenty-three, eighteen and thirteen times over a period of only three years.[27] Assuming that it is impossible for the underlying circumstances to have changed so radically so quickly, a number of questions are raised with regard to the need for so many and so frequent amendments and the ways in which target audiences are expected to keep track of them.

Another important concern relates to implicit amendments or repeals. While in principle, Amending Acts should explicitly state the provisions amended, other provisions are often affected, or insufficient care is taken in performing the tedious task of identifying all provisions affected. This creates not only

---

[25] Ibid at 223–39.

[26] Anthony Lynch, Peter Ziegler, 'The Amendment of Legislation' (1991) 12:1 Statute Law Review 48–63 at 48, 50.

[27] Klaus H. Goetz and Radoslaw Zubek, 'Law-making in Poland: Rules and Patterns of Legislation', 2005, accessible at: http://citeseerx.ist.psu.edu/viewdoc/download?doi =10.1.1.579.2915&rep=rep1&type=pdf 8-10 (last accessed 07/12/2018).

uncertainty and confusion but also insecurity with regard to the law in force (what is applicable and what is not). Last but not least, the understandability and accessibility of amendments and the law as amended is another concern with significant impact on legal certainty that has been analysed in other parts of this study.

Amendments are too large and complex a topic to be exhausted here. Seen as most common mechanism for legal systems to react to and correct failure, they come with a number of weaknesses raising serious and important concerns. Control devices to check the necessity of amendments and their quality appear to be required.

2.2. Simplification

Simplification is another response mechanism that targets, in particular, failures of compliance, 'regulatory costs'[28] and implementation. The potential of simplification lies in reducing complexity by reviewing and simplifying information collection requirements,[29] reducing the burden of compliance by removing 'symbols' of bureaucracy[30] and making legislation more user-friendly. Simplification is a mechanism that can be used to intervene in the medium term. However, it is resource intensive and relatively narrow in scope as it can address only very specific types of failure.

Simplification exercises have proven effective in correcting non productive costs and responding to complaints of businesses about administrative burdens[31] although their efficiency is not unequivocal.[32] Although, benefits were sometimes impressive, narrow simplification and administrative cost reductions proved to be counterproductive.[33] In several cases, the achievement of simplification targets did not satisfy businesses and citizens, because the changes introduced had limited impact, results were not visible or the percep-

---

[28] OECD, 'Cutting Red Tape: National Strategies for Administrative Simplification' (OECD 2006) 9; Commission, 'Measuring administrative costs and reducing administrative burdens in the European Union' (Working Document) COM(2006) 691 final.

[29] OECD, 'Why Is Administrative Simplification So Complicated? Looking Beyond 2010' (OECD 2010) at 15ff.

[30] Jacopo Torriti, 'The Standard Cost Model: When "Better Regulation" Fights against Red Tape' in Stephen Weatherill (ed), *Better Regulation* (Hart Publishing 2007) 106.

[31] Ibid at 89–90.

[32] P. Coletti, 'Standard Cost Model' in C. Dunlop and C. Radaelli (eds), *Handbook of Regulatory Impact Assessment* (Edward Elgar 2016) 93–107 at 104.

[33] Jonathan Wiener, 'Better Regulation in Europe. Current Legal Problems' [2006] Duke Law School Legal Studies Paper No. 130, 498.

tion of the subjects of regulation on burdensome obligations was not taken into account.[34]

2.3. Codification

Codification (and initiatives like consolidation, recasting, rewrite, etc.) is a response mechanism to failures associated with the stock of legislation, its accessibility and the removal of contradictions and inconsistencies. Terminology is often jurisdiction-specific but the essence of the tasks is to a great extent similar. Consolidation, codification and recasting indicate varying 'degrees' of codification ranging from the compilation of legislation with no formal legal effect (consolidation), the replacement of obsolete provisions without substantive changes (codification) and codification with changes in content (recast). In the UK, statutory mechanisms include consolidation, repeal, rewrite, restatement, reprint and revision.[35] In Western civil law jurisdiction, large-scale codification programmes or institutions are common.

Codification is a diverse and flexible instrument in form and substance, whose functions may range from formal simplification, to systematisation or drastic reform of the law.[36] Its main contribution is on the clarity, accessibility, coherence and foreseeability of the law and the reduction of its volume.[37] Consolidation is a more flexible tool promoting accessibility that responds, in particular, to the frequency of amendments.

In its traditional civil law meaning, codification brings together new and existing rules under a common structure and coherent principles.[38] Explicit programmes or institutions that systematically deal with codification of legislation are common.[39] Although codification is traditionally linked to civil law

---

[34] OECD, 'Administrative Simplification' (n 28) 15ff.

[35] J. Teasdale, 'Statute Law Revision: Repeal, Consolidation or Something More?' (2009) 11 European Journal of Law Reform 157, 195; Helen Xanthaki, *Drafting Legislation. Art and Technology of Rules for Regulation* (Hart Publishing 2014) at 226–89.

[36] Denis Tallon, 'Codification and Consolidation of the Law at the present time' (1979) 14:1 Israel Law Review 3.

[37] Eva Steiner, 'Codification in England: The need to move from an Ideological to a Functional Approach – A Bridge too Far?' (2004) 25 Statute Law Review 209; Wim Voermans, Chris Moll, Nico Florijn and Peter van Lochem, 'Codification and Consolidation in the European Union: A Means to Untie Red Tape' (2008) 29:2 Statute Law Review 65ff; Edward Donelan, 'European Approaches to Improving Access to and Managing the Stock of Legislation' (2009) 30:3 Statute Law Review 149.

[38] P. Popelier, 'Codification in a Civil Law Jurisdiction: A Northern European Perspective' (2017) 19:4 Journal of Law Reform 253–63.

[39] OECD, Better Regulation in Europe: France (OECD Publishing 2010) 129; OECD, Better Regulation in Europe: Germany (OECD Publishing 2010) 114; OECD

traditions, it is not unknown to common law ones.[40] The Law Commission in England and Wales has the mandate to review all the law of its jurisdiction, including codification, the elimination of anomalies, repeals, simplification and modernisation.[41] Although several ambitious codification efforts failed mainly because of its inflexible nature that required reform before codification and made the process burdensome, long, impractical and not particularly appealing to politicians,[42] there are several examples of functional and formal codifications like the Tax Law Rewrite project, and currently the sentencing law and the law of criminal evidence.[43]

Codification as a response mechanism has obvious benefits for clarity and accessibility of legislation. Yet, its solution is inevitably imperfect: complete codification is not possible, it is a resource intensive, complex and extremely time consuming mechanism that cannot eliminate uncertainty generated from consecutive revisions of the law, and cannot per se guarantee the intelligibility of the final text. Further, in many cases, codification places more emphasis on the procedure or the ways of organising legislation, hence addressing errors of form and structure, rather than substance.

2.4. Law reform – looking at the whole picture

The modern lawmaker oversees a two-fold task: lawmaking and law 'maintenance'. The latter refers to the processes of review, revision and update of rules and the evaluation of their quality and effectiveness.[44] The need to review existing law to ensure it remains fit for purpose and relevant to the needs of government and society is common in all jurisdictions and exacerbated by the number of laws and their complexity. Broadly defined, law reform indicates

---

Better Regulation in Europe: Spain (OECD Publishing 2010) 104; OECD, Better Regulation in Europe: Portugal (OECD Publishing 2010) 80; OECD, Better Regulation in Europe: Belgium (OECD Publishing 2010) 138.

[40] E. Steiner, 'Codification in England: The need to move from an Ideological to a Functional Approach – A Bridge too Far?' (2004) 25 Statute Law Review 209.

[41] Law Commissions Act 1965, s 3.

[42] J. Teasdale, 'Codification: A Civil Law Solution to a Common Law Conundrum?' (2017) 19:4 European Journal of Law Reform 247–52 at 250.

[43] H. O'Sullivan and David Ormerod, 'Time for a Code: Reform of Sentencing Law in England and Wales' (2017) 19:4 European Journal of Law Reform 285–305; Ian Dennis, 'Codifying the Law of Criminal Evidence' (2014) 35:2 Statute Law Review 107–19.

[44] M. De Benedetto, 'Maintenance of Rules' in U. Karpen and H. Xanthaki (eds), *Legislation in Europe. A Comprehensive Guide for Scholars and Practitioners* (Hart Publishing 2017) 215–27.

both the process of introducing legislative change to deal with problems in existing law[45] as well as the process through which reform is carried out.[46]

Law reform can respond to a broad range of situations from laws that are outdated, to areas of law requiring revamping or novel approaches or more specific need for change. Its main features, which are particularly relevant to the response to failure, are its systemic and systematic nature. It moves beyond opportunistic short term changes to grasp the greater picture and correct what needs to be corrected. Whether it is a group of laws (e.g. commercial laws) or an area of law (e.g. family law) or a specific Act that has been severely amended, the task at hand is to revisit the rationale, the intention and the function of the law.

The means employed to reform the law vary especially between common and civil law jurisdictions. In the UK, common modes of law reform include general legislative action, legislative action following a report of the Law Commission, judicial action in the courts and academic contribution.[47] In civil law systems, where the concept of law reform per se is less common, review mechanisms are often conflated with codification, consolidation, repeal, law revision and restatement.[48] Despite the differences in terminology, in their majority the mechanisms are a combination of techniques aimed to reorder the whole or parts of the statute book in a way to make it more effective and accessible.[49]

Law reform projects are flexible in their focus. They can address either specific areas of law or specific challenges that have been identified. For example, in East African states, national law reform programmes in commercial legislation aimed to adjust laws that originated from legal transplants or transnational commercial law to domestic needs and socioeconomic circumstances.[50] Law reform can also aim to make law more accessible through the use of plain language and the transfer of common law to statutes[51] or undertake

---

[45] J. Teasdale, 'Prologue: The IALS Law Reform Project' (2016) 18:3 European Journal of Law Reform 253–63.

[46] G. Palmer, 'The Law Reform Enterprise: Evaluating the Past and Charting the Future' (2015) 131 Law Quarterly Review 402.

[47] P. Sales, 'Law Reform Challenges: The Judicial Perspective' (2018) 39:3 Statute Law Review 229–43.

[48] E. Albanesi, 'The Mechanisms Used to Review Existing Legislation in the Civil Law System. Case Study – Italy' (2016) 18:3 European Journal of Law Reform 275–95.

[49] J. Teasdale, 'Prologue: The IALS Law Reform Project' (2016) 18:3 European Journal of Law Reform 253–63.

[50] A. Mugasha, 'The Reform and Harmonization of Commercial Laws in the East African Community' (2017) 19:4 European Journal of Law Reform 306–36.

[51] D. Ahern, 'Codification of Company Law: Taking Stock of the Companies Act 2006' (2014) 35:1 Statute Law Review 230–43.

a comprehensive review of legislation in relation to important milestones. For example, in Ireland, independence triggered an examination of all primary legislation on the statute book prior to it (Statute Law Revision (Pre-1922) Act 2005).[52] Law reform can also assess the performance of legislation in specific areas, eliminate unnecessary provisions and simplify the operation of the law removing unnecessary burdens.

Law reform in its distinct forms involves a systematic and systemic reflection on the success or failure (or particular aspects of failure) of legislation, the reasons behind it and the way forward. It is an important strategic mechanism to identify, respond and correct failure.

2.5. Effectiveness of the responses

The reactive mechanisms presented above can intervene in the short (amendments), medium (simplification, fitness checks) or long term (codification and law reform). How well can these ad hoc mechanisms respond to failure? How effective are they in correcting failure and improving learning?

Much depends on how these tools are used. Hasty and ill-thought-out amendments might create more problems than the ones they solve and even 'ruin' the design of a well-prepared Act. Amendments put forward to pacify an angry public or reach compromises with political opponents hide political motivations and are not always contributing to effective legislation. On the other hand, simplification exercises can prove successful or disappointing. Stretched out reform or codification projects may be outdated the moment they are completed. In other words, the effectiveness of ad hoc mechanisms relies to an important extent on how carefully and strategically legal systems use them, how much emphasis is placed in ensuring the health and sanity of the legal order and how much effort is invested in their quality. Correcting failure is one thing. But is there a way to anticipate, prevent or even avoid future failure?

3. ANTICIPATING AND AVOIDING FUTURE FAILURE

Even if failure is part of the human condition, and remedies can partly or entirely address it, is there a remedy to anticipate future failure? How can the 'immune system' of the legal order be strengthened in a way to be resistant to failure? How can lawmakers avoid being ineffective, when designing the

---

[52] K. Mooney, 'The Statute Law Revision Project and Statute Law Revision in Ireland 2003 to 2015' (2017) 38:1 Statute Law Review 79–97.

laws by which they govern themselves? Responding to failure is one thing, preventing it is a completely different matter.

A revolutionary recipe for fail-safe lawmaking would be delightful. Unfortunately, there is nothing even remotely resembling it. Instead, a systematic and strategic approach to the diagnosis and analysis of failure, an effort to strengthen and improve the 'immune' system and the response mechanisms of the legal order, using failure as a learning mechanism and investing in proactive lawmaking appear to be feasible responses to the need to sharpen lawmakers' reflexes and equip them against future failures.

3.1. Strategic approach to the diagnosis and analysis of legislative failure

Failure for whatever reason is not a comfortable topic. Legal systems have a number of mechanisms to respond, partly or more comprehensively, to failure yet often it looks better and more convenient to direct resources and effort to design new initiatives rather than engage in esoteric and introvertive analysis of what went wrong. This important function is not always consistently pursued and the actual moment when or the method according to which failure is diagnosed and analysed are not always evident.

However, the only way to prevent failure is firstly, by addressing it in a systematic way, and secondly, by adopting a strategic approach. Short sighted, knee jerk reactions are no sustainable solution. Grabosky notes the need for scepticism and analysis.[53] Scepticism raises hard questions while analysis provides answers and makes sense of what went wrong. This process leads to accumulated wisdom about the ways in which interventions can backfire and is the only way to improve the performance of the law but also improve the lawmaking method.

A systematic approach to failure requires, first of all, a method. The typology of legislative failure proposed above provides a framework for analysis from the perspective of the lawmaker. By separating the conceptual, communication and implementation aspects of legislation, it allows one to place the sources of errors, identify the type of corrective action required and direct it at the right level.

For the diagnosis of failure, the 'effectiveness test' proposed in the previous chapter, in its ad hoc dimension, can provide useful insights. The 'effectiveness test' is a logical exercise that scrutinises (proactively or reactively) the

---

[53] S. Sieber, *Fatal Remedies: The Ironies of Social Intervention* (Plenum Publishing 1981).

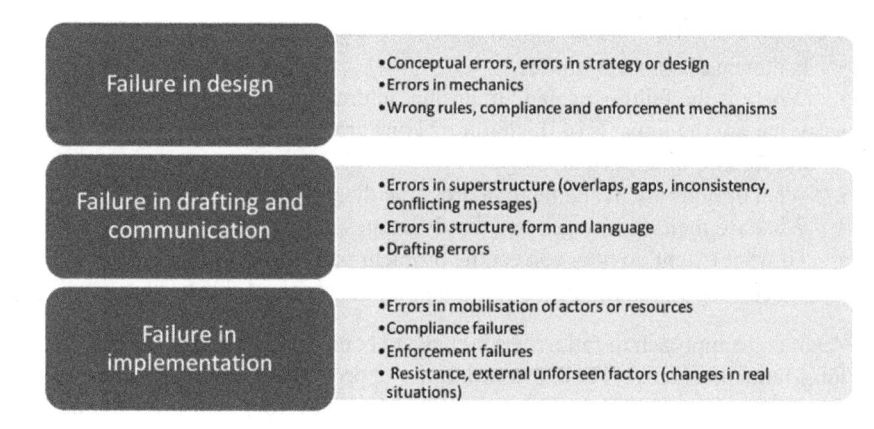

Failure in design	• Conceptual errors, errors in strategy or design • Errors in mechanics • Wrong rules, compliance and enforcement mechanisms
Failure in drafting and communication	• Errors in superstructure (overlaps, gaps, inconsistency, conflicting messages) • Errors in structure, form and language • Drafting errors
Failure in implementation	• Errors in mobilisation of actors or resources • Compliance failures • Enforcement failures • Resistance, external unforseen factors (changes in real situations)

Figure 7.1   A matrix for the analysis of legislative failure

purpose, content, context and results of legislation and can provide valuable insight on the sources of conceptual, communication or operational problems.

A tentative questionnaire for the diagnosis of legislative failure could include:

Design

- Were the initial goals of the Act well conceived? Were the objectives possible?
- Was the choice of mechanism appropriate?
- Was the overall design or solution appropriate to the problem?
- Did compliance unfold as expected?
- Was the design of the enforcement mechanism appropriate?

Communication

- Is the law accessible?
- Is it clear?
- Are contradictory rules in place?
- Are provisions unclear or ambiguous?

Implementation

- Has the law been implemented as planned?
- Have resources been mobilised?
- Have actors taken the required action?

Overarching questions on responses to failure

- Is there a diagnosed failure?
- Where is the failure located? In design, in drafting, in implementation?
- What are the impacts of this failure? How are these evaluated (significant, indifferent, unimportant, etc.)?
- What options are available to address the diagnosed failure?
- What are their advantages and disadvantages, costs and benefits?
- To what extent do they correct the problem partly or entirely?
- What are the mechanisms for introducing the required changes?

A strategic approach to failure would have to consider both short, medium and long term mechanisms and determine the appropriate level of intervention. Amendments are useful for correcting some kind of errors, while others might require a longer term approach. Selecting the right mechanism is an important aspect of 'mature' response to failure. Further, a response to failure requires a clear vision on what the limits of the law are. Legislating in respect to a problem amounts to setting a legal framework for action[54] rather than acting. Failure prompts consideration of the limits of intended action and law as a specific instrument of change. Norms may often be the reason behind oddities or anomalies in human behaviour, yet changes in norms might or might not be the best way to improve social well-being.[55] Acknowledging the limits of the law and drawing a clear line, and expectations, between what the law can and cannot do is important to prevent future failure.

Another aspect has to do with timing. The response mechanism should be immune to pressure from media, the public or politicians. React in haste will allow to repent at leisure. React too late and any sense of responsiveness might be lost. *Every legal system needs to determine the points in time, the method and the actors that will engage in a systematic diagnosis and analysis of failure.*

3.2. Strengthen the 'immune' system of the legal order

The response mechanisms examined above are the 'immune system' that can be mobilised to address and correct different types of failure. Despite its focus to correct errors or more entrenched pathologies through short, medium or long term interventions it cannot make the legal system immune to pathologies, many of which I attempted to highlight, although briefly. Strengthening

---

[54] G. Thornton, *Legislative Drafting* (2nd edn Butterworths, London 1979) at 112.
[55] C.R. Sunstein, 'Social Norms and Social Roles' (1996) 96 Colum. L. Rev. 903–68.

the response mechanisms and introducing control devices to ensure that they are used appropriately is necessary to prevent future failure or 'chain' failure.

Control devices or quality checks on amendments are an important measure in this direction. Amendments have become a pathogeny of the system themselves. Amendments should follow the exact same steps as lawmaking 'from scratch'. Identifying goals, alternative options, costs and benefits, compatibility with the overall design of the Act and other relevant acts would be in order. Amendments need to be subjected to impact assessments and the effectiveness test. Further, amendments should clearly mark the changes they introduce by listing in detail all provisions amended (even in different Acts) to avoid implicit changes or repeals.

Simplification exercises need to be pursued in a targeted way and with clear aims. Codifications should be timely and flexible, making use of new technologies that allow them to be up to date. Consolidation is a powerful tool to ensure accessibility of the law and its use needs to become more widespread.

However, law reform is the most important strategic 'cleansing mechanism' of legal systems. The concept of law reform needs to be clarified in all legal systems and move away from its limited focus, especially in civil law jurisdictions. A clear approach to law reform, law reform mechanisms that are equipped to perform their functions is critical for the sanity of the statute book and the prevention of future failure.

3.3. Learn from failure

Criticism and pronouncement of failure often come too easily, too lightly, in catastrophic language and listing a bric-a-brac of problems in an undifferentiated way. If failure is a way to learn, understanding it requires looking attentively at the details, separating relevant from irrelevant factors and analysing what went wrong and why. Looking at failure ex post is a source of learning. And even though there are no definite solutions to the prospective enterprise of lawmaking, trial and error, past experience and reflection offer useful lessons both on how to correct pathologies but also on mistakes to be avoided and legislative patterns that do not work.

John Dewey noted that 'we do not learn from experience, we learn from reflecting on experience'.[56] Reflection is a specialised form of thinking that involves 'serious thought', 'persistent and careful consideration of any belief or supposed form of knowledge' and 'a conscious and voluntary effort to

---

[56] J. Dewey, *How We Think. A restatement of the relation of reflective thinking to the educative process* (Revised edn Boston: D.C. Heath 1933).

establish belief upon a firm basis of evidence and rationality'.[57] This approach is fully in line with the rational turn in lawmaking and applies fantastically to lawmaking. Reflective thinking on success or failure or lawmaking practice needs to be strengthened both as a sign of maturity of lawmaking systems but also as a resource for improving future performance. Reflection is key to effective lawmaking.

The lawmakers' reflective cycle would include the emphasis on experience, its analysis, the lessons learnt and their projection to the future. It could be organised in at least five steps: reflecting on experience, evaluation and analysis of failure and projection of the conclusions and learning to the future. The reflective cycle involves reflection on specific Acts and the reactions to it, positive and negative aspects, making sense of what worked and what did not work, concluding on what could have been done differently and deciding on what needs to be done in the future. This is the thinking process of a reflective legislator.

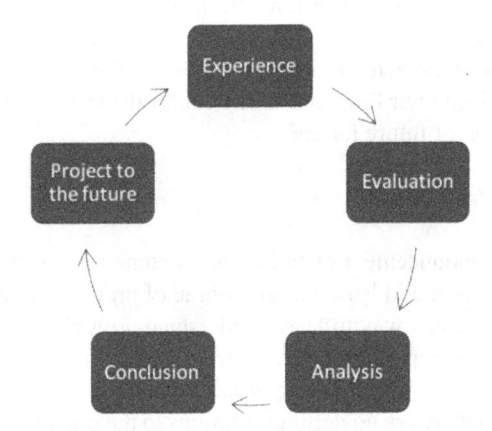

Source: G. Gibbs, *Learning by Doing:* A guide to teaching and learning methods (Further Education Unit, Oxford Polytechnic (1988)).

Figure 7.2 *The lawmakers' reflection cycle (adapted from Gibbs)*

---

[57] Ibid.

3.4. Invest in effective lawmaking

However, the only way to prevent failure, to the extent that this might ever be possible, is by investing effort in the proactive aspects of effective lawmaking. It has already been established that effective law does not materialise magically. Instead, it is the result of complex mechanics in the conceptualisation, design and drafting of legislation. If consistently addressed early on, and if effectiveness is a clear decision making criterion in lawmaking choices, the rationality and the workability of legislation can be improved. In other words, anticipatory diagnosis[58] that involves forward thinking about what could go wrong is the only way to soften the hard blows of unintended consequences. Investing the proactive quality mechanisms of lawmaking in the direction of effective legislation is the only feasible option.

4. CONCLUSION

Failure is partial or entire ineffectiveness of the law. Whether in the form of 'unanticipated consequences', 'miscarriages', 'counterproductiveness' or pure 'fiasco', legislative failure indicates the mismatch between legislative objectives and results. Acknowledging failure and learning from it are necessary steps for the learning legislator. Three types of failure are particularly relevant: failure in legislative design (the mechanism and rationale of the law), failure in drafting (in the expression and communication of the law), failure in implementation (in the application of the law), or, most commonly, combinations of the above pathologies. Failure needs to be identified at a moment in time when the law had sufficient time to mature, not too early, not too late. Scrutiny exercises are the ideal moment and scrutinisers, if equipped with the right tools, the ideal actors. A checklist for the diagnosis of failure would examine where the failure lies, what are the causes behind it and how can it be addressed.

Lawmakers respond to failure by amending the law, simplifying its implementation mechanism, improving accessibility and through broader mechanisms of law reform. The effectiveness of these solutions varies depending on the pathologies targeted but also on the way that these mechanisms are used in practice. Avoiding future failure, however, requires a more proactive approach that includes a careful diagnosis and analysis of previous failure, correcting the weaknesses of response mechanisms, learning from failure using reflective practice as a learning tool and reaffirming the emphasis towards the proactive elements of lawmaking.

---

[58] S. Sieber, *Fatal Remedies: The Ironies of Social Intervention* (Plenum Publishing 1981).

8. On lawmakers, lawmaking and effectiveness

1. SO WHAT ABOUT EFFECTIVENESS?

What lawmakers have to do is simple and very complex at the same time: they have to translate abstract notions into law, achieve coherent and comprehensive legal formulations, choose appropriate implementation mechanisms, set in place sufficient incentives for people to comply and establish a framework simple, clear and sophisticated enough to address complex issues. Can effectiveness help them in this task? And if yes, how?

Effectiveness, as the capacity of legislation to do the job is meant to do (to achieve its results), adds a purposive dimension to legislative decision making. It does not tell lawmakers what to do or how to do it but highlights the systemic nature of their choices. Further, it is something that lawmakers can realistically pursue within their autonomous decision making space. Other values that compete for the job are either too broad, like efficacy that connects the law with broader regulatory (policy) goals, or too narrow, like efficiency, that looks at legislation from the specific perspective of resources versus outcomes. However, all three values are useful. They work well as a triad to capture the multiple functions of legislation as an instrument operating in the legal, social and economic arena. Yet, out of the three, effectiveness is the one tailored closer to the measure of the law and reflects its *mechanics* and capacity to work as a system.

Lawmaking is not science but purposive decision making in a context of uncertainty. In a context where the correctness of concrete outcomes cannot be unambiguously determined, emphasis turns to procedural rationality and maximisation.[1] The primary usefulness of effectiveness is that it raises intriguing questions and triggers the lawmaker to think. Rather than a deterministic method to achieve outcomes it triggers reflection on what is possible. When a law is designed, effectiveness asks 'how to make it conducive to the desired

---

[1] Giandomenico Majone, 'Foundations of Risk Regulation: Science, Decisions-Making, Policy Learning and Institutional Reform' (2010) 1 European Journal of Risk Regulation at 5.

results'? When a law is implemented, on the other hand, effectiveness asks whether, and to what extent, the real attitudes, behaviours, results and outcomes of the law correspond to those initially prescribed and whether the law has achieved the desired results. The willingness or the effort to design and draft an effective law does not mean that the law will actually be effective. Even the rationality and irrationality of choices do not necessarily identify with success and failure.[2] But this is not the issue: what a lawmaker works for is to ensure that the law has the *potential to be effective* and that the factors they can control are in place.

This thinking process is not restricted to the generic working of the law. Effectiveness can be 'deconstructed' into four elements, present in every law: objectives, content, context and results. Each describes a different aspect of legislation: purpose is an internalised benchmark of what legislation aims to achieve; content determines how it will be achieved; context indicates how the law integrates the legal system and interacts with it and results indicate what has been achieved. Through more detailed probing questions on each of these elements and their alignment (for example, what aspects of an issue can the law address? What are its specific and broader objectives? How do they translate into expected results, outcomes and effects? What rules are necessary? Do they reflect the reality on the ground? What are the main audiences of the law? How are they expected to comply? What are the main regulatory messages? How are they organised and structured? How will the law integrate the legal order? What are the specific results, outcomes and impacts to be expected? How will the implementation of the law be monitored?), which I call the '*effectiveness test*', lawmakers are encouraged to *reflect* on specific lawmaking choices from the perspective of effectiveness. What the effectiveness test concretely offers is to highlight the potential of a solution, including its strengths and weaknesses. Even if the solution finally chosen is far from optimal but selected due to other reasons, like normative or political commitment, in response to different goals or deontological positions, the lawmaker is aware of its weaknesses, can do the best they can with them and, most importantly, knows what to expect. Big dramas, fiascos or disasters will not come as crude surprises.

In other words, effectiveness adds to rational lawmaking a layer of pragmatism and a concrete decision making criterion with a painfully straightforward logic: does it work? Does it have the capacity to work? How can it be designed to work? Where rational lawmaking offers no clear criterion for selecting solutions, or offers multiple criteria, effectiveness makes anticipation and retrospection more specific, focused and tailored to the measure of the legislative

---

[2] R.K. Merton, 'The Unanticipated Consequences of Purposive Social Action' (1936) 1:6 American Sociological Review at 896.

text. And while the joint assessment of efficacy, effectiveness and efficiency might be necessary to decide on the best course of action, effectiveness needs to come into play when the selected solution takes concrete shape and form.

Further, the process of 'deconstructing' effectiveness initiates a new line of thinking around lawmaking. The four elements are concepts familiar to lawmakers (purpose, rule types, enforcement provisions, etc.) compared to those used by policy makers (problem, options, cost-benefits, etc.). Looking at their theoretical and practical dimensions, especially the latter, initiates a process of 'reverse engineering' where reflection is oriented towards points of tension. This new way of looking at lawmaking brings theory and practice in a mutually reinforcing relationship (rather than parallel lives) whose potential is worth exploring.

Taking a closer look at the elements of effectiveness in their theoretical and practical dimensions reveals in real life colours their unique features – but also the tensions inherent in all of them, and their limitations. Purpose is the 'compass' and the internalised benchmark of legislation whose function is limited by the challenges involved in confining the objectives and multidimensionality of broad or complex interventions in (meaningful) legislative form. The 'hybrid' nature of purpose between policy and the law makes it an awkward concept, whose potential remains largely unexploited. Content raises different issues. Unquestionably the 'heart' of legislation, it delineates the licit from the illicit, the desirable from the undesirable and sets up a structure of rules, procedures, incentives and mechanisms to steer reality (and behaviour) in the desired directions. A (means-end) rationality is openly challenged by the complexity of situations to be addressed, limited information or analysis, wrong or incomplete assumptions or choices dictated by intuition or unquestioned automatisms (more on this later). The content of legislation exemplifies the tension between 'doing one's homework', designing solutions on paper and responding to external pressures, often all three of them to different degrees. Context on the other hand, determines the broader framework within which legislation operates. The capacity of the law to work *as* a system needs to coexist with its capacity to work *within* a system (the legal system). Tensions emerge in the coherence with other legislative messages; in the accessibility of the messages themselves; and on how identifiable and measurable they are. Last, but not least, results are the outcome of the law. They are the proof of whether and what has changed and in which direction. Results are the connecting point between the law and social reality and exemplify the difficult relationship between law and facts and the conceptual and methodological challenges inherent in trying to anticipate, capture and measure phenomena that often go beyond measurement.

So, even if we accept that effectiveness is, to a certain extent, the result of lawmaking craft, what is it that lawmakers need to do?

Firstly, lawmakers need to focus more on *legislative design*. A law is not a collection of random rules organised in elegant patterns but a micro system with a unique logic and goal and it needs to work. The more elaborate the social changes sought, the more delicate the provisions and machinery required to carry it out. Lawmaking cannot begin with a Bill or a draft but with reflection on what needs to be there. Legislative design is the process of making decisions on the fundamental elements of new legislation and fitting the pieces of the puzzle together. It is not about microscopic detail but about the broader picture: the type of problem to be addressed and its features, the available techniques, the legislative strategy. A clear phase of design is missing from the lawmaking process or is overshadowed by the emphasis placed on producing drafts. Thornton alludes to this need in the second stage of his methodology where he describes the need for a legislative report that presents the drafters' response to policy initiated instructions.[3] However, at the moment, legislative design holds an uncertain and obscure place in the lawmaking process.

Secondly, lawmakers need to make sure that the *mechanics* of the law are in place. This involves a clear *strategy* on what the law is there to do and how it intervenes, a clear purpose, appropriate and consistent content, a smooth relationship with the broader legal environment and measurable results. All elements need to be in place but also need to work well together. If the elements are aligned and consistent, the mechanics are solid. If ambiguous, complex, fragmented, they 'sabotage' rather than reinforce each other. Laws often fail, partly or entirely, because their conceptual design is poorly considered or their mechanics are not well articulated.

Thirdly, legislative decision making requires a clear thinking process. Rubin claimed that 'current methods of legislative design are fossils of a bygone era, which cannot be effectively applied to modern regulatory efforts'.[4] In their place, he proposed the use of techniques of public policy analysis and their well-known steps of identifying a problem, defining and ranking goals, specifying options, collecting data, predicting consequences and choosing the option that best achieves the goal. This 'problem solving' approach brings discipline to the process, allows a systematic approach and a separation of facts from values.

I am not sure that the fluid, contextual and dynamic process of lawmaking would not suffocate within a method. This is why I believe that what legislative decision making requires is a thinking process, and a decision making

---

[3] Helen Xanthaki, *Thornton's Legislative Drafting* (5th edn, Bloomsbury Professional 2013) at 151 ff.
[4] Edward L. Rubin, 'Legislative Methodology: Some Lessons from the Truth-in-Lending Act' (1991) 80 The Georgetown Law Journal 233 at 234.

criterion, that effectiveness can offer. It is thinking about effective lawmaking, before the actual drafting of provisions, that allows perspective. Between a choice of legislative strategy and a final draft lie many critical decisions: which requirements will best achieve the basic goal? What kind of rules? What kind of standards? What kind of incentives or deterrents? How specifically should requirements be framed? Who should be responsible for implementation? What sort of enforcement strategy? Effectiveness provides the thinking process and the effectiveness test suggests the questions. Its four elements are concepts familiar to lawmakers (purpose, rule types, enforcement provisions, etc.) compared to those used in public policy analysis and more common to policy makers (problem, options, cost-benefits, etc.), are inherent in every law, and allow one to look not only at the choices but also at their consistency.

At the level of design and drafting, there are several things that lawmakers can do. They can make the objectives of the legislative intervention explicit, specific and traceable to assist interpreters and implementers to locate and use them and avoid the confusion between instrumentalities and goals; they can formulate substantive provisions paying attention to all their aspects and dimensions, including rules, compliance incentives, expression and enforcement, being aware of the strengths and limitations of their choices, the cognitive biases that might impose them and allowing room, where pertinent, for experimentation; they can identify the points of conflict with other laws and make choices of superstructure that minimise them; they can anticipate the expected results and implementation and provide for a clear mechanism for monitoring, reviewing and evaluating results and learning from them.

Is that all? Attention to design, mechanics and drafting is all that is needed to make legislation effective? Of course not. Such a view, apart from the heyday of legislative optimism, would also be extremely naïve. The law is no miracle worker and laws cannot intervene like the crow flies. Reality is complex, dynamic and multidimensional and there is more to effective lawmaking than the elements of effectiveness or good mechanics. Only a few factors are highlighted below.

A first aspect is external: the limits of the law. Lawmaking is a flourishing industry invested with high hopes. Yet, legislating on a problem is not the same as addressing a problem. This fundamental misconception determines to an important extent the great expectations vested on legislation and the big drama that follows when these are not fulfilled. Discriminatory behaviours are embedded in attitudes, mentalities, even institutional processes. They will not disappear magically because a law was enacted. What a law can do is to define prohibited behaviours, determine procedures and remedies to respond, and, in the long term, hopefully influence perceptions, ideas and behaviours. But expecting discriminatory attitudes to be eliminated (as eloquently suggested in some of the examples presented in the earlier parts of this study) would be an exaggerated expectation. The machinery of legislation must not be given credit for more than it can accomplish.[5] Making these borders clear sets the limits for what legislation can do, and the limits of legislative effectiveness.

A second aspect is commitment to make the law work throughout its life-cycle. Legislation is too important to be abandoned to its fate or addressed by serendipity and this statement does not concern only design and drafting. Phantom, latent or frustrate norms[6] are norms that have been deserted. A genuine commitment to invest effort in producing effective laws pre- and post enactment, to monitor and correct, to listen to the courts and learn from them, in other words to care for legislation across its life cycle, is required for legislation to be effective.

A third aspect is the openness of lawmakers to learn from experience, failure, trial and error and the capacity of the legal system to institutionalise and share this knowledge. Einstein qualified experience as the only source of knowledge, the rest 'is just information'. This applies perfectly to lawmaking as a 'phronetic' discipline where general rules apply only in principle and have the function to guide the subjective empirical and concrete choices that lawmakers have to make.[7] There are three ways to improve lawmaking: through the accumulated knowledge born from experience, through conscious reflection on what is done and why and through a consistent discourse between theory and practice. Effective lawmaking requires all three.

2. LAWMAKING IN PRACTICE: TOP DOWN OR BOTTOM UP?

The previous chapters considered several examples from jurisdictions around the world. Apart from adding colour and flavour to some 'dry' topics, the perspective gained from observing post-enactment performance of legislation vividly highlights another issue: that the starting point of lawmaking can differ significantly.

The observation of legislative practice demonstrates two distinct approaches to lawmaking: *a 'bottom-up' and a 'top-down' approach*. The former starts from a specific issue, problem or question in its real context and with real dimensions; the latter starts with an idea that it aspires to transform into rules. The former addresses an existing problem, for example, inequalities, *through*

---

[5] B.A. Wortley, 'The Mechanics of Law Making Today', lecture delivered in the John Rylands Library on 18 January 1956.
[6] A. Allot, *The Limits of Law* (Butterworths 1980) at 38–9.
[7] Helen Xanthaki, *Drafting Legislation. Art and Technology of Rules for Regulation* (Hart Publishing 2014) at 15.

rules, while the latter attempts to operationalise or transform an abstract ideal, for example, equality, *into* specific rules.

There are several critical differences between the two: firstly, their connection to reality. In the top down approach the link to specific real life situations is not a priori obvious, thus favouring more abstract and 'intuitive' choices or solutions. On the contrary, bottom up is more 'grounded', attached to examples and paradigms and closer to information and data. Secondly, the thinking process is different: a bottom up approach starts from '*how things are*' and considers their potential to move forward with the use of the law. A top down approach thinks mostly about '*how things should be*' and assumes that the transformative power of the law is sufficient to lead there. The first invests in pragmatism, the second in symbolism. The former is in a dialectic discourse with reality, the latter attempts to 'tame' reality. Both might be necessary for different laws or circumstances. Laws need to regulate but they also need to inspire or educate. However, it is important to know where one stands in order to know what questions are to be considered.

The two approaches sketched here require much more research and empirical validation than what this study can offer. Yet one observation that emerges is that laws whose purpose, structure and content are shaped on the basis of a close observation of reality (the regulated phenomena, behaviours, implementation, trial and error) have more chances to achieve the desired results. Legislative solutions which are either in tension with reality or too far distanced from it inevitably run a greater risk of basking in the sun or remaining trapped in a vicious circle of correcting irreconcilable rationales. As far as effectiveness is concerned, the closer the link to reality, hence to situations or behaviours or phenomena that can be studied and understood, even partially, the better the potential to 'engineer' results. The less evident this connection, the more abstract the problems and the choices and the more 'intuitive' the solutions.

3. A TYPOLOGY OF LAWMAKERS?

And what about lawmakers? Laws are made by real people. What does getting in their shoes and walking around tell us about them? About their dilemmas and their reactions to them? We know very little about the anthropogeography of lawmakers in jurisdictions around the world, not to mention their culture, ethos, status, circumstance, resources and training, to be in the position to sketch a representative profile. However, with the perspective and advantage of hindsight, and admittedly, to a great extent intuitively, three distinctive 'personalities' of lawmakers emerge: the intuitive lawmaker, the reflective lawmaker and the one that muddles through.

3.1. The intuitive lawmaker

In the book *Simpler*, Cass Sunstein claims that pleading for empirical foundations seems obvious, as relying on sense rather than nonsense. But the temptation to favour intuition over information is strong.[8] It is easier to decide on a fine of €10,000 'because it seems right' rather than engage in tedious and complicated research around how similar fines have worked before, their deterring power over specific audiences, etc., and questions of what would work best. Intuition is not a bad thing, nor will asking all the right questions safeguard in any way that more effective rules will be produced. In fact, intuition and creativity are important qualities for lawmaking. The 'issue' with intuition is that, as problems become more complex 'the likelihood of guessing the right answers rapidly decreases'.[9]

The intuitive lawmaker is an 'idealist' of sorts. Led by values rather than facts, they are more policy makers or politicians rather than skilled craftspersons sculpting the law to its finest detail. Aspirations are grandiose, disturbing thoughts about whether reality has the capacity to reach the desired state are rapidly dismissed, the choices are the ones that 'seem right' and the rest (implementation, etc.) is 'detail' that has to be figured out by others. Lawmaking is a conceptual exercise. Even when dressed with evidence, this is often manipulated to justify choices already made, rather than show the best way forward. The intuitive lawmaker only thinks about effectiveness retrospectively and is mainly encountered in legal systems where the political 'aura' of legislation is strong.

3.2. The reflective lawmaker

The reflective lawmaker is 'serious' about legislation and diligent in their homework. Lawmaking is specialised problem solving, approached methodically with whatever tools are available. They are led by facts but take into account values and experience. The approach is systematic and based on reflection on what to do and why. They examine and question policy, the law and reality, reflect, test, learn, fail and try again. This is a mature lawmaker, aware of their role, their responsibility to make conscious decisions and the inherent limitations of their task. The reflective legislator gives serious consideration to effectiveness and lingers on the questions rather than hurry to provide an answer. Reflective lawmakers are 'neutral' actors within the legal

---

[8] Cass Sunstein, *Simpler* (Simon & Schuster 2013) at 5.
[9] E.L. Rubin, 'Legislative Methodology: Some Lessons from the Truth-in-Lending Act' (1991) 80 Geo. L.J. 233 at 301.

system, whose function is to balance competing influences, political or other, with legistic and legal concerns. Effectiveness holds a prominent place in their thinking.

3.3. The lawmaker that 'muddles through'

Charles Lindblom described the process of practical decision making as 'mudding through' by using incremental, limited comparisons among readily available choices.[10] I use the term 'muddler' in its literal meaning to depict a lawmaker who manages despite not being prepared, organised or particularly knowledgeable about how to do things. The 'muddler' is a bureaucrat, who drafts what they are asked to draft, without questioning choices and relies on whatever help is available, from comparative knowledge, to external drafts, to copy and paste practices. The target is to produce a draft as quickly as possible. Their draft might lack vision but it will include a wealth of minuscule administrative detail. The muddler is a formalist, that considers evidence, reflection and analysis a luxury and is not very convinced about their usefulness in actual lawmaking. Effectiveness is good as a 'slogan' but stretches no further.

These caricatures are not meant as criticism. Their usefulness is in highlighting, admittedly in an exaggerated way, that beyond the different stances towards lawmaking, there are also distinct levels of sensitivity and awareness towards the intricacies of lawmaking, which determine to an important extent the stance of lawmakers towards distinct type of automatisms present in lawmaking.

4. COGNITIVE BIASES IN LAWMAKING?

The fact that lawmakers operate in a context of bounded rationality[11] is well known. Limitations originate from limited information and analysis, political or other pressures but also lack of time, skills and resources. But are these the only ones? Or are lawmakers affected, in their capacity as decision makers, by more subtle and often imperceptible influences?

Behavioural economists highlighted, against the tide of traditional economics, that heuristics and cognitive biases influence decision making to an important extent. Rules of thumb like anchoring, availability, representativeness, loss aversion or status quo bias often lead towards 'intuitive' rather than

---

[10] Charles E. Lindblom, 'The Science of Muddling Through' (1959) 19:2 Public Administration Review at 79–88.
[11] Luc Wintgens, 'The Rational Legislator Revisited. Bounded Rationality and Legisprudence' in Luc Wintgens and A. Daniel Oliver-Lalana (eds), *The Rationality and Justification of Legislation* (Springer 2013) at 14–15.

reflective decisions.[12] Does this apply to lawmakers as decision makers? Are they also driven by (intuitive) rules of thumb – or the equivalents in their trade – that lead to automatic (rather than reflective) decisions? This exploratory, yet highly intriguing, question, would require extensive research and empirical validation before a fully proven answer could be possible. What this study humbly brings in this discussion is awareness of some automatisms present in lawmaking that dangerously resemble cognitive biases.

4.1. Legislative styles, drafting conventions and regulatory culture

Legal systems affect both perceptions about rules and their form and function.[13] Distinct regulatory cultures and traditions are linked to distinct legislative styles. Common law systems have a more informal, cooperative and voluntary culture[14] and prioritise precision, clarity and casuistic remedies, while civil law systems have a stronger attachment to legalism[15] and strive for concision and rules that set abstract principles.[16] Style is an 'inherent quality' of legislation[17] that includes wording, structure, superstructure and legal-cultural identity,[18] hence both what is legislated and the choices of words, arrangement and structure it finally gets. Drafting conventions on the other hand are born from experience and prescribe principles upon which structure, form and style are

---

[12] R.H. Thaler and C.R. Sunstein, *Nudge* (Penguin Books 2009) at 21–3.

[13] James Gibson and Gregory Caldeira, 'The Legal Cultures of Europe' (1996) 30 Law & Society Review 55–86; Konrad Zweigert and Hein Kötz, *An Introduction to Comparative Law* (trs Tony Weir, 3rd edn, OUP 2011) 67.

[14] Rob Baggott, 'Regulatory Reform in Britain: The Changing Face of Self-Regulation' (1989) 67 Public Administration 435–54, 438; Michael Moran, 'The Rise of the Regulatory State in Britain' (2001) 54 Parliamentary Affairs 19–34, 23, 24.

[15] Sénat, *La Qualité de la Loi* (Les Documents de Travail Du Sénat 2007) at 7; Karine Gilberg, 'Une production du droit mieux raisonnée? La diffusion de la légistique en droit français' [2008] Courrier juridique des finances et de l'Industrie 47–54.

[16] Christian Dadomo and Susan Ferran, *The French Legal System* (Sweet & Maxwell 1993) 11, 12; Louis-Philippe Pigeon, *Drafting and Interpreting Legislation* (Carswell 1988) 7, 8; Timothy Millet, 'A Comparison of British and French Legislative Drafting (with particular reference to their respective Nationality Laws)' [1986] 7:3 Statute Law Review 157–8.

[17] G.C. Thornton, *Legislative Drafting* (4th edn, Butterworths, 1996) at 46.

[18] W. Voermans, 'Styles of Legislation and Their Effects' (2011) 32:1 Statute Law Review at 41.

based[19] with the aim to capture best drafting practice and bring coherence and consistency. They can be definite and easily traceable, obtuse or hidden.[20]

Legislative styles and conventions are influential in the way legislation is designed and drafted, especially when it comes to choices of overarching structure, substantive content and language. Is the choice to disperse non-discrimination provisions in codified legislation a 'solution' imposed by the structure of the legal system or a conscious lawmaking choice selected for facilitating coherence and accessibility? Several similar questions can be asked. There is no doubt that good style is important[21] as it reinforces the continuity, homogeneity and 'ownership' of the law. Yet both are there to help communication – not to dictate substantive choices. Are lawmakers aware of whether and how conventions and style influence them? Do they consciously think about it?

4.2. Path dependence, habitual action and legislative 'patterns'

The life of the law has not been logic: it has been experience,[22] and history, I would add. Path dependence[23] reflects the relation between law and its historical path and shows that 'the past matters'. From an economic point of view, path dependence describes how a set of arrangements reinforced over time raises the cost of changing them.[24] From a political science perspective, path dependence highlights how 'history matters'.[25] Beyond costs and history, however, there is another dynamic attached to it: people learn and invest in a given way of doing things. As these add up, the (economic and social) impact of exploring alternatives – or changing the status quo – rises. Transferred in the world of lawmaking, this means that legislation is, to an important extent, bound to its historical evolution, and to its past. Substantive decisions made at some point might be difficult to change, even if necessary. Entrenched

---

[19] A. Quartey Parafio, 'Drafting Conventions, Templates and Legislative Precedents, and their Effects on the Drafting Process and the Drafter' (2013) 15:4 European Journal of Law Reform 376.

[20] J. Stark, *The Art of the Statute* (Littleton 1996) xi.

[21] Thornton (n 17) at 46.

[22] J. Dickinson, 13 August 1787, Assembly of the United States in Philadelphia (Farrand's Records Century of Lawmaking for a New Nation 1787/1991, vol. 2:278).

[23] O.A. Hathaway, 'Path Dependence in the Law: The Course and Pattern of Legal Change in a Common Law System' (2001) 86 Iowa L. Rev. 601.

[24] Paul Pierson, 'Increasing Returns, Path Dependence, and the Study of Politics' (2000) 94 Am.Pol.Sci.Rev. 251 at 252–7.

[25] Mariana Prado and Michael Trebilcock, 'Path Dependence, Development, and the Dynamics of Institutional Reform' (2009) 59 University of Toronto Law Journal 341–79.

legislation tends to persist.[26] But is this a 'healthy' attitude? How aware are lawmakers of path dependence? To what extent can history influence legislative decision making?

Another matter is habitual action. Merton highlights how 'mechanisms of habit' rely on assumptions that actions that led to the desired outcomes in the past will continue to do so.[27] These tend to become automatic, replicated through continued repetition, obscuring the fact that what was successful under certain circumstances need not be so under any and all conditions. To what extent does legislation repeat itself by force of custom? Or is legislation a set of patterns that lawmakers replicate without fully questioning? Are they even aware of them?

'Patterns' are a new way of looking at legislation. Research conducted by the National Archives in the UK[28] examined the existence of legislative patterns (defined as solutions that evolved over time) and attempted to map them. 'Pattern language' was expected to facilitate informed decisions, better understanding of legislation and promote 'good' design patterns,[29] or make us aware of their existence, I would add.

A legislative design pattern describes a problem that occurs repeatedly and a core legislative solution. For example, the 'protector pattern': to protect the public from a source of nuisance or harm, specify the harm and its instances, appoint an authority (the Protector), give powers (issue notices, mediate, sanction), create a claim-right to appeal, create an offence for failure to comply.[30] Patterns are present in the conceptual design of the law but also in language and expression, including the use of grammar and syntax. Is all legislation a set of patterns? Are lawmakers aware of them? Are they repeated consciously or unconsciously? Do they promote homogeneity and effective legislation? Or, coupled with path dependence and habitual action they obstruct reflection and resist alternative solutions and experimentation? Even worse, can they go unnoticed?

---

[26] Sofia Ranchordás, 'Time, Timing, And Experimental Legislation' (2015) 3:2 The Theory and Practice of Legislation 135–9.

[27] Merton (n 2) at 901.

[28] Council of the European Union (2015), Delegation of the United Kingdom, (OR. en) 14933/15 LIMITE JURINFO 43 EJUSTIC, Note on 'Patterns in legislation and work on big data' available at: http://data.consilium.europa.eu/doc/document/ST-14933-2015-INIT/en/pdf

[29] Ibid.

[30] Ibid.

4.3. Borrowed, imported and supranational rules

Transplants, borrowed or 'imported' rules are not a new phenomenon. Roscoe Pound wrote that 'history of a system of law is largely a history of borrowings of legal materials from other legal systems and assimilation of materials from outside of the law'.[31] Yet the mobility of rules between countries, regions or continents acquires nowadays breathtaking dimensions. 'Borrowing' is still considered a way to improve a legal system but is also the source of several concerns to the extent that imported concepts often fit awkwardly into the native politico-legal culture and might require parallel shifts in political cultures and structures. However, this is not the place to summarise an extensive discussion that has evolved over the years.[32] The point I want to raise is how these 'imported rules' affect lawmaking.

From transplants, to the influence of comparative law, to 'copy-out' technique,[33] rules 'external' to the system are common. It is also a fact that legal systems develop different reactions to them: from functionally 'adjusting' rules before incorporating them in national law, to 'resisting' them by developing tense relationships, to 'obedient' 'copy and paste' approaches. The influence of 'external' rules is a powerful 'automatism' in contemporary lawmaking. How do lawmakers deal with them? How pressured are they by them? And how do they react to them?

None of the questions raised in this section can be answered. Automatisms contradict, to a greater or lesser extent, the reflective aspects of lawmaking. Lawmakers need to be aware of them, their respective advantages and disadvantages but also of the fact that they are not 'mindless rules' to be carelessly followed but should go in hand with analysis, thought and flexibility.

---

[31] Roscoe Pound, *The Formative Era of American Law* (Little, Brown & Co. 1938) at 94.

[32] For an overview see Wim J.M. Voermans, 'From Legal Imposition to Legal Invitation' (2018) 20:1 European Journal of Law Reform 8–19; Alan Watson, *Legal Transplants* (University of Georgia Press 1974); R.B. Seidman, 'Law and Development; A General Model' (1972) 6 Law and Society Review at 338; Coen J.P. Van Laer, Helen Xanthaki, 'Legal Transplants and Comparative Concepts: Eclecticism Defeated?' (2013) 34:2 Statute Law Review 128–37.

[33] Lynn Ramsey, 'The Copy Out Technique: More of a "Cop Out" than a Solution?' (1996) 3:1 Statute Law Review 218–28.

5. EFFECTIVE LAWMAKING

This book came with some strong claims about effectiveness: that it is a concept with an important role to play in guiding lawmaking; that it has concrete operational content; and that effective laws can be consciously engineered.

Effective lawmaking is not science but purposive decision making in a context of uncertainty. It presents the challenge of having to anticipate – to the extent possible and in as much detail as possible – that the choices and solutions considered have the capacity to work. Effectiveness and its four elements, and the effectiveness test, provide a thinking process and a clear decision making criterion that can guide the lawmaking process towards concrete results.

I believe these claims have been proven. However, in the process, several other provoking questions were born regarding the nature of legislative design and decision making that I believe merit closer attention in the future.

Bibliography

Ahern D, 'Codification of Company Law: Taking Stock of the Companies Act 2006' (2014) 35:1 Statute Law Review 230–43.
Albanesi E, 'The Mechanisms Used to Review Existing Legislation in the Civil Law System. Case Study – Italy' (2016) 18:3 European Journal of Law Reform 275–95.
Alemanno A, 'A Meeting of Minds on Impact Assessment' (2011) 17:3 European Public Law 485–505.
Alemanno A, 'How Much Better Is Better Regulation? Assessing the Impact of the Better Regulation Package on the European Union – A Research Agenda' (2015) 3 European Journal of Risk Regulation 344–56.
Alexy R and Peczenik A, 'The Concept of Coherence and Its Significance for Discursive Rationality' (1990) 3 Ratio Juris 130–47.
Allan TRS, 'Legislative Supremacy and Legislative Intention: Interpretation, Meaning and Authority' (2004) 63:3 Cambridge Law Journal 685–711.
Allio L, 'On the Smartness of Smart Regulation – A Brief Comment on the Future Reform Agenda' (2011) 1 European Journal of Risk Regulation 19–20.
Allot A, *The Limits of Law* (Butterworths, 1980).
Andrews P, 'Are Market Failure Analysis and Impact Assessment Useful?' in Stephen Weatherill (ed) *Better Regulation* (Hart Publishing 2007) 49–81.
Arthuis J, 'La dégradation des finances publiques: la loi en échec, le contrôle et l'évaluation en recours' (2010) 3 Pouvoirs 83–95.
Atienza M, 'Reasoning and Legislation' in L Wintgens (ed) *The Theory and Practice of Legislation. Essays in Legisprudence* (Ashgate 2005) 297–318.
Ayres I and Braithwaite J, *Responsive Regulation. Transcending the Deregulation Debate* (OUP 1992).
Baggott R, 'Regulatory Reform in Britain: The Changing Face of Self-Regulation' (1989) 67 Public Administration 435–54.
Baldwin R, 'Why Rules Don't Work' (1990) 53:3 The Modern Law Review 321–37.
Baldwin R, *Rules and Government* (OUP 1995).
Baldwin R and Cave M, *Understanding Regulation. Theory, Strategy and Practice* (Oxford University Press 1999).
Baldwin R, 'Is Better Regulation Smarter Regulation?' (2005) Autumn, Public Law 485–511.

Baldwin R, 'Better Regulation: Tensions aboard the Enterprise' in Stephen Weatherill (ed) *Better Regulation* (Hart Publishing 2007) 27–47.

Baldwin R, Cave M and Lodge M, (eds) *The Oxford Handbook of Regulation* (OUP 2010).

Baldwin R, Cave M and Lodge M, *Understanding Regulation. Theory, Strategy and Practice* (2nd edn, OUP 2012).

Bar-Siman-Tov I, 'The role of courts in improving the legislative process' (2015) 3:3 The Theory and Practice of Legislation 295–313, 312.

Bar-Siman-Tov I, 'The dual meaning of evidence-based judicial review of legislation' (2016) 4:2 The Theory and Practice of Legislation, 4:2 107–33.

Barber NW, 'The afterlife of parliamentary sovereignty' (2011) 9:1 International Journal of Constitutional Law 144–54.

Bardach E, *The implementation game. What happens after a Bill becomes a Law* (MIT Press 1977).

Bardach E and Kagan R, *Going by the Book. The Problem of Regulatory Unreasonableness* (Temple University Press 1982).

Baugus B and Bose F, 'Sunset Legislation in the States: Balancing the Legislature and the Executive' (Mercatus Research, Mercatus Center at George Mason University, 2015) available at: https://www.mercatus.org/system/files/Baugus-Sunset-Legislation.pdf (accessed 1 December 2018).

Bécane J-C, Couderc M and Herin J-L, *La Loi* (2nd edn, Dalloz 2010).

Bennion Fr, *Bennion on Statutory Interpretation* (5th edn, LexisNexis 2008).

Bennion Fr, 'How They Do Things in France' (1995) 16:1 Statute Law Review 90–97.

Berry D, 'Techniques for Evaluating Draft Legislation' (1997) The Loophole.

Bertlin A, What works best for the reader? A study on drafting and presenting legislation, Loophole (2014) 2, 25–49.

Black J, 'Constitutionalising Self-Regulation' (1996) 59 Modern Law Review 24–55.

Black J, 'Critical Reflections on Regulation' (2002) 27 Australian Journal of Legal Philosophy 1–35.

Black J, 'Forms and paradoxes of principles-based regulation' (2008) 3:4 Capital Markets Law Journal 425–57.

Black J, 'The Rise, Fall and Fate of Principles-based Regulation' (2010) LSE Law, Society and Economy Working Papers 17/2010.

Blanc F and Ottimofiore G, 'Consultation' in Claire Dunlop and Claudio Radaelli (eds) *Handbook of Regulatory Impact Assessment* (Edward Elgar Publishing 2016) 155–76.

Bleich E, 'Social Research and Race: Policy Framing in Britain and France' (2011) 13 The British Journal of Politics and International Relations 59–74.

Bloch P, 'Diversity and Labor Law in France' (2005–2006) 30 Vanderbilt Law Review 717–47.

Blum A and Guerin-Pace F, 'From Measuring Integration to Fighting Discrimination. The Illusion of Ethnic Statistics' (2008) 26:1 French Politics, Culture & Society 45–61.

Bogdanor V, 'Imprisoned by a Doctrine: The Modern Defence of Parliamentary Sovereignty' (2012) 32:1 Oxford Journal of Legal Studies 179–95.

Bonnard-Plancke L and Verkindt P-Y, 'Egalité et Diversité: quelles solutions?' (2006) 11 Droit Social 968–80.

Borgetto M, 'Egalite, Différenciation et discrimination: ce que dit le droit' (2008) 148 Informations Sociales 8–17.

Borillo D, 'Les instruments juridiques français et européens dans la mise en place du principe d'égalité et de non-discrimination' (2002) 1 Revue française des affaires sociales 109–29.

Bowman G, 'The Art of Legislative Drafting' (2005) 7 European Journal of Law Reform 3–17.

Braithwaite J, 'The Essence of Responsive Regulation' (2011) 44 University of British Columbia Law Review 475–520.

Bradley A, 'The sovereignty of parliament – form or substance?' in Jeffrey Jowell and Dawn Oliver (eds) *The Changing Constitution* (7th edn, OUP 2011) 35–69.

Brown A and Erskine A, 'A Qualitative Study of Judgements in Race Discrimination Employment Cases' (2009) 31:1 Law & Policy 142–59.

Brunet P, 'Que-reste-t-il de la volonté générale? Sur les nouvelles fictions du droit constitutionnel français' (2005) 3 Pouvoirs 5–19.

Bundi P, 'Parliamentarians' strategies for policy evaluations' (2018) 69 Evaluation and Program Planning 130–138.

Burnier Fr and Pesquié Br, 'Test de discrimination et preuve pénale' (2007) 3:5 Horizons Stratégiques 60–67.

Bussmann W, 'Evaluation of Legislation: Skating on Thin Ice' (2010) 16:3 Evaluation 279–93.

Calvès G, 'La parité entre hommes et femmes dans l'accès aux fonctions électives. Faut-il réviser la constitution?' in CURRAPP, Questions sensibles (PUF 1998) 218–36 https://www.u-picardie.fr/curapp-revues/root/41/gwenaele_calves.pdf_4a09372a9019e/gwenaele_calves.pdf

Calvès G, 'La Parité entre Hommes et Femmes dans l'accès aux Fonctions électives. Faut-il réviser la constitution?' in CURRAPP, *Questions sensibles* (PUF 1998) 218–36.

Calvès G, 'Les politiques françaises de lutte contre le racisme, des politiques en mutation' (2000) 18:3 French Politics, Culture & Society 75–82.

Calvès G, 'Il n'y a pas de Race ici. Le modèle français à l'épreuve de l'intégration européenne' (2002) 4:17 Critique Internationale 73–186.

Calvès G, 'Les Politiques Françaises de Discrimination Positive: Trois spécificités' (2004) 4:111 Pouvoirs 29–40.

Calvès G, 'Refléter la diversité de la population française: naissance et développent d'un objectif flou', (2005) 1:183 Revue Internationale des Sciences Sociales 177–86.

Calvès G, 'Sanctionner ou réguler. L'hésitation des politiques de lutte contre les discriminations' (2008) 148 Informations Sociales 34–45.

Calvès G, 'L'égalité. Le cas du droit de la non-discrimination' in Jean Bernard Auby (ed), *L'influence du Droit Européen sur les catégories du Droit Public* (Dalloz 2010) 485–500.

Calvès G, *La Discrimination Positive* (PUF 2010).

Carcassonne G, 'The Principle of Equality in France: Perspectives on Equal Protection – Part I' (1998) St. Louis-Warsaw Transatlantic Law Journal 159–72.

Carcassonne G, 'Penser la loi' (2005) 3 Pouvoirs 39–52.

Cassiani U and Flueckiger A (eds), *De l'évaluation à l'action législatives: actes du colloque en l'honneur du Professeur Jean-Daniel Delley* (CETEL 2010).

Cave E, 'Determining Capacity to Make Medical Treatment Decisions: Problems Implementing the Mental Capacity Act 2005' (2015) 36:1 Statute Law Review 86–106.

Caygill T, 'A Tale of Two Houses?', (2019) 21:2 European Journal of Law Reform, 87–101.

Ciavarini Azzi G, 'Better Lawmaking: the Experience and the View of the European Commission' (1998) 4 Columbia Journal of European Law 617–28.

Cingranelli D and Richards D, 'The Cingranelli and Richards (CIRI) Human Rights Data Project' (2010) 32:2 Human Rights Quarterly 401–24.

Clapinska L, 'Post-Legislative Scrutiny of Legislation Derived from the European Union' (2007) IX:2 European Journal of Law Reform 321–54.

Clune W and Lindquist RE, 'What "Implementation" isn't: Toward a General Framework for Implementation Research' (1981) Wisconsin Law Review 1044–116.

Coglianese C and Evan Mendelson, 'Meta – Regulation and Self-Regulation' in R Baldwin, M Cave and M Lodge (eds), *The Oxford Handbook of Regulation* (OUP 2010) 146–68.

Coletti P, 'Standard Cost Model' in C Dunlop and C Radaelli (eds), *Handbook of Regulatory Impact Assessment* (Edward Elgar 2016) 93–107 at 104.

Cooper Th M, 'The Common and the Civil Law. A Scot's View' (1950) 63:3 Harvard Law Review 468–75.

Cormacain R, 'Legislative Drafting and the Rule of Law' (PhD Thesis, University of London 2017).

Costa-Lascoux J, 'Les Échecs de l'Intégration, un Accroc au Contrat Social' (2004) 4:111 Pouvoirs 19–28.

Cownie F, Bradney A and Burton M, *English Legal System in Context* (5th edn, OUP 2010).
Coxon B, 'Open to Interpretation: The Implication of Words into Statutes' (2009) 30:1 Statute Law Review 1–37.
Crabbe VCRAC, *Legislative Drafting* (Cavendish Publishing Ltd 1993).
Creighton WB, 'Enforcing the Sex Discrimination Act' (1976) 5 Industrial Law Journal 42–53.
Crouzatier-Durand F, 'Réflexions sur le concept d'expérimentation législative. (à propos de la loi constitutionnelle du 28 mars 2003 relative à l'organisation décentralisée de la République)' Revue française de droit constitutionnel 2003/4 56 at 675–95.
Cserne P, 'Introduction: Legislation, Legal Episteme, and Empirical Knowledge' (2013) 1:3 The Theory and Practice of Legislation 387–93.
Dadomo C and Ferran S, *The French Legal System* (Sweet & Maxwell 1993).
Dale W, 'Principles, Purposes, and Rules' (1988) 14 Statute Law Review 15–26.
David R and Brierley J, *Major Legal Systems in the World Today. An Introduction to the Comparative Study of Law* (3rd edn, Sweet & Maxwell 1985).
Deakin S, 'Editorial' (2011) 40:4 Industrial Law Journal 313–14.
De Benedetto M, 'Maintenance of Rules' in U Karpen and H Xanthaki (eds), *Legislation in Europe. A Comprehensive Guide for Scholars and Practitioners* (Hart Publishing 2017) 215–227.
De Benedetto M, 'Effective Law from a Regulatory and Administrative Law Perspective' (2018) 9:3 European Journal of Risk and Regulation 391.
Delley J-D, Derivaz R, Mader L, Morand C-A and Schneider D, *Le droit en action: étude de la mise en œuvre de la législation fédérale sur l'acquisition d'immeubles par des personnes domiciliées à l'étranger: rapport final au Fonds national* (CETEL, 1981).
Dennis I, 'Codifying the Law of Criminal Evidence' (2014) 35:2 Statute Law Review 107–19.
Denolle A-S, 'Les Etudes d'Impact: Une Révision Manquée?' (2011) 87 Revue Française de Droit Constitutionnel 499–514.
Derber M, 'What the Lawyer can Learn from Social Science' (1963) 16:2 Journal of Legal Education 145–54.
Destais N, Marigeaud M, Battesti J-P and Bondaz M, *Guide Cadrage méthodologique de l'évaluation des politiques publiques partenariales* (La Documentation Française 2012).
Dewey J, *How We Think. A restatement of the relation of reflective thinking to the educative process* (Revised edn, Boston: D.C. Heath 1933).
Dickerson R, *Legislative Drafting* (Little & Brown 1954).

Dickerson R, 'Statutory Interpretation in America: Dipping into Legislative History – II' (1984) Statute Law Review 141–56.

Donelan E, 'European Approaches to Improving Access to and Managing the Stock of Legislation' (2009) 30:3 Statute Law Review 147–83.

Driese D, 'Alternatives to Regulation? Market Mechanisms and the Environment' in R Baldwin, M Cave and M Lodge (eds) *The Oxford Handbook of Regulation* (OUP 2010) 203–22.

Drinoszi T, 'Legislative Process' in U Karpen and H Xanthaki (eds) *Legislation in Europe. A Comprehensive Guide for Scholars and Practitioners* (Hart Publishing 2017).

Drummond B, 'A purposive approach to the drafting of tax legislation' (2006) 6 British Tax Review 669–676.

Dunlop C and Radaelli C, 'The politics and economics of regulatory impact assessment' in Claire Dunlop and Claudio Radaelli (eds) *Handbook of Regulatory Impact Assessment* (Edward Elgar Publishing 2016) 8–14.

Duprat J-P, 'The Judicial Review of *ex ante* Impact Assessment in France: an Attempt to Fuse the Principles of Legal Certainty and Institutional Balance' (2012) 6:3 Legisprudence 379–96.

Ekins R, 'The Intention of Parliament' (2010) Public Law 709–26.

Epstein R, 'Evaluation of Public Policies' (2007) Report for the Seminar 'Legislative Evaluation' organised by the European Commission for Democracy through Law (Venice Commission), CDL-UDT(2007)002.

Evans C and Evans S, 'Evaluating the Human Rights Performance of Legislatures' (2006) 6:3 Human Rights Law Review 545–69.

Fassin D, 'L'Invention française de la Discrimination' (2002) 52 Revue française de science politique 403–23.

Fassin D, 'Une brève histoire des discriminations' in Eric Fassin and Jean-Louis Halpérin (eds), *Discriminations: Pratiques, Savoirs, Politiques* (Documentation Française 2009).

Faure M and Blanc F, 'Smart Enforcement. Theory and Practice' (2018) 20:4 European Journal of Law Reform 78–104.

Favell A, *Philosophies of Integration: Immigration and the Idea of Citizenship in France and Britain* (Palgrave Macmillan 1998).

Favennec-Héry F, 'Non-discrimination, égalité, diversité, la France au milieu du gue' (2007) 1 Droit Social 687.

Favoreu Louis, 'The Principle of Equality in the Jurispudence of the Conseil Constitutionnel' (1992) 21 Capital University Law Review 165–97.

Feldman D, 'Legislation Which Bears No Law' (2016) 37:3 Statute Law Review 212–24 at 214.

Finucane L, 'Definitions – A Powerful Tool for Keeping and Effective Statute Book Louise Finucane' (2017) 1 The Loophole 15–32, available at: http://

www.calc.ngo/sites/default/files/loophole/Loophole%20-%202017-01%20 %282017-02-02%29.pdf (accessed 11 May 2019).

Florijn N, 'The Instructions for Legislation in the Netherlands: A Critical Approach' (2010) IV:2 Legisprudence 171–91.

Flückiger A, 'Le droit administratif en mutation: l'émergence d'un principe d'efficacité' (2001) 57:(1–2) Revue de droit administratif et fiscal (RDAF) 93–119.

Flückiger A, 'L'obligation jurisprudentielle d'évaluation législative: une application du principe de précaution aux droits fondamentaux' in Andreas Auer, Alexandre Flückiger and Michel Hottelier (eds), *Les droits de l'homme et la constitution: études en l'honneur du Professeur Giorgio Malinverni* (Schulthess 2007) 155–70.

Flückiger A, 'L'évaluation législative ou comment mesurer l'efficacité des lois' (2007) XLV:138 Revue européenne des sciences sociales 83–101.

Flückiger A, 'Qu'est-ce que "mieux légiférer"?: enjeux et instrumentalisation de la notion de qualité législative' in Flückiger, A et al. *Guider les parlements et les gouvernements pour mieux légiférer: le rôle des guides de légistique* (Schulthess 2008) 11–32.

Flückiger A, 'Why Do We Obey Soft Law?' in Stephane Nahrath and Frederic Varone (eds) *Rediscovering Public Law in Comparative Policy Analysis: a Tribute to Peter Knoepfer* (Presses Polytechniques Romandes 2009) 45–62.

Flückiger A, 'Effectiveness: a new Constitutional Principle' (2009) 50 *Legislação: cadernos de ciência de legislação* 183–98.

Flückiger A, 'Can Better Regulation be achieved by guiding Parliaments and Governments? How the definition of the quality of legislation affects law improvement methods' (2010) VI:2 Legisprudence 213–218.

Fouquet A, 'L'évaluation des politiques publiques en France' in Anne-Marie Brocas (ed), *Méthodes d'évaluation des politiques publiques. Actes du séminaire* (Ministère du travail, de l'emploi et de la santé, Ministère du budget, des comptes publics, de la fonction publique et de la réforme de l'Etat, Ministère des solidarités et de la cohésion sociale 2011).

Fredman S, *Discrimination Law* (Clarendon Law Series, Oxford University Press 2002).

Fredman S, *Discrimination Law* (2nd edn, OUP 2011).

Freund E, 'The use of Indefinite Terms in Statutes' (1921) XXX:5 Yale Law Journal 437–55.

Friedman L, *The Legal System* (Russell Sage Foundation 1975).

Friedman L, *Law and Society. An Introduction* (Prentice-Hall 1977).

Friedman L, *Impact. How Law Affects Behaviour* (Harvard University Press 2016).

Friedman D, *Law's Order* (Princeton University Press 2000).

Fuller L, *Anatomy of the Law* (Penguin 1968).

Fuller L, *The Morality of Law* (Rev edn, Yale University Press 1969).

Fuller L, 'Law as an Instrument of Social Control and Law as a Facilitation of Human Interaction' (1975) 1 Brigham Young University Law Review 89–96.

Galligan D, 'Legal Failure: Law and Social Norms in Post-Communist Europe' in D Galligan and M Kurkchiyan *Law and Informal Practices: The Post-Communist Experience* (Oxford Scholarship Online 2012) 1–25.

P García-Escudero Márquez, *Técnica legislativa y seguridad jurídica: ¿hacia el control constitucional de la calidad de las leyes?* (Cuadernos Civitas Thomson Reuters 2011).

Gibbs G, *Learning by Doing:* A guide to teaching and learning methods (Further Education Unit, Oxford Polytechnic (1988)).

Gibson J and Caldeira Gr, 'The Legal Cultures of Europe' (1996) 30:1 Law & Society Review 55–86.

Gilberg K, 'De l'Art de Mieux Légiférer' (*Le Monde*, 17 February 2010).

Gilberg K, 'Une production du droit mieux raisonnée? La diffusion de la légistique en droit français' (2008) (special issue) Courrier juridique des finances et de l'Industrie 47–54.

Gilbert M, 'Insincere Rules' (2015) 101 Virginia Law Review 2185–223.

Goetz K and Zubek R, 'Law-making in Poland: Rules and Patterns of Legislation', 2005, accessible at: http://citeseerx.ist.psu.edu/viewdoc/download?doi=10.1.1.579.2915&rep=rep1&type=pdf 8–10 (last accessed 07/12/2018).

Graëfly R, 'Vers une unification des politiques publiques de lutte contre les discriminations' (2005) Actualité Juridique Droit Administrative 934–41.

Green M, 'What we talk about when we talk about indicators: Current approaches to human rights measurement' (2001) 23:4 Human Rights Quarterly 1062–97.

Greenberg D, 'The nature of legislative intention and its implications for Legislative Drafting' (2006) 27:1 Statute Law Review 15–28.

Greenberg D, (ed) *Craies on Legislation. A Practitioners' Guide to the Nature, Process, Effect and Interpretation of Legislation* (9th edn, Sweet & Maxwell 2008).

Greenberg D, *Laying down the Law* (Sweet & Maxwell 2011).

Grabosky P, 'Counterproductive Regulation' (1995) 23 International Journal of the Sociology of Law 347–69.

Grantham R and Jensen D, 'Coherence in the Age of Statutes' (2016) 42.2 Monash University Law Review 360–82.

Griffiths J, 'The Social Working of Legal Rules' (2003) 48 Journal of Legal Pluralism & Unofficial Law 1–84.

Griglio E, 'Post-Legislative Scrutiny as a Form of Executive Oversight' (2019) 21:2, European Journal of Law Reform, 118–136.

Gubler Z, 'Experimental Rules' (2014) 55 Boston College Law Review 129–79.

Gunningham N, 'Enforcement and Compliance Strategies' in R Baldwin, M Cave and M Lodge, *The Oxford Handbook of Regulation* (OUP 2010) 120–45.

Gunningham N and Grabosky P, *Smart Regulation* (Clarendon Press 1998).

Gunningham N and Sinclair D, 'Regulation and the Role of Trust: Reflections from the Mining Industry' (2009) 36:2 Journal of Law and Society 167–94.

Hage J, 'The (Onto)logical Structure of Law: A Conceptual Toolkit for Legislators' in M Araszkiewicz and K Pleszka (eds) *Logic in the Theory and Practice of Lawmaking* (Legisprudence Library Vol. 2, Springer 2016), 3–49.

Hathaway OA, 'Path Dependence in the Law: The Course and Pattern of Legal Change in a Common Law System' (2001) 86 Iowa Law Review 601.

Hart HLA, 'Positivism and the Separation of Law and Morals' (1958) 71 Harvard Law Review 593–629.

Hart HLA, *The Concept of Law* (2nd edn, OUP 1997).

Hauser J, 'Le Juge et la Loi' (2005) 3 Pouvoirs 139–56.

Heldeweg MA, 'Experimental legislation concerning technological and governance innovation – an analytical approach' (2015) 3:2 The Theory and Practice of Legislation 169–93.

Héritier A, 'New Modes of Governance in Europe: Policy-making without Legislating?' in A Héritier (ed) *Common Goods: Reinventing European and International Governance* (Rowman & Littlefield Publishers 2002).

Hepple B, 'Race Relations Act 1965' (1966) 29:3 The Modern Law Review 6–14.

Hepple B, 'Race Relations Act 1968' (1969) 21:2 The Modern Law Review 181–6.

Hepple B, 'Have Twenty-five years of the Race Relations Act in Britain Been a Failure?' in Bob Hepple and Erika Szyszczak, *Discrimination: The Limits of the Law* (Mansell 1992).

Hepple B, Coussey M and Choudhury T, *Equality: A New Framework. Report of the Independent Review of the Enforcement of UK Anti-Discrimination Legislation* (Hart Publishing 2000).

Hepple B, 'The Aims of Equality Law' (2008) 61:1 Current Legal Problems 1–22.

Hepple B, 'The New Single Equality Act in Britain' (2010) 5 The Equal Rights Review 11–24.

Hepple B, 'Enforcing Equality Law: Two Steps Forward and Two Steps Backwards for Reflexive Regulation' (2011) 40 Industrial Law Journal 315–35.

Hepple B, *Equality. The New Legal Framework* (Hart Publishing 2011).

Humphreys L, Santos C, di Caro L, Boella G, van der Torre L and Robaldo L, 'Mapping Recitals to Normative Provisions in EU Legislation to Assist Legal Interpretation' in A. Rotolo (ed) *Legal Knowledge and Information Systems* (ebook, series Frontiers in Artificial Intelligence and Applications IOS Press), Volume 279, 2015.

Hutter B, *The Reasonable Arm of the Law? The Law Enforcement Procedures of Environmental Health Officers* (Clarendon Press 1988).

Hood C, Baldwin R and Rothstein H, 'Assessing the Dangerous Dogs Act: When does a regulatory law fail?' (2000) (Summer) Public Law 282–305.

Irresberger K and Jasiak A, 'Publication' in U Karpen and H Xanthaki *Legislation in Europe* (Hart 2017), 165–185.

Issmer R and Meßerschmidt K, 'Evidence-based judicial review of legislation: some introductory remarks' (2016) 4:2 The Theory and Practice of Legislation 91–106.

Jacobs S, 'Towards a simpler and practical approach' in Dunlop and Radaelli (eds) *Handbook of Regulatory Impact Assessment* (Edward Elgar Publishing, 2016), 78–90.

Jacobzone St, Chang-Wong Choi and Claire Miguet, 'Indicators of Regulatory Management Systems' (2007) 4 OECD Working Papers on Public Governance http://www.oecd.org/dataoecd/38/10/39954493.pdf (accessed 11 May 2019).

Jamieson N, 'The Pathology of Legislation' (1984) 2 Statute Law Review 87–101.

Jestaz Ph, *Le Droit* (7th edn, Dalloz 2012).

Jolls C, Sunstein C and Thaler R, 'A Behavioral Approach to Law and Economics' (1998) 50 Stan. L. Rev. 1471.

Jones H, *The Efficacy of Law* (Rosenthal Lectures, Northwestern University Press 1968).

Jorion B, 'Egalité et Non-discrimination en Droit Public Français' in G Guglielmi and G Koubi (eds) *L'Egalité des Chances* (La Découverte 2000).

Jowell J, 'The Administrative Enforcement of Laws Against Discrimination' (1965) Public Law 119–86.

Jowell J, 'Is Equality a Constitutional Principle?' (1994) 47 Current Legal Problems 1–18.

Jowell J, 'The Rule of Law and its Underlying Values' in J Jowell and D Oliver (eds) *The Changing Constitution* (7th edn, OUP 2011) 11–34.

Kagan P, Gunningham N and Thornton D, 'Fear, duty and regulatory compliance: lessons from three research projects' in C Parker and VL Neilsen (eds) *Explaining Compliance* (Edward Elgar 2011), 37–58.

Karpen U, 'Giving Effect to European Fundamental Rights Through Evaluation of Legislation', (2002) 23 Statute Law Review 191–202.

Karpen U, (ed) *Evaluation of Legislation* (Broschiert 2002).

Karpen U, 'Implementation of Legislative Evaluation in Europe: Current Models and Trends' (2004) VI:1/ 2 European Journal of Law Reform 57–85.

Karpen U, 'Improving Democratic Development by Better Regulation' in C Stefanou and H Xanthaki, *Drafting Legislation. A modern approach* (Ashgate 2008) 151–64.

Karpen U, 'Efficacy, Effectiveness, Efficiency: from Judicial to Managerial Rationality' in K. Messerschmidt and AD Oliver-Lalana (eds) *Rational Lawmaking under Review. Legisprudence According to the German Federal Constitutional Court* (Springer 2016).

Karpen U, 'Introduction' in U Karpen and H Xanthaki, *Legislation in Europe. A Comprehensive Guide for Scholars and Practitioners* (2017) 1–16.

Karpen U and Delnoy P (eds), *Contributions to the Methodology of the Creation of Written Law* (European Association of Legislation (EAL) 1996.

Kavanagh A, 'Pepper v Hart and Matters of Constitutional Principle' (2005) Law Quarterly Review 98–122.

Kealy S and Forney A, 'The Reliability of Evidence in Evidence-based Legislation' (2018) 1 European Journal of Law Reform 40–66.

Kelemen D and Menon A, 'The Politics of EC Regulation' in Stephen Weatherill (ed), *Better Regulation* (Hart Publishing 2007) 175–90.

Kellermann A, 'Proposals for Improving the Quality of European and National Legislation' (1999) 1 European Journal of Law Reform 7–30.

Kelsen H, 'Law as a Specific Social Technique' (1941) 9 University of Chicago Law Review 75–97.

Kelsen H, *Pure Theory of Law* (translated from the 2nd revised and enlarged German edition by Max Knight, The Lawbook Exchange 2009).

Kiendl Krišto I and Poutouroudi V, *Review Clauses in EU Legislation: A Rolling Check-List* (European Parliament, European Parliamentary Research Service 2018), available at: http://www.europarl.europa.eu/RegData/etudes/STUD/2018/621821/EPRS_STU(2018)621821_EN.pdf (accessed 1 December 2018).

Klimas T and Vaitiukait J, 'The Law of Recitals in European Community Legislation' (2008) 15:1 ILSA Journal of International & Comparative Law 65–93 at 62.

Kouroutakis A, *The Constitutional Value of Sunset Clauses: An Historical and Normative Analysis* (Routledge 2016).

Kress K, 'Coherence' in D Patterson (ed) *A Companion to Philosophy of Law and Legal Theory* (2nd edn, Blackwell Publishing 2010) 521–38.

Kuehnhenrich D and Michalik S, 'Are Citizens and Businesses (Dis)satisfied with the Public Administration in Germany?', Paper at the 34th IARIW General Conference Dresden, Germany, 21–27 August 2016, accessible at: https://bscw.bund.de/pub/bscw.cgi/d41513289/Aufsatz%20Lebenslagenbefragung%20englisch.pdf? nonce=dc600a08f456d340cb6ef8071631625967f805ad (last accessed 8 December 2018).

Landis J, 'Statutes and the Sources of Law in Harvard Legal Essays', Written in Honor and Presented to Joseph Henry Beale and Samuel Williston (Harvard University Press, Cambridge MA 1934).

Landman T, 'Measuring Human Rights: Principle, Practice and Policy' (2004) 26:4 Human Rights Quarterly 906–31.

Lanquetin M-Th, 'L'égalité des rémunérations entre les femmes et les hommes, réalisée en cinq ans?' (2006) 6 Droit Social 624–35.

Latraverse S, 'Tradition Française et Politique Européenne de Lutte contre les Discrimination. A la lumière de trois directive européennes récentes' (2005) 125 Informations Sociales 94–102.

Lavery U, 'The "Findability" of the Law' (1943) 27 Journal of the American Judicature Society 25.

Laws S, 'Drawing the line' in C Stefanou and H Xanthaki (eds), *Drafting Legislation. A Modern Approach* (Ashgate 2008) 19–34.

Laws S, 'Giving Effect to Policy in Legislation: How to Avoid Missing the Point' (2011) 32:1 Statute Law Review 1–16.

Lee A and Leslie J, 'Judicial Review of Target-Setting Legislation' (2010) 15:3 Judicial Review 236–41.

Leigh I and Masterman R, *Making Rights Real. The Human Rights Act in its First Decade* (Hart Publishing 2008).

Leyland P, *The Constitution of the United Kingdom. A Contextual Analysis* (Hart Publishing 2007).

Lindblom C, 'The Science of Muddling Through' (1959) 19:2 Public Administration Review 79–88.

Lodge M, 'The Wrong Type of Regulation? Regulatory Failure and the Railways' (2002) 22:3 Britain and Germany Journal of Public Policy 271–97.

Luchaire F, 'Un Janus Constitutionnel: l'Egalite' (1986) 5 Revue du Droit Public et de la science politique en France et a l'etranger 1229–75.

Luhman N, *Law as a Social System* (tran. Klaus Ziegert, Oxford University Press 2004) 162–63.

Lynch A and Ziegler P, 'The Amendment of Legislation' (1991) 12 Statute Law Society, 48–57.

Lynch-Fannon I, 'Legislative Policy, Law and Competitiveness: a Mysterious and Difficult Relationship in the EU' (1999) 15:1 European Law Journal 98–120.

Mader L, 'Evaluating the Effects: A Contribution to the Quality of Legislation' (2001) 22:2 Statute Law Review 119–31.

Mader L, 'L'évaluation législative en Suisse: la "longue marche" d'une idée a travers les institutions étatiques', in U Cassiani and A Flückiger (eds), *De l'évaluation a l'action législatives: actes du colloque en l'honneur du Professeur Jean–Daniuel Delley* (CETEL 2010) 15–26.

Mader L and Schäffer H, (eds), *Text and Context – The Development of Legal Techniques and Legal Culture in the New Context of Europe* (Broschiert 2010).

Majone G, 'Foundations of Risk Regulation: Science, Decisions-Making, Policy Learning and Institutional Reform' (2010) 1 European Journal of Risk Regulation at 5.

Mandelkern Group on Better Regulation, 'Final Report', 2001 (Mandelkern Report).

Mathieu B, *La Loi* (2nd edn, Dalloz 2004).

Mathieu B, 'La part de la Loi, la part du Règlement. De la limitation de la compétence réglementaire a la limitation de la compétence législative' (2005) 3 Pouvoirs 73–87.

McAllister L, 'Dimensions of Enforcement Style: Factoring in Regulatory Autonomy and Capacity' (2010) 32:1 Law and Policy 61–78.

McBarnet D and Whelan C, 'The Elusive Spirit of the Law: Formalist and the Struggle for Legal Control' (1991) 54 MLR 848.

McColm H, 'Smart Regulation: The European Commission's Updated Strategy' (2011) 1 European Journal of Risk Regulation 9–13.

McCrudden Ch, 'Institutional Discrimination' (1982) 2 Oxford Journal of Legal Studies 303–67.

McCrudden Ch, 'Equality Legislation and Reflexive Regulation: A Response to the Discrimination Law Review's Consultative Paper' (2007) 36:3 Industrial Law Journal 255–66.

Megret B, *Méthodologie pour le suivi des recommandations résultant des évaluations de politiques publiques* (Ministère des transports, de l'équipement, du tourisme et de la mer Conseil général des ponts et chaussées 2006) http://www.ladocumentationfrancaise.fr/rapports-publics/ 064000568-methodologie-pour-le-suivi-des-recommandations-resultant -des-evaluations-de-politiques (accessed 9 December 2018).

Melin-Soucramanien F, 'Le Droit a l'Egalite' in L Favoreu, P Gaïa, R Chevontian, J-L Mestre, O Pfersmann, A Roux, G Scoffoni (eds), *Droit Constitutionnel* (9th edn, Dalloz 2006).

Merton R, 'The Unanticipated Consequences of Purposive Social Action' (1936) 1:6 American Sociological Review 894–904.

Meuwese A, 'Impact Assessment in EU Lawmaking' (Phd Thesis, University of Leiden 2008).

Meuwese A, 'Embedding Consultation Procedures: Law or Institutionalization?' (2011) 17:3 European Public Law 527–38.

Meuwese A, 'Regulatory Review of European Commission Impact Assessments. What Kind for Which Better Regulation Scenario?' (2017) 19:1 European Journal of Law Reform 16–33.

Meuwese A and van Voorst S, 'Regulatory Impact assessment in legal studies' in C. Dunlop and C. Radaelli (eds) *Handbook of Regulatory Impact Assessment* (Edward Elgar Publishing 2016) 21–32.

Meyer W, 'Human Rights and MNCs: Theory versus Quantitative Analysis' (1996) 18:2 Human Rights Quarterly 368–97.

Millard E, 'Les limites des guides de legistique: l'exemple du droit français' in A Flückiger and C Guy-Ecabert (eds) *Guider les Parlements et les Gouvernements pour mieux légiférer – Le rôle des guides de legistique* (Schulthess 2008) 117–128.

Millett T, 'A Comparison of British and French Legislative Drafting (with particular reference to their respective Nationality Laws)' (1986) 7:3 Statute Law Review 130–58.

Monaghan K, *Equality Law* (OUP 2007).

Mooney K, 'The Statute Law Revision Project and Statute Law Revision in Ireland 2003 to 2015' (2017) 38:1 Statute Law Review 79–97.

Moran M, 'The Rise of the Regulatory State in Britain' (2001) 54 Parliamentary Affairs 19–34.

Mousmouti M, 'Operationalising Quality of Legislation Through the Effectiveness Test' (2012) 6:2 Legisprudence 191–205.

Mousmouti M, 'Effectiveness as an Aspect of Quality of EU Legislation: Is it Feasible?' (2014) 2:3 The Theory and Practice of Legislation 309–27.

Mousmouti M, 'Introduction to the Symposium on Effective Law and Regulation' (2018) 9:3 European Journal of Risk Regulation 387–39.

Mousmouti M, 'Making Legislative Effectiveness an Operational Concept: Unfolding the Effectiveness Test as a Conceptual Tool for Lawmaking' (2018) 9:3 European Journal of Risk Regulation 445–64.

Mousmouti M, and Crispi G, 'Good Legislation as a Means of Ensuring Voice, Accountability, and the Delivery of Results in Urban Development' (2014) 6 World Bank Legal Review 257.

Mugasha A, 'The Reform and Harmonization of Commercial Laws in the East African Community' (2017) 19:4 European Journal of Law Reform 306–36.

Munday R, 'Bad Character Rules and Riddles: "Explanatory Notes" and the True Meanings of s. 103 (1) of the Criminal Justice Act 2003' (2005) Criminal Law Review 337–54.

Munday R, 'Explanatory Notes and Statutory Interpretation' (2006) 170:8 Justice of the Peace 124–32.

Munday R, 'In the wake of "Good Governance": Impact Assessments and the Politicisation of Statutory Interpretation' (2008) 71:3 Modern Law Review 385–412.

Munday R, 'Interpretation of Legislation in England: The Expanding Quest for Parliamentary Intention' (2011) 75:4 Rabels Zeitschrift für ausländisches und internationales Privatrecht 764–86.

Naundorf S, 'Beyond compliance costs: How do you experience the law? Perception surveys as a complementary tool for Better Regulation', accessible at: https://bscw.bund.de/pub/bscw.cgi/d33672063/160614%20survey%20life%20events.pdf?nonce=863f3d4ccc7f2fcb841656474684658f265d0208 (last accessed 1 December 2018).

Naundorf S and Radaelli C, 'Regulatory Evaluation Ex Ante and Ex Post: Best Practice, Guidance and Methods', in U Karpen and H Xanthaki, *Legislation in Europe. A Comprehensive Guide for Scholars and Practitioners* (Hart Publishing 2017) 187–211.

Nelken D, 'Can Law Learn from Social Science?' (2001) 35:2–3 Israel Law Review 205–24.

Noll P, *Gesetzgebungslehre* (Rowohlt, Reinbeck 1973).

Obradovic D and Alonso Vizcaino J, 'Good Governance Requirements Concerning the Participation of Interest Groups in EU Consultations' (2006) 43 Common Market Law Review 1049–85.

OECD, 'Background Note on the Reference Checklist for Regulatory Decision Making' (OECD Publishing 1995).

OECD, 'Recommendation of the Council on Improving the Quality of Government Regulation 9 March 1995' – C(95)21/FINAL.

OECD, 'Report on Regulatory Reform: Synthesis' (1997) available at: http://www.oecd.org/regreform/regulatory-policy/2391768.pdf (accessed 8 December 2018).

OECD, 'Implementing Administrative Simplification in OECD Countries: Experiences and Challenges' http://www.oecd.org/dataoecd/0/37/37026688.pdf (accessed 8 December 2018).

OECD, *Regulatory Impact Analysis: Best Practices in OECD Countries* (OECD Publishing 1996).

OECD, *Regulatory Reform in Greece* (OECD Publishing 2001).

OECD, *Citizens as Partners. Information, Consultation and Public Participation in Policy-Making* (OECD Publishing 2001).

OECD, *Background Report on Government Capacity to Assure High Quality Regulation* (OECD Publishing 2002).
OECD, *Regulatory Reform in the United Kingdom. Government Capacity to Assure High Quality Regulation* (OECD Publishing 2002).
OECD, *Regulatory Policies in OECD Countries: From Interventionism to Regulatory Governance.* (OECD Publishing 2002).
OECD, 'Building Capacity for Regulatory Quality: Stocktaking Paper', GOV/PGC (2004) 11.
OECD, 'Guiding Principles for Regulatory Quality and Performance' (2005) http://www.oecd.org/dataoecd/24/6/34976533.pdf (accessed 8 December 2018).
OECD, *From Red Tape to Smart Tape. Synthesis Report: Administrative Simplification in OECD Countries* (OECD 2003).
OECD, *Cutting Red Tape: National Strategies for Administrative Simplification*, (OECD Publishing 2006).
OECD, *Cutting Red Tape: Comparing Administrative Burdens across countries* (OECD Publishing 2007).
OECD, *Building an Institutional Framework for Regulatory Impact Analysis (RIA): Guidance for Policy Makers* (OECD 2008).
OECD, 'Introductory Handbook for Undertaking Regulatory Impact Analysis (RIA)' (OECD 2008).
OECD, *Why Is Administrative Simplification So Complicated? Looking Beyond 2010* (OECD Publishing 2010).
OECD, *Better Regulation in Europe. United Kingdom* (OECD Publishing 2010).
OECD, *Better Regulation in Europe: Portugal* (OECD Publishing 2010).
OECD, *Better Regulation in Europe: Spain* (OECD Publishing 2010).
OECD, *Better Regulation in Europe: Germany* (OECD Publishing 2010).
OECD, *Better Regulation in Europe: France* (OECD Publishing 2010).
OECD, *Better Regulation in Europe: Belgium* (OECD Publishing 2010).
OECD, *Greece: Review of the Central Administration* (OECD Public Governance Reviews, OECD Publishing 2011).
OECD, *Report on Alternatives to Traditional Regulation*, available at: http://www.oecd.org/dataoecd/17/5/42245468.pdf (accessed 9 December 2018).
OECD, 'Proceedings from the OECD Expert Meeting on Regulatory Performance: Ex Post Evaluation of Regulatory Policies' (2003) http://www.oecd.org/dataoecd/34/30/30401951.pdf> (accessed 9 December 2018).
OECD, 9th OECD Conference on Measuring Regulatory Performance. Key Findings and Conference Proceedings, available at: http://www.oecd.org/gov/regulatory-policy/Proceedings-9th-Conference-MRP.pdf (last accessed 8 December 2018).

Oliver D, 'Pepper v Hart: a suitable case for reference to Hansard?' (Case Comment) (1993) Public Law 5–13.

Oliver H, 'Sexual Orientation Discrimination: Perceptions, Definitions and Genuine Occupational Requirements', (2004) 33:1 Industrial Law Journal 1–21.

Oliver-Lalana D, 'Due Post-Legislative Process? On the Lawmakers' Constitutional Duties of Monitoring and Revision' in K Messerschmidt and AD Oliver-Lalana (eds) *Rational Lawmaking under Review. Legisprudence According to the German Federal Constitutional Court* (Springer 2016) 257–294.

Oliver-Lalana D, 'On the (judicial) method to review the (legislative) method' (2016) 4:2 The Theory and Practice of Legislation 135–53.

Oliver-Lalana D and K Messerschmidt, 'On the Legiprudential Turn in Constitutional Review: An Introduction' in K Messerschmidt and D Oliver-Lalana (eds) *Rational Lawmaking under Review Legiprudence According to the German Federal Constitutional Court* (Springer 2016), 1–16.

O'Sullivan H and Ormerod D, 'Time for a Code: Reform of Sentencing Law in England and Wales' (2017) 19:4, European Journal of Law Reform 285–305.

Page E, 'The Civil Servant as Legislator: Law Making in British Administration' (2003) 81:4 Public Administration 651–79.

Palmer G, 'The Law Reform Enterprise: Evaluating the Past and Charting the Future' (2015) 131 Law Quarterly Review 402.

Parker Ch and Lehmann Nielsen V, 'Introduction', in Ch Parker, V Lehmann Nielsen (eds) *Explaining Compliance. Business Responses to Regulation* (Edward Elgar 2011) 1–36.

Paulick-Thiel C, 'Summary of the expert findings on gathering, analysing and presenting information on organisational processes and structures in the context of national and international legislation' 2017, available at: https://bscw.bund.de/pub/bscw.cgi/d48976022/180111_SVB_CPT_EN_short.pdf?nonce=3e20b79a11f49326036ed4258546083708a568ca (accessed 8 December 2018).

Pedersen MJ, 'Defining Better. Investigating a New Framework to Understand Quality of Regulation' (2016) 18:2 European Journal of Law Reform 159–78.

Pélisson É, *Les Discriminations* (Transversalle Debats Ellipses 2007).

Perret B, *L'évaluation des politiques publiques* (La Découverte 2008).

Perrin J-F, *Introduction à la sociologie empirique du droit* (CETEL 1987).

Petersen N, *Proportionality and Judicial Activism. Fundamental Rights Adjudication in Canada, Germany and South Africa* (CUP 2017) at 2.

Pettiti Ch and Scalbert S, 'La loi du 30 décembre 2004 portant création de la Haute Autorité de Lutte contre les Discriminations et pour l'égalité' (2005) 25–26 Mars *Gazette du Palais*.

Peyvel P–A, 'La mise on œuvre de la réglementation' in D Madelkern, *La qualité de la réglementation* (Groupe de Travail Interministériel sur la qualité de la réglementation, Documentation Française 2001).

Pierson P, 'Increasing Returns, Path Dependence, and the Study of Politics' (2000) 94 Am.Pol.Sci.Rev. 251.

Pigeon L-P, *Drafting and Interpreting Legislation* (Carswell 1988).

Piris J-C, 'The legal orders of the European Union and of the Member States: Peculiarities and Influences in Drafting' (2006) IV:1/2 European Journal of Law Reform 1–14.

Pound R, *Jurisprudence* (2nd edn, The Lawbook Exchange 2000).

Pound R, *The Formative Era of American Law*, (Little, Brown & Co. 1938).

Popelier P, 'Legal Certainty and Principles of Proper Law Making' (2000) 2:3 European Journal of Law Reform 321–42.

Popelier P, 'Mosaics of Legal Provisions' (2006) VII:1/2 European Journal of Law Reform 47–57.

Popelier P, 'Five Paradoxes on Legal Certainty and the Lawmaker' (2008) 2:1 Legisprudence 47–66.

Popelier P, 'Governance and Better Regulation: Dealing with the Legitimacy Paradox' (2011) 17:3 European Public Law 555–69.

Popelier P, 'The Court as a Regulatory Watchdog: The Procedural Approach in the Case Law of the European Court of Human Rights' in P Popelier, A Mazmanyan and W Vandenbruwaene (eds), *The Role of Constitutional Courts in Multilevel Governance* (Die Keure 2013) 249–67.

Popelier P, 'Codification in a Civil Law Jurisdiction: A Northern European Perspective' (2017) 4 European Journal of Law Reform 253–61.

Popelier P, 'Management of Legislation' in U Karpen and H Xanthaki, *Legislation in Europe. A Comprehensive Guide for Scholars and Practitioners* (Hart Publishing 2017) 53–72.

Popelier P, 'Codification in a Civil Law Jurisdiction: A Northern European Perspective' (2017) 4 European Journal of Law Reform 253–61.

Popelier P, and Mazmanyan A, 'Constitutional Courts and Multilevel Governance in Europe. Editors' Introduction', in P Popelier, A Mazmanyan and W Vandenbruwaene (eds), *The Role of Constitutional Courts in Multilevel Governance* (Intersentia 2013), 1–18.

Posner E and Sunstein C, 'Moral Commitments in Cost-Benefit Analysis' (2017) Coase-Sandor Working Paper Series in Law and Economics 802.

Prado M and Trebilcock M, 'Path Dependence, Development, and the Dynamics of Institutional Reform' (2009) 59 University of Toronto Law Journal 341–79.

Prat M-P and Janvier C, 'La Cour des Comptes, Auxiliaire de la Démocratie' (2010) 3 Pouvoirs 97–107.

Quartey Parafio A, 'Drafting Conventions, Templates and Legislative Precedents, and their Effects on the Drafting Process and the Drafter' (2013) 15:4 European Journal of Law Reform 371–99.

Rachlinski J, 'Evidence-Based Law' (2011) 96 Cornell Law Review 901–23.

Radaelli C, 'Cracking Down on Administrative Burdens: Why Business is not Latching on' (2007) Occasional Paper Centre for Regulatory Governance 1–6.

Radaelli C, 'Desperately Seeking Regulatory Impact Assessments. Diary of a Reflective Researcher', (2009) 15 Evaluation 31–48.

Radaelli C, 'Rationality, Power, Management and Symbols: Four Images of Regulatory Impact Assessment' (2010) 33:2 Scandinavian Political Studies 164–88.

Radaelli C and de Francesco F, *Regulatory Quality in Europe. Concepts, Measures and Policy Processes* (Manchester University Press 2007).

Radaelli C and Meuwese A, 'Better Regulation in Europe: Between Public Management and Regulatory Reform' (2009) 87:3 Public Administration 639–54.

Radin M, 'Statutory Interpretation' (1929–1930) Harvard Law Review 863–85.

Ramsey L, 'The Copy Out Technique: More of a "Cop Out" than a Solution?'(1996) 3:1 Statute Law Review 218–28.

Ranchordás S, *Constitutional Sunsets and Experimental Legislation* (Edward Elgar 2014).

Ranchordás S, 'Time, Timing, And Experimental Legislation' (2015) 3:2 The Theory and Practice of Legislation 135–39.

Ranchordás S, 'Sunset Clauses and Experimental Regulations: Blessing or Curse for Legal Certainty?' (2015) 36:1 Statute Law Review 28–45.

Ranchordás S, 'Consultations, Citizen Narratives and Evidence-Based Regulation. The Strange Case of the Consultation on the Collaborative Economy' (2017) 19:1–2 European Journal of Law Reform 52–73.

Rangone N, 'Making Law Effective: Behavioural Insights into Compliance' (2018) 9:3 European Journal of Risk Regulation 483.

Raz J, 'The Identity of Legal Systems' (1971) 59:3 California Law Review, A Tribute to Hans Kelsen 795–815.

Raz J, *The Authority of Law* (2nd edn, OUP 1980).

Raz J, *The Morality of Freedom* (OUP 1987).

Renton L, 'The Preparation and Enforcement of Legislation in the Enlarged Community' (1996) 17:2 Statute Law Review 1–6.

Rivero J, 'Rapport sur les notions d'égalité et de discrimination en droit public français' in XIV Documents of the Henri Capitant Association of the Friends of French Legal Culture (Dalloz 1961–1962) 343–60.

Robinson W, 'Drafting EU Acts: A View from the European Commission' (2008) X 2 European Journal of Law Reform 151–62.

Robinson W, 'Manuals for Drafting European Union Legislation' (2010) IV:2 Legisprudence 129–155.

Rubin E, 'Legislative Methodology: Some Lessons from the Truth-in-Lending Act' (1991) 80 Geo. L.J. 233.

Rubin E, 'Review: The Conceptual Explanation for Legislative Failure' (2005) 30:3 Law & Social Inquiry 583–606.

Rutter J and Knighton W, *Legislated Policy Targets* (Institute for Government 2012).

Sabbagh D and Peer Sh, 'French Color Blindness in Perspective' (2008) 26:1 French Politics, Culture & Society 1–6.

Sales P, 'Law Reform Challenges: The Judicial Perspective' (2018) 39:3 Statute Law Review 229–43.

Samuels A, 'Statement of Purpose and Principle in British Statutes' (1998) 19:1 Statute Law Review 63–4.

Sanders AJGM, 'The characteristic features of the Civil Law' (1981) 14 The Comparative and International Law Journal of Southern Africa 196–207.

Sarat A, 'Legal Effectiveness and Social Studies of Law: on the unfortunate resistance of a research tradition', IX:1 Legal Studies Forum (1985) 23–31.

Savignac J-C and Salon S, 'Des mosaïques législatives?' (1986) 1 L'Actualité Juridique – Droit Administrative 3–9.

Schäffer H, 'Evaluation and Assessment of Legal Effects Procedures: Towards a More Rational and Responsible Lawmaking Process' (2001) 22 Statute Law Review 132–53.

Scharffs B, 'Law as Craft' (2001) 54 Vanderbilt Law Review 2243–347.

Schulze-Fielitz H, 'Paths Towards Better Legislation, Detours and Dead-Ends. An Appraisal of Consultation and Independent Experts, Justifications for Legislation, Impact Assessments and Controls of Efficacy' in K Messerschmidt and D Oliver-Lalana (eds) *Rational Lawmaking under Review Legiprudence According to the German Federal Constitutional Court* (Springer 2016) 33–57.

Seidman A, Seidman R and Abeyesekere N, *Legislative Drafting for Democratic Social Change. A Manual for Drafters* (Kluwer 2001).

Seidman R, 'Law and Development; A General Model' (1972) 6 Law and Society Review 311–42.

Senden L, 'Soft Law, Self-Regulation and Co-Regulation in European Law: Where Do They Meet?' (2005) 9:1 Electronic Journal of Comparative Law, 1–27.

Shavell St, 'The Optimal Structure of Law Enforcement' (1993) 36:1 Journal of Law and Economics 255–87.

Sieckmann J, 'Rational Lawmaking, Proportionality and Balancing' in K Messerschmidt and AD Oliver-Lalana (eds) *Rational Lawmaking under Review. Legisprudence According to the German Federal Constitutional Court* (Springer 2016) 349–72.

Sieber S, *Fatal Remedies: The Ironies of Social Intervention* (Plenum Publishing 1981).

Simon P, 'Discriminations: les contradictions françaises' (2006) 9 Les Grands Dossiers des Sciences Humaines 84–7.

Simon P, 'La discrimination: La définir pour agir' (2004) 368 Economie et Humanisme 10–14.

Simon P, 'La mesure des discriminations raciales: l'usage des statistiques dans les politiques publiques' (2005) 183 Revue Internationale des Sciences Sociales 13–30.

Simon P, 'L'ombre portée des discriminations dans les statistiques de l'emploi' (2000) 353 Economie et Humanisme 15–19.

Skinner C, 'Codification and the Common Law' (2009) 11:2 European Journal of Law Reform 225–57.

Slapper G and Kelly D, *The English Legal System* (12th edn, Routledge 2011–12).

Smismans S, 'The Politicization of ex post Policy Evaluation in the EU' (2017) 19:1–2 European Journal of Law Reform 74–96 at 74.

Smith T, 'Regulatory Reform in the USA and Europe' (1996) 8:2 Journal of Environmental Law 257–82 at 258.

Stame N, 'Governance, Democracy and Evaluation' (2006) 12:7 Evaluation 7–16.

Stark J, *The Art of the Statute* (Littleton 1996).

Stasi B, *Vers la haute autorité de lutte contre les discriminations et pour l'égalité: rapport au Premier ministre* (La Documentation Française 2004).

Steiner E, 'Codification in England: The need to move from an Ideological to a Functional Approach – A Bridge too Far?' (2004) 25 Statute Law Review 209–22.

Steiner E, *French Law. A Comparative Approach* (OUP 2010).

Stefanou C, 'Drafting as a form of communication' in Luzius Mader/ Marta Tavares de Almeida (eds), *Quality of Legislation. Principles and Instruments* (Nomos 2011) 308–20.

Stefanou C, 'Drafters, Drafting and the Policy Process' in C Stefanou and H Xanthaki (eds), *Drafting Legislation. A Modern Approach* (Ashgate 2008) 319–32.

Stefanou C, 'Comparative Legislative Drafting. Comparing across Legal Systems' (2016) 18(2) European Journal of Law Reform 123–34.

Stephenson P, 'Why Better Regulation Demands Better Scrutiny of Results, The European Parliament's Use of Performance Audits by the European

Court of Auditors in ex post Impact Assessment' (2017) 1–2 European Journal of Law Reform 97–120.

Stolyarenko K, 'Case-Study #1: National Evaluation Policy in Switzerland' (Parliamentary Forum for Development Evaluation 2017), available at: https://www.seval.ch/app/uploads/2017/07/case_study_Switzerland_kstolyarenko.pdf (accessed 1 December 2018).

Suk J, 'Procedural Path Dependence: Discrimination and the Civil-Criminal Divide' (2007–2008) 85 Washington University Law Review 1315–71.

Suk J, 'Criminal and Civil Enforcement of Antidiscrimination Law in Europe' (2012) 14 European Anti-Discrimination Law Review 11–20.

Summers R, 'The Technique Element in Law' (1971) 59 California Law Review 733–51.

Sunstein C, 'On Legal Theory and Legal Practice' (1995) 37 Nomos 267–87.

Sunstein C, 'Social Norms and Social Roles' (1996) 96 Colum. L. Rev. 903–68.

Sunstein C, 'Behavioral Analysis of Law' (1997) 64 U. Chi. L. Rev. 1175–1195.

Sunstein C, *Simpler* (Simon & Schuster 2013).

Tala J, 'Better Regulation through Programs and Quality Standards – Are new perspectives needed?' (2010) IV:2 Legisprudence 193–212.

Tallon D, 'Codification and Consolidation of the Law at the Present Time' (1979) 14:1 Israel Law Review 1–18.

Teasdale J, 'Statute Law Revision: Repeal, Consolidation or Something More?' (2009) 11 European Journal of Law Reform 157–212.

Teasdale J, 'Prologue: The IALS Law Reform Project' (2016) 18:3 European Journal of Law Reform 253–63.

Teasdale J, 'Codification: A Civil Law Solution to a Common Law Conundrum?' (2017) 19:4 European Journal of Law Reform 247–52.

Teubner G, 'Substantive and Reflexive Elements in Modern Law' (1983) 17:2 Law & Society Review 239–85.

Thaler R and Sunstein C, *Nudge* (Penguin Books 2009).

Thornton G, *Legislative Drafting* (4th edn, Tottel 1996).

Timmermans C, 'How can one improve the quality of Community Legislation?' (1997) 5 Common Market Law Review 1229–57.

Torriti J, 'The Standard Cost Model: When "Better Regulation" Fights against Red Tape' in Stephen Weatherill (ed) *Better Regulation* (Hart Publishing 2007) 81–106.

Trautmann S, 'Empirical Knowledge in Legislation and Regulation: A Decision Making Perspective' (2013) 1 The Theory and Practice of Legislation 533–42.

Tremper C, Thomas S and Wagenaar A, 'Measuring Law for Evaluation Research' (2010) 34(3) Evaluation Review 242–66.

Tuori K, 'Legislation Between Politics and Law' in Luc Wintgens (ed) *Legisprudence* (Hart Publishing 2002) 99–107.

Turnbull IML, 'Problems of Legislative Drafting' 1986 (67) Statute Law Review 67–77.

Twining W and Miers D, *How to Do Things with Rules* (5th edn, CUP 2010).

Uhlmann F and Konrath Ch, 'Participation' in U Karpen and H Xanthaki (eds) *Legislation in Europe. A Comprehensive Guide for Scholars and Practitioners* (Hart Publishing 2017) 76–81.

van Aeken K, 'From Vision to Reality: Ex post evaluation of legislation' (2011) 5:1 Legisprudence 41–68.

van Gestel R and van Dijck G, 'Better Regulation through Experimental Legislation' (2011) 17:3 European Public Law 539–53.

van Gestel R and de Poorter J, 'Putting evidence-based law making to the test: judicial review of legislative rationality' (2016) 4:2 The Theory and Practice of Legislation 155–85.

van den Hoogen Th and Nowak T, 'The Emergence and Use of Self-Regulation in the European Decision Making Process: Does it make a Difference?' (2010) IV:3 Legisprudence 343–83.

van der Meulen D, 'The Use of Impact Assessments and the Quality of Legislation' (2013) 1:2 Theory and Practice of Legislation 305–25.

van Laer C and Xanthaki X, 'Legal Transplants and Comparative Concepts: Eclecticism Defeated?' (2013) 34:2 Statute Law Review 128–37.

van Lochem P and Westerman P, 'Rules on Rulemaking' (2010) IV:2 Legisprudence 107–218.

van Voorst S and Mastenbroek S, 'Enforcement tool or strategic instrument? The initiation of ex-post legislative evaluations by the European Commission' (2017) 18:4 European Union Politics 640–57.

Varone F, Bundi P and Gava R, 'Policy evaluation in parliament: interest groups as catalysts' (2018) International Review of Administrative Sciences 1–17.

Veljanovski C, 'Economic Approaches to Regulation' in R Baldwin, M Cave and M Lodge (eds), *The Oxford Handbook of Regulation* (OUP 2010) 17–38.

Veil S, 'Redécouvrir le Préambule de la Constitution, Rapport du Comite préside par Simone Veil' (La Documentation Française 2009).

Verbruggen P, 'Does Co-Regulation Strengthen EU Legitimacy?' (2009) 15:4 European Law Journal 425–41.

Viswanathan M, 'Sunset Provisions in the Tax Code: A Critical Evaluation and Prescriptions for the Future' (2007) 82 N.Y.U. L. Rev. 656–88.

Voermans W, 'The Sisyphus Paradox of Cutting Red Tape and Managing Public Risk. The Dutch Case' (2008) Paper delivered to the 2nd ECPR Conference on Regulatory Governance, Netherlands, 5–7 June 2008.

Voermans W, 'Concern about the Quality of EU Legislation: What Kind of Problem, by What Kind of Standards?' (2009) 2:1 Erasmus Law Review 59–95.

Voermans W, 'Styles of Legislation and Their Effects' (2011) 32:1 Statute Law Review 38–53.

Voermans W, 'Motive-Based Enforcement', in Luzius Mader, Sergey Kabyshev (eds), *Regulatory Reforms; Implementation and Compliance, Proceedings of the Tenth Congress of the International Association of Legislation (IAL) in Veliky Novgorod, June 28th-29th 2012* (Nomos 2014) 41–61.

Voermans W, 'To Measure is to Know: the Quantification of Regulation' (2015) 3:1 The Theory and Practice of Legislation 91–111.

Voermans W, 'From Legal Imposition to Legal Invitation' (2018) 20:1 European Journal of Law Reform 8–19.

Voermans W and Schuurmans Y, 'Better Regulation by Appeal' (2011) 17:3 European Public Law.

Voermans W, Moll Ch, Florijn N and van Lochem P, 'Codification and Consolidation in the European Union: A Means to Untie Red Tape' (2008) 29:2 Statute Law Review 65–81.

Wahlgren P, 'The Legitimacy Sphere: Between Law, Culture, Politics and Enforceability' (2010) 56 Scandinavian Studies in Law 428–42.

Waldhoff C, 'On Constitutional Duties to Give Reasons for Legislative Acts' in K Messerschmidt and AD Oliver-Lalana (eds) *Rational Lawmaking under Review* (Springer 2016) 129–51.

Waller J, 'The Expenditure Effects of Sunset Laws in State Governments' (All Dissertations 2009) 381.

Ward R and Akhtar A, *Walker & Walker's English Legal System* (11th edn, OUP 2011).

Watson A, *Legal Transplants* (2 edn, University of Georgia Press 1974).

Weatherill S (ed), *Better Regulation* (Hart Publishing 2007).

Wegrich K, 'Which Results? Better Regulation and Institutional Politics' (2015) 6:3 European Journal of Risk Regulation 369–71.

Westerman P, 'Who is Regulating the Self? Self-Regulation as Outsourced Rule-Making' (2010) IV:3 Legisprudence 225–41.

Westerman P, 'Breaking the Circle: Goal-legislation and the Need for Empirical Research' (2013) 1:3 The Theory and Practice of Legislation 395–414.

Westerman P, *Outsourcing the Law. A Philosophical Perspective on Regulation* (Edward Elgar Publishing 2018).

Whelanová M, 'Quo Vadis, Europa? Loopholes in the EU Law and Difficulties in the Implementation Process' (2016) 2 European Journal of Law Reform 179–208.

White R, '"It's Not a Criminal Offence"—or Is It? Thornton's Analysis of "Penal Provisions" and the Drafting of "Civil Penalties"' (2011) 32:1 Statute Law Review 17–37.

Wiener J, 'Better Regulation in Europe, Current Legal Problems' (2006) Duke Law School Legal Studies Paper No. 130.

Wintgens L (ed), *Legislation in Context: Essays in Legisprudence* (Ashgate 2007).

Wintgens L, 'The Rational Legislator Revisited. Bounded Rationality and Legisprudence' in L Wintgens and AD Oliver-Lalana (eds), *The Rationality and Justification of Legislation* (Springer 2013), 1–31.

Wintgens L, 'Legisprudence as a New Theory of Legislation' in Luc Wintgens (ed) *The Theory and Practice of Legislation* (Routledge 2016).

Wirths D, 'Procedural Institutionalization of the Evaluation Through Legal Basis: A New Typology of Evaluation Clauses in Switzerland' (2017) 38:1 Statute Law Review 23–39.

Woehrling J-M, 'Le droit français de lutte contre les discriminations a la lumière du droit comparé' (2008) 148 Informations Sociales 58–71.

Wortley BA, 'The Mechanics of Law Making Today', lecture delivered in the John Rylands Library on 18 January 1956 available at: https://www.escholar.manchester.ac.uk/api/datastream?publicationPid=uk-ac-man-scw:1m1919&datastreamId=post-peer-review-publishers-document.pdf (accessed 11 May 2019).

Wright J and Ginsburg D, 'Behavioral Law and Economics. Its origins, fatal flaws, and implications for liberty' in A Hatzis and N Mercuro (eds), *Law and Economics. Philosophical issues and fundamental questions* (Routledge 2017) 297–331.

Xanthaki H, 'The Slim Initiative' (2001) 22:2 Statute Law Review 108–18.

Xanthaki H, 'The Problem of Quality in EU Legislation: What on Earth is Really Wrong?' (2001) 38 Common Market Law Review 651–76.

Xanthaki H, 'On the Transferability of Legislative Solutions: the Functionality Test' in C Stefanou and H Xanthaki (eds), *Drafting Legislation. A Modern Approach* (Ashgate 2008) 1–18.

Xanthaki H, 'Drafting Manuals and Quality in Legislation: Positive Contribution towards Certainty in the Law or Impediment to the Necessity for Dynamism of Rules' (2010) IV:2 Legisprudence 111–128.

Xanthaki H, 'Quality of Legislation: an achievable universal concept or an utopia pursuit?' in L Mader, M Tavres de Almeida (eds), *Quality of Legislation. Principles and Instruments* (Nomos 2011) 75–85.

Xanthaki H, *Thornton's Legislative Drafting* (5th edn, Bloomsbury Professional 2013).

Xanthaki H, 'European Union Legislative Quality After the Lisbon Treaty: The Challenges of Smart Regulation' Statute Law Review Advance Access published 13 May 2013, 1–15.

Xanthaki H, 'The Regulatory Reform Agenda and Modern Innovations in Drafting Style' in L Mader (ed) *Regulatory Reform* (Nomos Baden-Baden 2013).

Xanthaki H, 'Legislative Drafting: The UK Experience' in F Uhlmann and S Hoefler (eds) *Professional Legislative Drafters. Status, Roles, Education* (DIKE 2016) 15–38.

Xanthaki H, 'An Enlightened Approach to Legislative Scrutiny: Focusing on Effectiveness' (2018) 9:3 European Journal of Risk Regulation 431–44.

Young A, *Parliamentary Sovereignty and the Human Rights Act* (Hart Publishing 2009).

Zander M, *The Law Making Process* (2nd edn, Weidenfeld and Nicolson 1985).

Zamboni M, *The Policy of Law: A Legal Theoretical Framework* (Hart Publishing 2007).

Zamboni M, 'Goals and Measures of Legislation: Evaluation' in U Karpen and H Xanthaki, *Legislation in Europe. A Comprehensive Guide for Scholars and Practitioners* (Hart Publishing 2017) 97–107.

Zamboni M, 'Legislative Policy and Effectiveness: A (Small) Contribution from Legal Theory' (2018) 9:3 European Journal of Risk Regulation 416–30.

Ziegler P, 'Information Collection: Techniques for the Evaluation of the Legislative Process' (1988) 160 Statute Law Review 160–85.

Zumbansen P, 'Law's Knowledge and Law's Effectiveness: Reflections from Legal Sociology and Legal Theory' (2009) 5:2 CLPE Research Paper 11/2009 11.

Zweigert K and Kötz H, *An Introduction to Comparative Law* (trs Tony Weir, 3rd edn, OUP 2011).

Zwaan P, S van Voorst and E Mastenbroek, 'Ex post legislative evaluation in the European Union: questioning the usage of evaluations as instruments for accountability' (2016)82:4 International Review of Administrative Sciences 674–93.

Index

accessibility 6, 48, 66, 67, 149, 152, 160
    amendments 80–81, 139
    clear messages 59, 60
    codification 109, 140, 141
    consolidation 140, 147
    context 66, 80–81, 83, 127
        'all-in-one' messages 67
        'diffuse' messages 70–71, 78
        'fragmented' messages 73, 74
        'patchwork' messages 74, 78
    law reform 142
    OECD checklist 110
    tradition and style 50
air pollution 132
'all-in-one' messages 67–9, 78, 82, 83
amendments 74, 75–8, 79
    accessibility 80–81, 139
    legislative failure 137–9, 143, 146, 147, 149
anchoring 158–9
apartheid 42
Australia 60, 80, 94, 99
automatisms 56, 79, 152, 158–62
availability 80, 158–9

behavioural economists 158–9
behavioural insights 61
behavioural law and economics 4
Belgium 75
benchmarks 11, 102, 118, 125
    objectives as 36–7, 38
bias(es) 137
    cognitive *see separate entry*
    confirmation 56
    selection 117
    status quo 158–9
bottom up or top down approach 155–6
bounded rationality 44, 158

Canada 23, 36, 111
    preambles 27–8
    purpose clauses 26
    Regulatory Impact Analysis 114
China 21
civil law countries 62, 140, 142, 147, 159–60
    see also individual countries
climate change 102
codification 71, 79, 80, 109
    legislative failure 140–141, 142, 143, 147
    non-discrimination provisions 160
    'patchwork' messages 76–8
cognitive biases 4, 56, 154, 158–9
    borrowed, imported and supranational rules 162
    legislative styles, drafting conventions and regulatory culture 159–60
    path dependence, habitual action and legislative 'patterns' 160–161
coherence 6–7, 11, 53–4, 124, 126, 152
    codification 109, 140, 160
    context 65–6, 67, 71, 74, 78, 81–2, 83, 123, 127
    impact assessments 112
    simplification 109

styles and drafting conventions 160
common law countries 27, 62, 141, 142, 159
  see also individual countries
communicating the law 4, 48–51, 54, 64, 83, 118, 124
  clear messages 59–60
  effective message delivery 79–82
  equality legislation 52, 53
  failure, legislative 133–4, 135, 145
  superstructure and transmission of messages 66–79
comparative law 162
competitiveness 115
complexity and fragmentation 74
compliance 45, 46–7, 48, 74, 116, 118, 124, 139
  anticipating 57–8
  costs 47, 57–8, 99, 113
confirmation bias 56
consolidation 79, 80, 140, 142, 147
  'patchwork' messages 76–8
Constitutional Courts 6, 7
  France 44
  Germany 6–7, 18
  purpose 18, 19
constitutional law/rules 5, 19, 81
constitutional principles 42
constitutionality
  purpose 18
Constitutions 5, 19, 42, 80, 98, 99, 109, 125, 133–4
consultation 57, 109, 110, 116–19
  effectiveness 120
content 16, 151, 152
  balance opposing dynamics 44
  challenges 40
    communicating the law 48–51
    compliance and enforcement 45–8
    selecting substantive rules 41–4
  conclusions 61–3

effective mechanics 51
  anticipating compliance 57–8
  clear legislative strategy 52–3
  clear mechanics 53–4
  clear messages for clear communication 59–60
  enforcement and implementation 58–9
  experimentation 60–61
  informed by evidence 54–6
  selected on basis of effectiveness 56
effectiveness test 122–3, 124–5, 126, 127
heart of effectiveness 14–15
context 15, 16, 83, 151, 152
  effective message delivery 79
    accessibility 80–81
    coherence 81–2
    how will changes to appraised 82
    informed choices on superstructure 79
  effectiveness test 123
  superstructure and messages 66, 78–9
    'all-in-one' messages 67–9, 78, 82, 83
    'diffuse' messages 69–71, 78–9, 83
    'fragmented' messages 71–4, 78, 79, 82, 83
    'patchwork' messages 74–8, 83
  why context matters 64–6
conventions, legislative styles and regulatory culture 159–60
'copy-out' technique 162
cost(s) 10, 11, 19, 29, 42, 59, 108
  compliance and enforcement 45, 46, 47, 57–8, 62, 99, 113
  cost-benefit analysis 28, 42, 56, 57, 110, 119, 146, 147, 152, 154

impact assessments 113, 114, 115, 118, 119
review obligation 93
evaluation: cost-efficiency 95, 97
failure, legislative 133, 146, 147
impact assessments 113, 114, 115, 116, 118, 119
implementation 99, 102
evaluation 95, 97
learning from results 106
plan 59, 102
review 93, 104
path dependence 160
simplification 139

definitions 60, 74, 124–5, 134
existence or placement 59
'diffuse' messages 69–71, 78–9, 83
disabled people 73
see also equality
discrimination *see* equality
drafting conventions, legislative styles and regulatory culture 159–60
due legislative process 75

East African states 142
Kenya 133–4
Mozambique 134
economics 160
effectiveness 59, 62, 97, 109, 119, 149, 150–155, 163
efficacy or efficiency 9–12
functional link 56
intuitive lawmaker 157
lawmaker that 'muddles through' 158
potential to be effective 151
reflective lawmaker 158
test *see* effectiveness test
see also content; context; purpose; results

effectiveness test 16, 119–21, 128, 151, 154, 163
advantages of 127–8
amendments 147
case studies 124–6
content 122–3, 124–5, 126, 127
context 123
failure, legislative
diagnosis of 144–5
limitations of 128
overarching questions 124
purpose 121–2, 124, 125, 126
results 123–4, 125, 126, 127
usefulness and relevance 127–8
effects/impacts, outcomes and direct results 86–7
efficacy 97, 109, 118, 119–20, 150, 152
effectiveness or efficiency 9–12
efficiency 4, 59, 97, 118, 119, 120, 150, 152
effectiveness or efficacy 9–12
'patchwork' messages 76
enforcement 45–8, 52–3, 54, 116, 124, 125, 126, 127, 135
equality 110, 118, 154–5
content 49–50
clear legislative strategy 52–3
enforcement 47–8
selecting substantive rules 41–4
context
'all-in-one' messages 67–9, 82
'diffuse' messages 69–71, 79
'fragmented' messages 71–3, 82
'patchwork' messages 75–7, 78
effectiveness test: three case studies 124–6
purpose
benchmarks 36, 37
long title of Act 27, 30, 124
tactical and strategic goals 21
too much information 30–33

vague language 22–5
results
    outcomes, impacts and 87
    reviews 93, 99, 100–101
    top down or bottom up approach 155–6
equality before the law 61
European Union 135
    Better Regulation Guidelines 110
    costs 58
    Court of Justice 27, 30
    equality laws 43, 44, 52, 126
        'fragmented' messages 72–3
    evaluation 106
        clauses 97–8, 106
        impact assessments 113, 114–15
        monitoring clauses 89
        Parliament: evaluations 99–100
        practical guide 110
        purpose clauses 26
        recitals 27
        tax law 58
evaluation of draft legislation: usability tests 60
evaluation or post-legislative scrutiny 84–5, 87–8, 95–8, 125, 126, 137
    clauses 97–8, 104–6
    'diffuse' messages 71
    framework 103–4
    learning from results 106–7
    purpose 18
    when, how and who 98–101
evidence-based
    lawmaking 8–9, 54–6, 108
    policy making 112
    review of legislation 7
experimentation 60–61, 154
extraneous or preparatory material and purpose 28, 37–9

failure, legislative 129, 149
    anticipating and avoiding future 143–4
    'immune' system of legal order 146–7
    invest in effective lawmaking 149
    learn from failure 147–8
    limits of law 146
    overarching questions 146
    questionnaire for diagnosis of 145
    scepticism 144
    strategic approach to analysis of failure 144–6
    responding to 137
        amendments 137–9, 143, 146, 147, 149
        codification 140–141, 142, 143, 147
        effectiveness of responses 143
        law reform 141–3, 147
        simplification 139–40, 143, 147
        timing 146
    timing and actors of diagnosis of 136–7
    typology of 131–2, 144
        combinations 135–6
        drafting and communication 133–4
        implementation 134–5
        legislative design 132–3
    understanding 130–131
feedback 57, 116
'fragmented' messages 71–4, 78, 79, 82, 83
France 80
    Council of State
        'patchwork' messages 75
    equality legislation 24–5, 36, 52
        'diffuse' messages 69–71
    effectiveness test 125–6
    enforcement 47, 125, 126

'patchwork' messages 76
pay equality evaluation
    100–101
selecting substantive rules 41,
    42–4
strategy 52, 54
    impact assessments 113–14
    'patchwork' messages 75, 76
    practical guide 110–111
    purpose clauses 26
    results 100–101, 102–3, 125
        monitoring 89, 125
        National Assembly 99
Fuller, L. 17, 19
fundamental rights 15, 84, 115

gender 20–21, 72–3, 79, 86
    impact assessments 115
    pay gap 21, 24–5, 36, 93
        evaluation 100–101
    recognition 89
general principles of law 19
Germany 6–7, 18, 23, 36
    communicating the law 48
    compliance costs 57–8, 99
    explanatory memoranda 28–9
    human-centred development
        approaches 61
    impact assessments 113
    results 99, 100
goals, justifications and reasons 18–20
Greece: equality legislation 24, 36, 44,
    47
    effectiveness test 126
    inconsistency 49–50
    strategy 52–3

habitual action 161
headings 59
heuristics 2, 158
historical legacies 42
housing 134–5

human-centred development approaches
    61
hybrid nature of purpose 22, 152

immigration 43
impact assessments 109, 110, 112–16,
    118–19, 120
    amendments 147
    effectiveness test 128
    functions 112
    purpose 28, 29–30, 31, 34
    questions considered by 113–14
    reviews required by 90
impacts/effects, outcomes and direct
    results 86–7
implementation 58–9, 116, 117, 118, 127
    failure in 134–6, 139, 145
    plan 59, 102–3
    results *see separate entry*
inclusivity 80
inconsistency 97
    content 49–50, 51, 54
    context 65–6, 74
    effectiveness test 126, 127
    legislative failure 134, 135
        codification 140
    purpose 30, 33
incrementalism 55, 62, 69, 79, 158
inequalities, elimination of *see* equality
information
    asymmetries 73
    disclosure 61
    inclusivity 80
    objectives: too much 30–33
international rules 81
Internet 80
intuitive lawmaker 157
Ireland 89, 143
Israel 75
Italy 100

jargon 50

judicial activism 7
judicial and legislative processes 3
judicial review 6, 7, 107
    Germany 6–7
    purpose 18
justifications, reasons and goals 18–20

Kenya 133–4

law and economics 4, 9
law reform 7, 141–3, 147
layered approach 60, 61
learning 155
    from failure 147–8
    from results 106–7
legal certainty 5, 6, 61, 75, 84, 95, 109, 115, 139
legal sociology 4, 12
legal theory 4
legal transplants 44, 142, 162
legalese 50
legalism 159
legislative studies or legisprudence 7–9
legitimacy 7, 17, 18, 19, 66, 117, 118, 131
LGBTI community 73
    see also equality
life cycle of legislation 155
limits of law 146, 154–5
Llewellyn, K. 1
long title to Act 27, 30, 75, 124
loss aversion 158–9

mapping 'user-journeys' 57
media 134–5, 136, 146
micro, meso and macro goals 21
monitoring 87–9, 106, 125, 126
    clauses 89, 104, 106
    framework 103–4
    when, how and who 98–101
moral values 115
morality 47, 56

Mozambique 134
'muddles through', lawmaker that 158

naming and shaming 61
narrative approach 60, 61
navigability 75, 80
Netherlands
    Table of Eleven 57
non-discrimination *see* equality
norms 3, 5, 6, 12, 46, 115, 130, 131, 146, 155
    effectiveness 9, 10
nudges 61

objective or purpose clauses 25–6, 32–3, 35, 37
OECD (Organisation for Economic Co-operation and Development) 109
    checklist 110
    reviews 89–90
optimal solutions 44
outcomes, direct results and effects/impacts 86–7

'patchwork' messages 74–8, 83
path dependence, habitual action and legislative 'patterns' 160–161
patterns 57–8, 161
perverse incentives 73
plain language 50–51, 142
Poland 138
policy 82, 95, 118, 150
    consultation 117
    objectives and purpose of law 22–3, 24–5, 35, 152
    translator 3–4
political science 4, 131, 160
post-legislative scrutiny *see* evaluation or post-legislative scrutiny
Pound, R. 162
power games 107

preambles 27–8, 31–3, 37
precedent 7
preparatory or extraneous material and purpose 28, 37–9
principles to guide lawmaking 4–9
privacy 110
problem-solving approach 153
proportionality 5, 10, 109, 124
    content 54, 122
    purpose 18, 19
'protector pattern' 161
public policy analysis 153–4
purpose 16, 17–18, 39, 85–6, 151, 152
    benchmark of effectiveness 13–14
    challenges 18
        (intended) goals and (real) effects 20–22
        location of legislative objectives 25–30
        too much information 30–33
        unclear boundaries between reasons, justifications and goals 18–20
        vague language 22–5
        what objectives 20–22
    effectiveness test 121–2, 124, 125, 126
    hybrid nature of 22, 152
    objectives 33
        as benchmarks 36–7, 38
        broader 34
        hierarchy 35, 36
        specific, measurable and well-formulated 35
        starting point in lawmaking 34
        traceable 37–9
purpose or objective clauses 25–6, 32–3, 35, 37
purposive interpretation 18

questionnaire for diagnosis of legislative failure 145

rationality 2, 5, 8, 11, 17, 18, 19, 108, 118, 148, 149, 151
    bounded 44, 158
    economic or 'managerial' 9
    means-end 152
    procedural 6, 150
    substantive 6
reasons, justifications and goals 18–20
reflective lawmaker 147–8, 157–8
regulatory culture, legislative styles and drafting conventions 159–60
repeals 75, 142
reports accompanying draft legislation 28–9
representativeness 158–9
responsive regulation 46
results 16, 84–5, 107, 151, 152
    challenges 85
        evaluation 87–8, 95–101
        horizontal questions 98–101
        how can results be anticipated and measured 87–9
        monitoring 87–9, 98–101
        results produced by legislation 85–7
        review 87–8, 89–93, 98–101
        sunsetting 94–5
    direct results, outcomes and effects/impacts 86–7
    in effective lawmaking 101
        anticipating implementation 102–3
        clauses 104–7
        clearly defined results 101–2
        framework 103–4
    effectiveness test 123–4, 125, 126, 127
    measure of effectiveness 15–16
    monitoring, review and evaluation 88–98, 102–3, 107, 137
        clear framework 103–4
        clear and specific clauses 104–6

differences between 87–8
learning from results 106–7
Parliaments 99–100
when, how and who 98–101
reverse engineering 57, 152
review 85, 87–8, 89–93, 106, 125, 137
    clauses 104
    framework 103–4
    sunset 94
    when, how and who 98–101
Rules of Procedure 19

sanctions, penalties or fines 46–7, 52, 56, 157
scepticism 144
scrutiny of law *see* evaluation or post-legislative scrutiny
simplification 109, 139–40, 143, 147
simplified outline 60
single/'all-in-one' messages 67–9, 78, 82, 83
smart regulation 46
social construction 45
South Africa
    objects clause 32–3
    preambles 27, 31–3
    selecting substantive rules 42
Spain 26, 27
specialisation of law 73
specific, measurable, achievable, relevant and time-bound objectives 35
stakeholders 57, 110, 116–17
status quo bias 158–9
statutory interpretation 3, 74
    Explanatory Notes in UK 29
    impact assessments 30
    purposive 18
story-telling approach 60, 61
strategic approach to analysis of legislative failure 144–6
strategic or tactical objectives 21
style(s) 50, 59, 79

drafting conventions and regulatory culture 159–60
sunsetting 94–5, 99
Sweden 23, 100
Switzerland 22–3, 36
    dispatches on Bills 28
    evaluation 107
        clauses 97
    Federal Assembly
        impact assessments 99
    preambles 27
    purpose clauses 26

Table of Eleven 57
tactical or strategic objectives 21
tax law 58, 141
tools 108–9, 128
    consultation 57, 109, 110, 116–19, 120
    effectiveness test *see separate entry*
    impact assessments *see separate entry*
    toolkits and lawmaking 109–12, 118–19
top down or bottom up approach 155–6
traffic codes 61
transnational commercial law 142
transparency 19, 22, 112, 116, 117, 118
transplants 44, 142, 162
typology of lawmakers 156
    intuitive 157
    'muddles through' 158
    reflective 157–8

United Kingdom 80
    codification 141
    consultation 117
    equality legislation 52
        'all-in-one' message 67–9
        clear legislative strategy 52
        effectiveness test 124–5
        enforcement 47

'fragmented' messages 71–2
long title to Act 27, 30, 124
'patchwork' messages 75,
    76–7, 78
reviews 93, 99, 100
selecting substantive rules 41,
    43
too much information on
    objectives 30–31
Explanatory Notes to Acts 29, 31,
    124
failure, legislative 140
    Dangerous Dogs Act 1991 136
    housing 134–5
    Law Commission in England
        and Wales 141, 142
    law reform 141, 142
    Mental Capacity Act 2005
        135–6
impact assessments 30, 31, 113, 115
legislative patterns 161
long title of Act 27, 30, 75, 124
'patchwork' messages 75, 76–8

practical guide 110
readers of legislation 48
results 102–3
    Parliament 100
    post-implementation reviews
        85, 90–93, 99, 100, 106,
        125
    target: net carbon account in
        2050 102
United States 42
    Americans with Disabilities Act 73
    Clean Air Act 1970 132
    purpose clauses 26
    selecting substantive rules 42
    sunset reviews 94
    Truth-in-Lending Act 1968 61–2
usability tests of draft legislation 60

vague language 49
    of legislative objectives 22–5
VAT legislation 58
visual aids 59, 61